Creative Church Leadership

A MODEM Handbook

Edited by
John Adair and John Nelson

CANTERBURY
PRESS

N o r w i c h

© MODEM 2004

First published in 2004 by the Canterbury Press Norwich
(a publishing imprint of Hymns Ancient & Modern Limited,
a registered charity)
St Mary's Works, St Mary's Plain,
Norwich, Norfolk, NR3 3BH
www.scm-canterburypress.co.uk

British Library Cataloguing in Publication data

A catalogue record for this book is available
from the British Library

ISBN 1-85311-502-9

Typeset by Regent Typesetting, London
Printed and bound by
Biddles Ltd, www.biddles.co.uk

Contents

Introduction

JOHN NELSON

This is MODEM's third book. Its first – *Management and Ministry* (1996) – tackled the issue of churches needing to manage their resources properly. Its second – *Leading, Managing, Ministering* (1999) – explored the wider issues of managing in ministry; ministering in management and of both in leading organisations – churches and secular organisations. This book, its third, focuses on leadership – church leadership – and incidentally celebrates MODEM's tenth anniversary, its coming of age as a torch-bearer for the importance of considering issues of leadership and management in relation to those of ministry.

How the idea for a third book on church leadership came about – and grew and grew

In July 2001 John Adair came up to Lancashire to talk to several MODEM meetings. During our conversations he suggested that MODEM should consider a third book in what had clearly been a much valued and successful series, and I welcomed the idea whole-heartedly. We discussed possible titles and when I came up with 'Creative Church Leadership' he said that it sounded absolutely right – we should look no further. And nor did we. John offered to help in any way as contributor and as editorial advisor; and latterly as Joint Editor with me, and may I say how grateful I have been for his help and advice.

Not that MODEM had not been wrestling with the theme of leadership before our meeting. During that summer our quarterly newsletter *MODEM Matters* carried a series of articles and letters on such topics as selecting senior leaders in the Church of England (the experience of strategic leadership in Exeter Diocese, episcopal leadership for a new millennium, 'Incarnational Leadership' and others – so you can see that leadership was on my mind!

But John felt – and I positively agreed – that the introduction of the adjective *Creative* opened a whole set of new windows and maybe, too, some doors for action. And so we began to explore the new idea in further depth.

A milestone on this road was MODEM's annual conference in September 2002, at Whirlow Grange in Sheffield. Our reasoning was that first a foundation needed to be laid. For many people in the churches are uncomfortable with the idea of leadership in the church context, let alone *creative leadership*. Before we could commend the latter we needed to establish the credibility and relevance of leadership as such. So we chose Belief in Leadership as the conference theme.

The paper that Sir Philip Mawer gave to the conference, bearing the same title, is reproduced below, and it speaks for itself. And the key ideas that our other principal contributor John Adair expressed are fully reflected in the opening sections of his closing chapter. Encouraged by the thoughtful and constructive way that MODEM members built on the armature of the idea during the conference, MODEM's Management Committee decided to push ahead with the book. With encouragement from Christine Smith, editorial director of Canterbury Press, who had been midwife to our two previous books, we began to approach possible contributors.

Our team of contributors – our choice and our rationale

Not least because of our sense of the importance of the subject encapsulated in our title, we decided to abandon our previous policy of limiting ourselves to MODEM members as contributors and to invite a wider cross-section of views from those whom we thought would have interesting, stimulating and thought-provoking things to say. As you will, I hope, agree, we have not been disappointed. It would be hard to find a better selection of writers on the subject.

Our policy has been to choose the individual person; so none of our contributors is speaking for any body, party or section of the church – simply for themselves. The balance that you see between, say, 'academics' and 'practitioners', clergy or lay, male or female, senior and less senior, believers and non-believers, is almost entirely fortuitous. It is the voice of this person we invite you to hear.

Not that it was difficult to attract contributors. All those we approached were extremely positive about the project – it was as if our title struck a chord in their hearts. Perhaps inevitably some we invited could not, with sincere regret, accept our invitation for reasons beyond their control. Among those who could not thus accompany us on the journey were a distinguished Catholic theologian in

Germany, a leader in the Conference of European Churches in Germany and a leading Lutheran bishop in Norway. The latter wrote:

> The title of the book immediately tickled my thinking and reflection – not to say creativity. The theme will stay with me in my work and writing later in the summer as I pursue the study and the actual challenge of ministerial and lay leadership in our church.

I mention these 'near misses' to make the point that the book was not intended to be either Anglican or insular in its perspectives. We felt – and still feel – that *Creative Church Leadership* is for all churches in all countries as we move forwards with this challenging new millennium. Indeed we hope that the book will serve as a model or template for similar explorations throughout the world.

Is the contributor list too churchy?

It could still be argued that the list of contributors is *too churchy*, that is, consisting mainly of people inside or sympathetic to the Church, beholden to it or too close to it and hence blinkered in their views. Maybe it is, but it seemed right to me that such people – providing they were in a position to know the realities, burdens, responsibilities and powers of church leadership at all levels – should be invited *first* to interpret their vision of the need for creative church leadership and the form it should take. What can't be sustained, however, is the argument that the list is too clerical. Lay contributors actually outnumber clergy contributors.

It would be nice to entertain the hope that the response to this book is such that we can follow it with one wherein the contributors were thinkers of eminence with little or no direct experience of the church nor sympathy necessarily for it. We could then compare their findings with those that have emerged from this one. (Other successors in similar vein might focus on the European, American, Asian or African perspective!)

Guidelines to contributors

John Adair drew up guidelines for the contributors. They were, however, non-directive and offering help if wanted:

> First, may I say how delighted I am to hear that you have agreed to contribute to this book. Please do not hesitate to get in touch with

me should you wish to bounce ideas off me or show me any drafts if you think it would help.

I am looking forward to reading what you have to say. The unpredictable variety and range of the contributions is what will give most value to this book, and it will be my job at the end to see if I can discern any pattern in them, or perhaps a few threads that I can pull together. What I trust may happen is that the contributions, widely as they differ, may somehow hang together and have some kind of coherence.

But putting anything editorial on paper at this stage would, I feel, threaten the very creativity – the freedom and opportunity to think outside the box – which makes this book such an unusual, interesting and exciting project. So the only guideline lies in the title itself, and it will guide us in different ways. Yet I am very confident that a harmony will emerge, and that the book will prove to be immensely worthwhile.

So we decided not to issue guidelines, or rather to make them non-directive. We left it to each contributor to interpret – creatively – our title – *Creative Church Leadership* – in the light of their own experience, expertise and vision for the church. Clearly, this approach as such could result in a collection of individual contributions lacking any cohesion. I was only able to adopt it through John Adair's generosity in agreeing to act as sweeper – to search for and gather up convergent ideas/themes and to cover issues we felt were important but which hadn't been covered. In this way we hoped to get the best of both worlds – a coherent overview of a wide variety of views.

Criteria for success

Christopher Mayfield, who recently retired as Bishop of Manchester and is a patron of MODEM, wrote a letter to me expressing his hopes for this book.

After saying how delighted he was to hear about the new book *Creative Church Leadership* in the making, he added that it looked very exciting. He also pointed out that the term 'leadership' resonates more with church people than does the term 'management', while 'creativity' is always much sought after. These are his hopes for the book:

That it will be helpful to those who seek to offer creative church leadership among people who live in inner-city or outer-estate communities as well as in suburban communities.

That it will help people to get started in thinking who they are and what they could/should be about. Some are frightened of 'management speak' while others feel that it is unhelpful. But others would like some help that makes few rather than many assumptions and is pitched at the level of people learning to drive for the first time. Later they can swap their red L plate for green ones and eventually become Grand Prix drivers, but initially they need to get started!

That it will help people who have got started to resolve some of the difficulties they will encounter on the way such as apathy among those whom they seek to lead, the absence of consensus about the way forward, conflict, etc.

That it will help people who have got started to review their journey and to plan the next stage.

That it will help church leaders to find creative ways of resourcing church members both to worship and pray, and to run their churches well, etc., and also to think and act creatively in their domestic life and their daily work, the latter area being totally neglected by most church leaders!

That it will offer some models (stories) of how people have discovered and given creative church leadership – not only historically but also in today's world. Some people thrive on intellectual, reasoned argument; but many learn as much or more from reading about contemporary experiments and initiatives, some of which have blossomed, others having stumbled or failed. Stories often tell us more than rhetoric!

I'm happy to go along with this. If the book proves to be helpful in these ways, it will have been well worthwhile producing it.

A new foundation for church leadership

One of the risks of a book like this one is that they inspire enthusiasm but without creating a following. But fortuitously the publication of this book coincides with the launch by the Church of England of a Foundation for Church Leadership, itself an example of the very kind of creative church leadership we are talking about. It shows it can be done! I am delighted that the Chairman of the Foundation's Trustees, Michael Turnbull CBE, lately Bishop of Durham, accepted my invitation to outline the purpose and aims of this new foundation.

The pillars we build on

Too often the churches are accused of being ill informed and amateur when they address subjects. To guard against this danger we have attempted to establish the 'state of play' intellectually both in the study of leadership in general and in the more specialised area of church leadership and management.

To that end, and through the good offices of John Marks, both a member of MODEM and Trustee of the Foundation for Church Leadership, the Mulberry Trust provided some funds for research. For this benefaction we are most truly grateful.

We divided this research into two. We commissioned the Centre for Leadership Studies at the University of Exeter to give us an annotated list of 'best books' on leadership – no easy task – and a brief guide to the chief centres of advanced studies in leadership and leadership development.

Simultaneously we commissioned the Lincoln Theological Institute at the University of Manchester to carry out a similar survey on church leadership and development. The results can be found below. Although far from exhaustive and inevitably to some extent subjective, both surveys give us a starting point for further research and development.

Finally

Finally, I thank everyone who has helped to make this book possible, not least Malcolm Grundy, immediate past Chairman of MODEM, and our fellow members of the Management Committee for entrusting me with the editorship of this book: I hope it proves a worthy third volume in MODEM's (first) trilogy of publications and that it helps to produce not just creative church leadership but also a stronger belief in a creative God of love. That is the note I wish to be uppermost. David Jenkins, latterly Bishop of Durham, also a contributor to this book, expressed it well in these sentences in his autobiography *The Calling of a Cuckoo* (New York and London, Continuum, 2002, p. 170):

> The churches seem determined to trap the dynamics of God within the self-centred constructions of religion. Even the church cannot keep a good God down. God has not stopped. As creator he calls us to be co-creators with him and contributors to the untrammelled energy of God's unending agenda of love.

Part 1

1 Overview: passing the ball to you

JOHN ADAIR

There are two kinds of servants, Pascal once said. The servants who carry torches and go ahead to light the way, and the servants who come behind carrying the luggage and picking up the bits. No prizes for guessing in what role John Nelson has cast me! Given that the torches of my fellow contributors have so illuminated the subject, the task of pulling the threads together is going to be fun.

My plan is to reflect here upon each of the elements on components – LEADERSHIP, CREATIVE and CHURCH – that make up our title, so that by way of summary we are all more-or-less clear about what they mean. The result should be a rough-and-ready framework. The significance of rolling them together into one concept is, of course, precisely what each contributor has been invited to explore. Rather than attempting to identify some general themes in the collection as a whole, I have chosen to offer later a few comments on each of the chapters which I hope will reveal an underlying unity.

I have called that section 'Points to ponder or take away'. As you will see, they are really no more than some random points I have picked out for my own reflection and to develop further. You are better off if you have been making your own list of such points.

Let me say up-front, too, that both John and I hope that you will take away some 'action points' to implement from your acquaintance with this book. It is not a book *about* creative church leadership, it is a book *for* creative church leaders – of all ages, in all churches and at all levels – especially those occupying senior leadership roles now who are aged fifty years or over. There is a tendency for this age group to be written off. Field Marshal Lord Montgomery once wrote a letter to me stressing the importance of leadership development 'at Sandhurst, in our universities and especially among the young in general, *for it is wasted on the old*' (my italics). That is not quite the way we see things now! Learning for leadership is the journey of a lifetime. Unless you are one of those few geniuses born to lead you will find here a wealth of philosophy, principles, lessons and practical tips that will keep you singing until you reach the end of the road.

Speaking for myself I found something else I know I need –
inspiration. Plato once said, 'those who have torches will hand
them on to others'. What I catch from these leaders and thinkers is a
light from their torches which I hope I may be able to hand on to
others.

Leadership

Leadership comes from an old North European word meaning a path,
road, way or course of a ship at sea. It's a journey word. A leader is
someone who shows the way, characteristically by leading from in
front, and taking people with them. In a looser sense it is used about
those who step out in front of others in order to speak on their behalf,
such as the foreman of a jury. Those with the authority to speak are
often the chief ones, those in charge. Such presumably are the church
'leaders' (Greek *hegoumenoi*) mentioned twice in the Epistle to the
Hebrews.

In this more general sense every society, institution, organisation
and group has its leaders. They are known under a variety of titles.
These are people who occupy the role of leadership. Whether or not
they are true leaders – that is, those who perform the necessary functions of leadership – is, of course, another matter. A ship's figurehead
looks like a person and goes first, ahead of everyone else on board, but
it is merely a painted wooden effigy. Many so-called leaders are
almost as useless figureheads, but rather more expensive.

We now know a great deal about the role of leadership in working
groups and organisations. We know what kinds of personal qualities
or characteristics, professional or technical knowledge and social
skills someone needs if they are going to be perceived by others to be
a leader, especially an excellent leader. At the core of our modern
understanding of that role, in my opinion at least, lies a breakthrough
in thinking achieved around the middle of the last century. Present in
all working groups, it suggests, are three areas of overlapping need:
the need to achieve the common task, the need to be held together as
a working harmonious unity, and the needs which individuals bring
with them by virtue of being persons. These are interactive for good or
ill, and can be represented as three circles (see Figure 1.1).

In order to meet these requirements, certain *functions* have to be
performed, such as *defining* the task, *planning*, *briefing*, *controlling*, *supporting* and *evaluating*. Broadly speaking, a function is what you do as
opposed to a quality which is what you are. But there isn't a hard-and-
fast distinction. Some qualities suggest capacity for providing actions

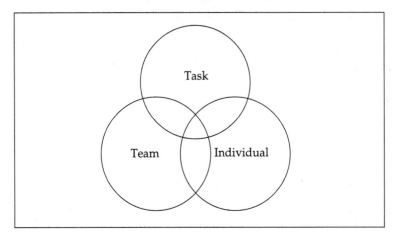

Figure 1.1

that are necessary and appropriate; others may be like adverbs describing or informing *how* a function is carried out.

The Semitic or biblical version of the three-circle model (which stands in the Greek tradition of impersonal or abstract thought) is the *shepherd-and-flock* metaphor of leadership. The shepherd leads his flock in front over ten or more miles to pasture; he maintains the unity of his flock; and he cares for each individual sheep. Almost all the elements of our modern functional model are available in the ancient pastoral model.

'I am the good shepherd,' says Jesus. The Greek word for *good* here is not *agathos* (morally good) but *kalos*, skilled, proficient, professional. This self-description takes on even more resonance when it is known that the Jewish rabbis of his day apparently regarded professional shepherds as being technically sinners in the same category as the tax-collectors or publicans and harlots.

Leadership and management

Until about twenty years ago *management* was the dominant concept, and leadership – if considered at all – was regarded as merely a part of it, a synonym for staff-management. But a revolution has taken place. Leadership is now seen as equal if not more important than management. Why?

The answer lies in one word – *change*. Change throws up the need for leaders and leaders bring about change. The first condition is much stronger than the second. In times of change and crisis people look for leadership, but even the best leader will struggle to bring about change in an organisation or institution which is insulated from and averse to change. Would you place churches in that category?

Leadership is about providing direction on the journey – all changes are journeys of one kind or another, and all journeying implies change. Leaders also create teams, inspire others, lead by example and do some of the work themselves. Management, by contrast, has overtones of day-to-day running of things in a steady state, controlling (a financial word by origin), administration – virtually a synonym for management – systems, and the husbanding of scarce resources. Managers traditionally manage at one remove from the actual work: they don't get their hands dirty.

Levels of leadership

Leadership exists on three broad levels: *team* (about ten people), *operational* – where you are running a significant part of the organisation – and *strategic*, the whole organisation. *Strategic* is made up of two Greek words: *stratos*, a large spread-out body of people and *egy*, the root of leader, which we have already encountered in the Epistle to the Hebrews and find again in our English word *hegemony* (in Greek it has a rough breathing that gives the *h* sound).

As organisations have downsized or delayed, cutting out unnecessary levels of management, this bony structure of the three domains becomes more apparent. In the Metropolitan Police in London, for example, we find Police Sergeants (team), 32 Borough Commanders (operational) and the Commissioner (strategic). You will find, too, the same three levels in the much smaller community of a Benedictine monastery[1] or in a large global institution like the Roman Catholic Church – every practising Catholic knows the name of their parish priest, their bishop and the Pope.

There is a useful distinction between line and staff leadership. The *line* is there to deliver the goods and the *staff* are there to give specialist help and support. Sometimes role confusion follows when an organisation imposes a new level on an old. In the Church of England, for example, the widespread introduction of suffragan bishops on the one hand and of diocesan secretaries with their professional staffs on the other seriously eroded the traditional role of archdeacons. The solutions were to abolish or merge the office of archdeacon or to redevelop it as a staff leadership role, a course which I proposed with some success to the Diocese of York in 1974.[2]

The same principles of leadership apply at all levels, which simplifies things. At the strategic level, however, greater complexity is encountered in the interaction of the institution with its environment, which includes other similar organisations or bodies within its field. The mental equipment a strategic leader needs to cope with the complexity is roughly what the Greeks called *phronesis*, practical wisdom. It was the quality that leaders such as Pericles and Themistocles displayed. I have suggested that it has three elements in its make-up: intelligence, experience and goodness. The word occurs, incidentally, in the New Testament, as well as playing a significant part in Aristotelian ethics.[3]

Leadership and vision

The linking of *leadership* and *vision* emerged in American studies in the 1980s. It was a useful prompt, because although the connection between the two concepts is already there in the tradition about leadership, speaking for myself I had completely overlooked it. It was associated with a new emphasis on the personal qualities of leaders, especially giving inspiration. Charisma was in vogue.

Yet not all leaders are visionaries; not all visionaries are leaders. What is vision? Literally it means eyesight. You cannot lead others on a physical journey if you are unable to see, as Jesus said in a proverb he quoted: 'If a blind man leads a blind man, both will fall into the pit.'

In a more metaphorical sense, *vision* means a sharpness of understanding – thoughtfulness, provision or foresight, acuity. *Sight* is a less formal term for the same concept, and both these words apply to something seen. *Vision*, here, would indicate something seen as in a dream or hallucination, or something that may be illusory, imaginary, ideal or supernatural. Not necessarily unreal, though. 'An ideal is a flaming vision of reality,' said Joseph Conrad.

A vision in this latter, imaginary or ideal sense is often dressed in familiar clothes as merely the restoration of some vanished state of affairs or 'golden age', but it always introduces something new into the picture. An artist with vision (and skill) produces a work of art; a leader with vision (and skill) may, if the conditions are right, be a catalyst for change. Both artist and leader are exhibiting creative imagination and, in their different ways, bringing something new and of value into existence which was not there before. Vision without task is a dream, it has been said, just as task without vision is merely a form of drudgery. Someone expressed much the same idea thus:

> Vision without action is merely a dream
> Action with vision just passes the time
> Vision with action can change the world.

So a leader with vision has to break the gold coin down into the silver of tasks and the small change of daily steps or actions while still keeping the spirit of 'going for gold'.

The vision of Jesus

What is immediately clear to anyone with the above knowledge about leadership in reading the Synoptic Gospels is that Jesus is a visionary leader *sans pareil*. His vision was expressed in that difficult Aramaic phrase which we render in English as the *Kingdom of God*. What it means can only be learnt by studying the Synoptic Gospels, for there are virtually no other sources. It is a combination of two ideas: the power of God already at work and intervening decisively in the here-and-now; and, secondly, the concept of a new age as foretold by the prophets as having dawned, its consummation being imminent. The key point is that Jesus' vision of the Kingdom of God – both now and soon – is a vision of the Kingdom *on earth*. He is not speaking of a kingdom which people might experience in heaven, entered by the gate of death.

It is better to think of it as God's vision. Jesus offered himself – and he was 'called' – to be the leader in its realisation. Our general knowledge of leadership now illuminates much of what Jesus does. He communicates the vision and he lives it; he sets a task for himself, calls others, teaches them the leadership appropriate to the Kingdom and he leads them, from in front. He shares their dangers and hardships, and ultimately he gives his life, literally, in the common cause.[4]

You can kill a man but you cannot kill a vision. The seeds of that vision had already taken root in the minds and imaginations of those around Jesus, the seedlings of the Church. In his lifetime Jesus had pointed to healings, exorcisms, the power of his words and, above all, the forgiveness of sins as signs of the Kingdom; these were eclipsed by the greatest sign of all, God's act in raising him from the dead. Inspired by their vision of the 'Risen Lord' and with hope burning anew that the Lord would soon lead in the Kingdom, the disciples went back to work with renewed energy. Now they proclaimed not only the message *of* Jesus but the message *about* Jesus. The soon-expected coming of the Kingdom and the *Parousia*, the Second Coming, had fused in their imaginations into a single world-shattering and world-transforming event.

Creative

Until the Renaissance, the word *create*, from the Latin verb *creare*, was reserved for the original divine creation of the world. Since then, 'to create' or to be 'creative' (an eighteenth-century word) came to be applied to the human faculty for making or producing in present and future. It sits now with a set of other words that apply to the active and explorative mind, such as *imaginative, inventive, original* and *resourceful*.

But Genesis still hovers in the distinctive senses of *creative*. For it is suggestive of creators or creations that employ ordinary materials in extraordinary ways. *Creative* is also the most appropriate word for situations where the raw materials and the finished product are very different from each other.

Creative leadership

The word *creative* and its cognates are now so overused as positive noises that their coinage is now debased. As John Tusa writes:

> Stripped of any special significance by a generation of bureaucrats, civil servants, managers and politicians, lazily used as political margarine to spread approvingly and inclusively over any activity with a non-material element to it, the word 'creative' has become almost unusable.[5]

How, then, does the adjective *creative* properly qualify leadership? As a general principle, I suggest, *the more specified the task is, the less room there is for creativity*. We don't expect a surgeon removing our appendix or a captain of an airliner to be creative – they are taking us on a highly specified journey.

In contrast, if the teacher gives children some materials and a canvas and says 'Paint a picture', that is certainly an invitation to be creative. Note that the necessary condition of freedom is also there. Freedom, of course, can paralyse as well as liberate. In order to get going, a child may want to say to the teacher: 'Give me a clue. What sort of picture do you have in mind?'

What Jesus does, I suggest, is to give us a clue – or a set of clues – but Jesus leaves us to work out for ourselves the mystery of the Kingdom. The best way of understanding how Jesus worked (and works) in this respect, to my mind, bizarre as it sounds, is to consider the case of one of the greatest misleaders of history, Adolf Hitler. It's an extreme case of studying *black* in order to know the meaning of *white*!

Hitler gave no orders, enunciated no tasks. He talked. He shared his vision of an empire on earth purged of the 'unclean' Jews. His listeners, his unholy band of spellbound disciples, were expected – or persuaded themselves that they were so constrained – to take action. They had to identify the tasks; they had to build the extermination camps and manage the whole ghastly business of the killing of six million people. There were no directives, nothing on paper – just a rambling, incoherent, nightmare vision and a group of powerful, ruthless and over-mighty subordinates and efficient middle-ranking bureaucrats vying with each other to give effect to the ideas of the *Führer*, Leader, as a means of being close to him, to enjoy his favour, to bask in his power and glory, and – one day – to expect great rewards when the empire was complete.

Hitler's personal leadership style, in this respect, has been linked to the current German military system known as *Augsfrautactik*, which has long since been adopted by the British and American armies as 'Mission Command'. In essence the general sets the *mission* and gives out no more than an outline plan. Well-trained operational leaders, working as a team, are expected to break it down into *tasks, aims, objectives* and *time-lines*, co-ordinating their plans with each other. It is actually a military form of the principle of subsidiarity so clearly described by Charles Handy and Gillian Stamp in their chapters. In other words, it is as if through Jesus we are given the vision or the 'big picture' but God is not going to do what we can and should be doing. That sounds rather bare and uncompromising, but it means that we are expected to use all our initiative, creative imagination, discernment, practical wisdom and skill. The worst policy is to bury all these in the ground and wait for God to appear. That is to misunderstand the situation. For as Jesus reveals, our actions and God's actions are not two distinct things: they are together as hand in glove.

Creativity and vocation

The coupling of creativity with vocation may seem an odd one. Yes, artists, writers, sculptors and composers are creative, but what is the warrant for arguing that vocation is creative? There is a link, I suggest. All creative people tend to be vocational, and vocational people are often the more creative ones in their field. Leadership is best understood as a second calling which emerges from the first.[6]

The relation of creativity and vocation was first suggested by Dorothy Emmett, Emeritus Professor of Philosophy at Manchester University. In *Function, Purpose and Powers* (1958) she explored the interrelationships between the three elements readily identified in the three-circle model: *Task* (Purpose), *Team Maintenance* (Function) and *Individuals* (Powers). She argued that the 'innersprings' or creative powers of individuals, which she associated with religious calling, were essential for the life and vitality of institutions, especially for their purpose. And administrators, the functional maintainers of equilibrium in an organisation, would transcend their function in such organisations and be far more than bureaucrats.

'The Christian calling is to love,' writes Gary Badcock.

> The ideal of love alone can reflect the whole of the teaching of Jesus and the ethic of the kingdom of God; it is also love alone that can provide an adequate answer to the question, 'What will I do with my life?'

It is, moreover, in the context of 'the kingdom as something present . . . that the Christian doctrine of vocation is ultimately located'.[7]

So, to put it simply, Christian vocation – both the general call to love and the more specific call to use our particular talents in the service of others – has everything to do with the Kingdom of God on earth. Calling to the ordaining ministry of the churches is only one small part of a much bigger picture. Yet, at present, the churches don't appear to see it that way.

Church

I come to the last of the three elements in our title, the Joker between two Kings. What is its significance or value? Is *Church* simply a field in which leadership or management is exercised, like *military*, *education*, *health* or *local government* – a segment of the *voluntary sector*? Or is this kind of thinking an unconscious product of the long process of secularisation?

Church is our English equivalent to the Greek/Latin *ecclesia*, a secular word that meant a gathering of citizens especially for the purpose of an election or public business. But the northern European word *church* is much more specific than the Greek: it was coined for the job. It derives from the Greek *kuriakos*, 'of the lord'. The lord in question is, of course, Jesus surnamed 'the Christ'.

Lord, in turn, is another old English word that stems, appropriately enough, from the Anglo-Saxon for a 'loaf-giver'. 'Acknowledged leader' is one of its several accepted senses, and the one most appropriate in this context. Jesus Christ is the acknowledged leader of the Church. By labelling any group, organisation or institution a *church*

(I shall use the lower-case initial letter) a claim is being implicitly or explicitly made that it belongs to the Church in the broad sense. The claim – which may be called into question – is that that church as an expression or part of the Church is 'of the Lord' and that Jesus Christ is its acknowledged leader. My argument would be that this entails an acceptance *in the heart*, not just on the lips, of the vision or purpose of the Founder. If I am wrong on this point I hope for correction.

Purpose and Church

From the Latin *proponere*, to propose, purpose has the primary sense of something set up as an object or end to be attained – or the object or result aimed at. It carries the overtones of a resolute, determined or deliberate movement towards a result, as well as the end towards which one chooses to direct activity. A result can be thought of as a consequence, issue or conclusion. It often comes at the end of a series of events.

The specific overtone of *purpose* in either use – movement towards or result – is that of significance. In other words, what we are talking about has meaning and importance.

An individual, group or organisation may pursue more than one thing at a time, may have a plurality of activities. Yet our natural tendency in such a situation is to try to identify a key overarching *purpose*, even if we have to take a step up into generality or abstraction in order to do so. Our minds are quite capable of these gear changes.

Take a university, for example. Its distinctive activities are *research* and *teaching*, to which you can add *administration*. Some will argue that the real purpose of a university is research; others that handing on knowledge to students comes first. Yet if we define the purpose one level up as *learning* – to advance, promote and pass on learning – we encompass both research and teaching. There may be tensions between them, but not conflict. If you want to use a different word, each could be expressed as aims, and – when it comes to strategic thinking and planning – cast in terms of goals, policies, objectives and programmes.

Can there be a similar expression of *purpose* for the Church (and therefore churches)? I do not know, but I believe so.

There is a general consensus that the Church does not exist for itself, just to survive. It is there *for* something. That for may be expressed in very different ways, inviting outsiders to conclude that the Church is possessed of seven purposes or none – or at least none that a clear majority can agree on.

Yes, there does seem to be a lack of clarity of thought here. It can be a strength. As Elizabeth Welch mentions, the Church always has to be wary of charismatic 'Missionaries' who claim to know both the destination and the exact route!

We may have difficulty in formulating the true purpose; sometimes you can have purpose without being able to put it into words even to yourself. At least we can falsify statements of the Church's purpose: we know what cannot gain acceptance.

No Christian church, for example, could accept a statement of purpose that left out the vision of Jesus, the Kingdom of God on earth. It would be tantamount to erasing the first petition from the Lord's Prayer: 'Your kingdom come; your will be done on *earth* as it is in heaven'.

To summarise:

- The Church (and churches) do, by universal agreement, have *purpose*. Like a university or college they are communities with a purpose beyond themselves. They do not just exist.
- And we know that it is a *creative* purpose. If it is God's purpose, how can it be otherwise?
- There is no authorised definition of what it is, and it would probably be dysfunctional if such a form of words existed. But we can say what it is not. Definitions, for instance, that leave out the vision of Jesus Christ, the acknowledged leader of the Church, will not last long.
- That vision is contained in the Gospels, which all Christians accept as guides in this respect.
- The first commandment in any institution, organisation or working community is to be clear about its purpose. Once purpose is seen clearly and agreed upon then other things tend to fall into place.

Notes

1. Kit Dollard, Anthony Marrett-Crosby OSB, Timothy Wright OSB, *Doing Business with Benedict: The Rule of Saint Benedict and Business Management, a Conversation*, London, Continuum, 2002.
2. See my *Report on the Diocese of York* (1970). About a decade later, Archbishop John Habgood wrote to inform me that the principles of the report were still being applied, albeit with modifications. A similar report on the Diocese of Chichester (1974) was never implemented, due to a change of bishop. See also my *The Becoming Church*, London, SPCK, 1976.
3. See my *Effective Strategic Leadership*, London, Pan, 2002 and, for a

further discussion of *phronesis*, *The Inspirational Leader*, London, Kogan Page, 2003.

4. These are themes explored in my *The Leadership of Jesus*, London, SCM-Canterbury Press, 2002.

5. John Tusa, *On Creativity: Interviews Exploring the Process*, London, Methuen, 2003.

6. These themes are explored in my *How to Find Your Vocation*, London, SCM-Canterbury Press, 2001.

7. Gary D. Badcock, *The Way of Life: A Theology of Christian Vocation*, Grand Rapids, MI, William B. Eerdmans, 1998, p. 52.

Part 2

2 A theological reflection

MALCOLM GRUNDY

The Resurrection of Jesus Christ fulfilled the purpose of his life and death. It deepens the ways in which individuals and communities understand how they live today. Any book about creative church leadership has to have at its heart this key experience of the Christian faith. Resurrection brings new life and hope from despair, often in surprising new ways. Such a deliberately optimistic and challenging title as 'Creative Church Leadership' for the contents of this book should arouse the interest of church leaders and many others. It might challenge us all to see how much ideas of Resurrection energise our faith, our thoughts and our actions.

Our Western culture tends towards a belief that any leadership exercised will eventually become discredited – it is more like crucifixion than a life-giving experience. There are ample grounds for disillusionment with all too many examples of new starts running into the sand. Hopes aroused by a new prime minister or government, a new senior manager or director of a charity, a bishop, moderator or chairman, and even of the local vicar or minister, seen in worldly terms can go the same way. Leadership seen through the filter of what God has given to us in the life, death and Resurrection of Jesus Christ can look very different. The contributors of chapters in this book, creative people in their own areas of achievement, point us to the implications for living with the experience of that divine creative event. In this chapter I want to set out my reasons for being sure that we must start with Resurrection.

Can church leadership be creative?

Church leadership has to be creative. I can make such a statement because the faith of the Christian churches is based on one all-consuming creative event – the Resurrection of Jesus Christ from the dead. The story of faith read either back through the Scriptures from the story of the initial act of creation, or forward through the experience of Christian people, demonstrates that a God of surprises perpetually takes us on to experiences of new life. This knowledge of new life often comes as a result of defeat, desperation and despair. It requires vision and responsible action to manage and supervise the particular kind of new life which it offers. Resurrection requires responsibility based on the model of how Jesus lived and what he taught. Handled well we can say that Resurrection experiences allow glimpses of God's Kingdom to be located and nurtured in the experiences of everyday life.

What will it look like?

Creative church leadership will have all the characteristics of our wrestling to understand and apply God's actions in Jesus Christ and those of the prophets and patriarchs before him for today. It will have at its core the central Resurrection event of this faith demonstrated in contemporary circumstances. Creative leadership of any kind, and particularly within the churches, will have a transforming newness about it. Through the eyes of this faith we shall see old situations which led us to near despair in new ways. We shall see new possibilities in what we are doing now and we shall bring renewed insights into the next set of problems which will face us. Experiences of living out a Resurrection faith will come through difficult and confusing situations being addressed in the light of a new way of seeing the purposes of life. These qualities and approaches need to be seen in all Christian people but they will be more openly apparent in those whose responsibilities are exercised in public.

The Resurrection life

To live a creative Christian life is not just to try to work with integrity and to follow, so far as they can be understood, the teachings of Jesus. It is to live with an understanding of an experience which gives a new interpretation to everything else. It is that from despair and darkness, betrayal and death, can come a new life whose characteristics are peace and reconciliation and an ability to forgive and overcome human failure and sinfulness. This invigorating task is understood as a lifelong commitment to redeem often hopeless situations. This is the Resurrection-based application of leadership that I want to see. Let it begin to be seen in the churches and then, through creative Christian leadership, flow out into the world. We may discover, however, that if we strengthen a listening and learning church, this will be a two-way traffic because we shall discover that God is just as active in the world.

Resurrection leadership in the New Testament

It might be tempting to think that Christian principles are all that are needed to lead a good life, that Christianity can stand on its own feet without the Resurrection. The first disciples did not find it so. For them the gospel without the Resurrection was not merely a gospel without a final chapter: it was not a gospel at all. Jesus Christ had, it is true, taught and done great things but he did not allow his disciples to rest on his achievements. He led them into paradox, perplexity and darkness, and there he left them. There they would have remained had he not been raised from death. The significance of his appearing and presence with the disciples after he had been crucified and buried was that his Resurrection threw new light backwards on the life and death that went before. It showed, to those who would see, a unity of purpose in God's way of reaching out to redeem the perplexing experiences of life (see Luke 24.13–end).

The emptiness of success

In human terms one of the things a person in any leadership position realises is not the privilege of elevated status, but the transitory nature of any achievement. Success has vacuous adulation which only lasts until the next crisis or change of public mood.

The preacher who gave the book of Ecclesiastes gave us also the despairing cry 'Vanity of vanities, all is vanity'. The same author has given a well-known series of 14 experiences of life when we are told, 'to everything there is a season' – 'a time to reap, a time to sow . . .' (Ecclesiastes 3). The creative leader knows all about timing. But an understanding that everything has its appointed time can lead only to confirm a tragic view. Things and actions may have their time. They pass and other things have their time. The most you can do is enjoy them while they are here. The creative leader who wonders if there can be any more to it than this asks, 'Can anything break this circle in which all life moves?' Can inspired or enlightened people enter into the mystery of this timing? Is even the desire for mystery all vanity and frustration? Or is there something else?

Timing and God's time

The modern manager, church leader or minister seems more conscious than ever before that they have no time. Life is a cascade of events which eat up working and leisure time and leave little time to think. This pressured, unreflective existence can lead to an awareness that the leader has not produced the right time. That their calculations and timings were wrong and that hopes raised by them have been dashed. The creative Christian leader can begin with the Ecclesiastes experience that all things are timed with birth and death, and that they are beyond human timing. Even creative leadership without faith can be put off by the experience of a cycle which cannot be broken. The point of the resurrection is that when Jesus went up to Jerusalem he pronounced that 'his hour had come, that the Kingdom of God was at hand' (Matthew 26.45).

The theologian Paul Tillich, writing an essay called 'The right time' in his book *The New Being*, says that 'He was pronouncing a victory over the law of vanity.'[1] He says that 'This hour is not subject to the circle of life and death and all the other circles of vanity.' The significance of Christ's death and Resurrection is that, although the moment passed, an eternal significance remains. It says to us that whatever in this moment happens to us has infinite significance. Our planning may seem to be from day to day, moment to moment, but the experience of the Resurrection says that the moments are not lost, they have eternal significance. This is because their meaning lies not ahead, where vanity will swallow it up, but above where eternity affirms it. This is the effectiveness of creative leadership and the use of timing. Tillich says to people of faith and discernment, 'Through our timing God times the coming of His Kingdom; through our timing He elevates the time of vanity to the time of fulfilment.'[2]

St Paul says the same thing and affirms the value of our attempts to transform failing situations,

> Though our outer nature is wasting away our inner nature is renewed every day – because we look not to things that are seen but to the things that are unseen. For the things that are seen are transient, but the things that are unseen are eternal. (2 Corinthians 4.16–18)

In these words and their resonances the everyday experience of the leader and the eternal message of a Resurrection which points beyond time become united. In our everyday language this is being excited about an idea, seeing the longest-term possibilities of our short-term actions, about goals and transforming visions which come with this

Resurrection faith. But our immediate concerns are not our ultimate concerns, therein lies the mistake. When eternity calls in time, activism gains a purpose. When a longer perspective is glimpsed, then creative leadership is transfigured from creative problem-solving towards leadership which transmits a vision which redeems and reunites. Through apparently transitory and sometimes vain activities we communicate something of a new life which will have different qualities and dimensions because familiar and challenging situations are seen in a different way.

Redeeming hopeless situations

The creative leader will face some of the same issues which the first Christians had to grapple with. They thought that Jesus would return within weeks or months and that there would be a rapid final judgement. They and their followers thought that there would be a quick solution! Like all those with responsibilities they had to learn to live with the reality of indifference and frustrating situations and with those who oppose them in a deliberate way. Living with integrity and working away at present problems brought them to see that a resurrection church was not escapist nor one which gave shallow, easy answers. It was one which was committed to facing real-life situations and to discover how to put faith into practice. Whatever else this faith meant its implications led to the need to continue, as Christ's disciples and part of his risen body, the work of redeeming situations with little hope in them. Creative Christian leadership will see divine possibilities in situations about which a faithless approach would despair.

Transformed communities

Seeing the possibilities for transforming communities will energise a creative leader. Whether in the workplace, in community work or in the churches, unless those who work or live in a situation can be accompanied towards a vision which gives them hope, no lasting achievement will be made. There have to be underlying beliefs about what is possible before hope can be restored. If employees think that a company is doomed, the quality of their work and the product they produce declines. If a congregation thinks it has no future it becomes demoralised and begins to defend ideas which belong to past solutions. Sometimes leadership requires a careful analysis of a situation and then acts on the possible solutions which emerge. Often an inspired leader acts on intuition. They bring renewal without a worked-out strategy. It seems to come from 'the spirit' of who they are. This is incarnational work. By coming alongside people in their distress and showing the divine possibilities open to them a transformation occurs. Sensitive leadership allows this to happen. It is what occurred when Jesus was with people in a crowd or while meeting them over a meal or in private. It is only after the Resurrection that they could understand the real significance of his teaching, his healing work and his life of ultimate self-sacrifice.

Open doors

A creative Christian leader will open doors so that those who are searching for faith or for solutions to the questions with which life presents them can make some progress. In religious terms churches and church leaders, bishops or ministers, can be the 'sacred arch' through which people travel to mark stages in their life's journey. Creative leadership takes a human experience and transforms it.

Often these doors of understanding are opened by personal pastoral contact. Sometimes they are made through introducing a searcher to a sympathetic group of people. The very first step towards any solution is to understand that there is a welcome for those who are searching. They bring their questions and we test out our faith as we dialogue with them. Creative leadership allows doors to open so that searching questions can be explored. Permissions are needed from the leader and from the atmosphere they create. Jesus pointed those enquirers who came to him with questions to the commandments. He encouraged them to go home, after a meeting with him, and work out what those commandments mean in a particular situation. Once the door of faith is opened then searchers and believers move on to creative new understandings of challenging situations. Creative leadership which gives permission for exploration and inspires, through example, opens doors to new possibilities of Resurrection.

Creative interfaith leadership

We now face new challenges in the leadership of our churches. The same question faces leaders of communities and nations. It is how to enable those who belong to different world faiths to live side by side. This work will go alongside, accompanying those who are moving along different stages in their own spiritual journey.

Creative church leadership will enable and encourage those whose route and faith journey has been different. It will help them to realise that they are in partnership with Christians on a journey of the spirit. It is perhaps between Christianity and Islam that new opportunities are being forced upon us. Creative leaders will see in this a sense of God's time presenting an opportunity. Here there is a new resurrection challenge. We are forced to look much more closely than before at what shape public and civic religion will take for the future. In Western countries where there are significant minorities of members of other faiths we have little choice but to discover that God is forcing us to forge new partnerships. There is just as great a challenge in other parts of the world where Christians are a minority group. Creative faith leadership will learn to take its own stand with majority faith partners who may in the recent past have been brutal and discriminatory against Christians.

MODEM's contributors are alive to the creative possibilities which will arise for their readers. None can be more pressing than to translate the experience of Resurrection which was the seedbed of the early church into contemporary experience. If this can be done with faith partners their contribution to building new societies with values which arise from world faiths will be all the greater. The one story is in the other.

At the second Building Bridges seminar between Christian and Muslim leaders in Qatar the final communiqué issued by Archbishop Rowan Williams used texts which speak of Resurrection.

> Muslims confess their faith in a God who 'brings the living out of the dead and he brings the dead out of the living' (Qur'an, Sura 30 v 19–30). Christians strive to 'live in the presence of the God who gives life to the dead and calls into existence the things which do not exist' (Romans Ch 4, v 17). Without compromising our respective convictions, we found it possible to listen to how each tradition of faith understood this fundamental vision of the creator's presence and action.

Notes

1. Paul Tillich, *The New Being*, London, SCM Press, 1964, p. 167.
2. Tillich, *New Being*, p. 168.

3 One question and ten answers

CHARLES HANDY

Imagine yourself as you contemplate your new job, one where you have been told that creative leadership is required. You will, if you are sensible, begin by asking yourself what sort of organisation you are entering and what your role will be. It's an innocent-sounding question, perhaps, but one fraught with confusions, particularly where church organisations are concerned. For, despite what some management texts imply, organisations are not all the same, and the rules that work in some are disastrous in others.

A religious organisation belongs to the class of voluntary, not-for-profit organisations. Even that does not tell you very much. Voluntary organisations, rather obviously, are not businesses, yet some of them do share some of the same characteristics. That is because voluntary organisations differ widely amongst themselves and the subset of religious organisations will also contain its own differences. You cannot begin to lead one effectively unless you understand how and why they differ and why this matters. To start with, every voluntary organisation will fall into one of three categories or some combination of them:

- Mutual support
- Service delivery
- Campaigning

Each category makes different assumptions about the purpose of the organisation, the motivations of those involved, the nature and location of power and authority, and the terms and conditions of involvement. Many voluntary organisations start off as mutual support groups, then move to providing organised services to their members or clients, ultimately supported by campaigning efforts. Church organisations have traditionally combined all three roles, giving them their own more religious titles such as fellowship, ministry and evangelism.

Mutual support

These organisations are made up of like-minded people, people with similar problems or with similar interests. They exist, as their name suggests, to offer support, friendship and comradeship. Some are support networks for people suffering from a common problem or disease. Alcoholics Anonymous is one of the best known of this type. Others include the parents of autistic children, the carers for Alzheimer sufferers or the ME Association. It would, in fact, be hard to find a problem that did not have its associated network of support. Other mutual support groups are bound together by a common leisure interest. In one study of a single suburban community, in Kingswood in Surrey, Jeff Bishop and Paul Hoggett found 300 leisure interest groups involving some 28,500 people. The early Christians were organised in this way and have their counterpart in the house groups and prayer meetings of the modern day.

Mutual-support groups need the minimum of organisation and resent hierarchy. They prefer what might be called low-profile organisation or management from underneath. The maintenance of the information base and the arrangement of places and times for meetings are the essential requirements. Leadership is an inappropriate concept for this type of organisation and were anyone to seek to take on the role it would probably be resented unless it was very discreet. Organiser or convenor are the words preferred. 'Manager' or 'Leader' are both words to be avoided.

Service delivery

Mutual-support organisations tend to start providing organised services to those of their fellowship in need. In time this aspect of their work comes to predominate. The RNIB, Mountain Rescue and The Royal National Lifeboat Institution are some of the largest. To these can be added an organisation such as The National Trust, now with twice as many members as the Church of England has regular attendees at its services. Some of these organisations are in fact so large, with so many fully paid staff, that it seems odd to include them as voluntary organisations.

The volunteer element in these organisations is largely devoted to fund-raising. Support comes in the form of subscriptions or, more actively, by soliciting funds from others, by manning the charity shops where they exist, mailing literature organising fund-raising events.

The service-delivery part of these organisations is run very much as are other organisations, in business or elsewhere. The crucial, and important, difference is that most of those working in this type of so-called voluntary organisations are there because they believe in the cause of the organisation. They are, therefore, more willing to be 'managed' than those in the mutual-support organisations, reckoning that the ends justify the means. They are even willing to accept lower than normal remuneration, which can mean, in places, that they are exploited by the management. At the same time, people cannot join the workforce of these organisations just because they share their aims. The organisations need competent, professional staff.

Governance is an important issue for these organisations. Typically they are accountable to a large and representative council. All the stakeholders, clients, government, both local and national, employees and relevant professionals are usually included. In this, councils are radically different from businesses where the board is directly responsible only to the shareholders, with a duty to take into consideration the needs of the other stakeholders who tend not to be represented. Leadership of a service-delivery organisation is exercised by both the chairperson of this council and the chief executive of the organisation.

Campaigning

Some organisations, CND in the past, The Countryside Alliance more recently, were created expressly to campaign for a cause. These organisations are led rather than managed. To be sure, they need their administration to be done effectively, their meetings to be arranged properly and their literature to be well designed and circulated, but it would be more true to talk of these activities as administration rather than management. The leader is often the dominant force in these organisations. His or her views and character shape the way things happen to a much greater degree than in the service-delivery organisations where he or she is much more a first among equals. The campaigning organisations often prefer to speak of themselves as movements rather than organisations.

The mixed organisation

Over time organisations have a tendency to include a bit of all three types. Just as the mutual-support organisations begin to arrange services for their members, so the campaigning types start to move backwards into service provision and elements of mutual support grow up among the members. Shelter started off as a campaigning organisation for the homeless, but soon saw it as its moral responsibility to put its organisation where its mouth was, and to give practical help to those whose cause it was fighting for.

This is all understandable. The problem is that the styles of leadership and management are very different for each type. A charismatic leader will be effective, may even be essential, in a campaigning organisation, but in what theorists call the machine bureaucracy of a service-delivery organisation too much charisma can be seriously disruptive.

An international-aid organisation was at one time led by a passionate and committed man who was also a galvanising speaker. He saw it as his priority to tour the country advocating his organisation's work and to visit the countries where the aid was spent. The actual management of the organisation he allocated to the Fridays when he was in town. On these days he spent most of the time going through his accumulated mail and dictating short peremptory memos to his staff. He was amazed when the staff began to mutter and finally to revolt over his long absences, his impersonal style of management and what they saw as his lack of concern for the organisation. 'Don't they understand,' he complained, 'that it is because I am so concerned that I am out and about? Why can't they grow up?' His first instinct was to replace the senior team with his own buddies, but in the end it was he who had to go. He was a great leader – of a campaigning organisation.

In contrast, when the efficient and effective head of a national service-delivery organisation accepted the decision of the council that it was necessary to supplement the service delivery with more advocacy, in order, quite sensibly, to work on the causes of the problems before they reached their doors, she applied her managerial skills to the campaigning task. But this task needed personal advocacy and the willingness to be the public face of the organisation. Her skills lay in other areas. She tried to delegate the task to others but, in reality, only she or the chair of the organisation would have been able to front the campaign. The organisation was criticised for wasting the subscriptions of its members on what they called 'unnecessary PR'.

A country parish in the Church of England fell apart when one of the churchwardens attempted to impose managerial disciplines, responsibilities and budgets on what had, up to then, been purely a fellowship organisation, a place where a dwindling number of ageing people came together of a Sunday to support and encourage each other in their daily lives. The churchwarden, quite reasonably, believed that this was not enough, that the church should have a broader purpose and that the congregation should go out, in the words of the liturgy, 'to love and serve the Lord' in the wider community and that, in the meantime, they should organise their own gatherings more systematically with proper accountabilities and standards. The organist, for instance, much loved but by now over eighty and nearly blind, should be replaced by a younger and better musician who should, if necessary, be paid. The churchwarden was fiercely resented and eventually resigned, embittered and angry, and never darkened the doors of the church again.

In all these cases well-meaning people who wanted to do the right thing failed just because they failed to understand what sort of organisation they were dealing with. It wasn't that they were wrong, just wrong for that type of organisation.

Church organisations are supposed to be a blend of all three types, something that presents a great dilemma to those who would aspire to lead them, at whatever level. The solutions are, however, clear, even if they are difficult to implement. There are, I suggest, ten principles to guide one.

First: distinguish the different functions of the organisation. The three types do not mix although they can usefully learn from each other and help each other. They will each need a different sort of organisation and management, leadership or coordination and, almost certainly, a different person or persons to do it.

Second: know thyself – the inscription carved over the old temple of Apollo at Delphi in Ancient Greece. Few of us are good at everything. It is only sensible to be clear about where one's strengths lie, what things one is good at and what things would best be done by others. Some of those others may be in the organisation, some above it, in the governing body, or outside it. The chairperson should complement the chief executive in their respective skills. Coordinators can often emerge from the surrounding corps of volunteers.

Third: put the right people in the right place. Most management devices are there because the people cannot be relied upon to do the right thing on their own. A colleague of mine was an expert in group behaviour which he taught at the university. He left to run a restaurant. One year later I met him. 'It must be great to have a chance to put all your ideas about groups to work in the real world,' I said to him. 'You know,' he said, 'I have discovered, after a lot of pain, that if you get the right people in the first place you don't need all those group techniques. It just happens.'

Fourth: remember that mixed organisations have to be a team effort. Effective teams, moreover, have a shifting leadership. Take, for instance, a rowing eight, which appears at first sight to be a group of people going backwards without speaking to each other led by the one person, the cox, who doesn't row – not too untypical of many a voluntary organisation, one might think. Closer investigation, however, reveals that they can only do that because they know each other so well, know their respective roles so well, know and agree on where they are trying to get to and, finally, are determined to do their very best to get there. If only all church organisations could say the same! Even more interestingly, the cox is only one of the leaders. There is also the official captain of the boat who is responsible for selection, morale and motivation. There is the stroke who sets the pace and, finally and sometimes most importantly, there is the coach on the bank who isn't even in the boat at all. All of them have a leadership role but, interestingly, none of them is called a leader, let alone *the* leader. What rowing crews do as a matter of course the rest of us have to work at. There are some clear messages for the churches in the parable of the rowing eight. You don't, for instance, have to be called a leader to have a leadership task. Indeed, it can be the seemingly weakest who has the most visible leadership task, while the role of the bishop should perhaps be more akin to that of the coach than to a traditional boss. Again, you don't need to discuss things if you trust each other and are clear about your tasks.

Fifth: be clear where you want to go, and how you will know if you get there. That rowing crew again! Too many church organisations aren't going anywhere. They are like a car with the engine running but without the gears engaged, a lot of noise and smoke but no progress. If you are clear in your own mind about where you are heading it will be easier to communicate that to others. But the goals must be related to the type of organisation. It is no use asking the fellowship arm to start campaigning, or a great preacher to be a bureaucratic manager, yet both will be needed. The final chart for the organisation will be a mix of goals. It helps, too, if there are some easy ways to keep the score. Numbers distort priorities, so one must take care. Bums on seats are easy to count, but that may not be, perhaps should never be, the main priority for the whole church. But if not, then what, and how do you keep the score?

Sixth: remember, however, that for things to stay the same things need to change. Everything declines after a while, projects outlive their usefulness, energies falter, people grow older, others get bored or disillusioned. Long-lived organisations reinvent themselves while still keeping their eyes fixed on the distant goals. The time to plan the new path is while the organisation is upbeat, when energies are strong and the teams committed. Left too late any reinvention is a response to a crisis when resources of money and people are at their lowest. Organisations left to themselves are reactive, they respond to external stimuli relying on their members to deal with in trays, telephone calls and emails. It is easy then to be busy without initiating anything. Wise leaders are counter-intuitive, stimulating new paths just when the current one seems to be working perfectly.

Seventh: be mindful of subsidiarity. This may be today a crucial feature of the constitution of the European Union but the principle was first enunciated by the Church, in this case Pope Leo X, who stated that it was 'against right moral order' for a higher order body to do what properly belonged to a lower order body. In more vernacular language, stealing people's choices is morally wrong. It is a sin that many organisations and governments are guilty of, largely because they don't trust the lower bodies to make what they would consider to be the right decisions. As a result many organisations reek of distrust. The churches are not guiltless. Many would like to see much more power invested once again in the parishes of the Church of England, dismantling the diocesan apparatus and returning the bishops to their role of spiritual leader without the encumbrances of the managerial duties that have been thrust upon them and for which they have been neither trained nor selected.

Eighth: don't do it unless you are passionate. You cannot lead others well unless you are totally committed to the purpose of the organisation and to the people whom you have chosen and who have themselves chosen to strive for it. If you cannot walk the talk, even live and breath your talk, you are not credible. Functionaries can do a job adequately in return for the money. They have a rational and calculative view of their psychological contract with the organisation. To lead a voluntary organisation, and particularly a religious one, requires that you draw a large part of your sense of identity from the work.

Ninth: take care, therefore, that the job does not consume you totally. Those leaders who do not invest in themselves are soon of less use to their organisations. It is not only time for recreation and renewal that is needed but also the opportunity to stand outside the organisation, to walk in other worlds, and to see your place as others see it. Even a good novel can lift you out of your too familiar space. Too much immersion blocks the ears and clouds the eyes. Creativity needs empty spaces to sprout, and is not self-fertilising. These intervals for refreshment and new thinking need to be planned and timetabled or they do not happen. Church leaders tend to be reactive in planning their years. Their culture inclines them to say 'yes' to all who ask. Bishops are known to carry two or even three years of diaries with them, mortgaging their time far in advance. Wise leaders know how to say 'no'. Asked to keep a diary for three months, one bishop divided all his days into three, morning, afternoon and evening. In three months he discovered that only seven of these periods, the equivalent of just over two days, had been free of tasks for the organisation. Shocked, he took charge of his life instead of letting others determine his diary.

Tenth: remember to keep learning. Learning is best described as experience understood in reflection. It is hard, psychologically, to stockpile learning, to learn something in advance of using it. We learn by working through problems, with help if need be, and then reflecting on the experience so that we can do it better next time. But this reflection needs help itself. We can all do with what Lord Young of Dartington once called a learning companion. Find one that you can trust, preferably outside the organisation. Leading is lonely. There are few in the organisation with whom one can share one's worries and fears, yet leaders need to possess what Keats called a negative capability, the ability to function whilst in the midst of doubts, mysteries and uncertainties.

Finally, you will need good luck. Successful people seem to create their own luck, but in reality they are the ones who see opportunity where others see problems. Apples seem to fall into their laps, but that is because they have taken the trouble to find an orchard to stand in and have shaken the odd tree.

4 Pathways to leadership

BILL ALLEN

Some years ago, a noticeboard outside one of the largest Free Church theological colleges in London bore the legend, 'TRAINING LEADERS FOR TODAY'S AND TOMORROW'S CHURCH'. The college was founded to offer training and education for the Baptist ministry, but today draws a clientele seeking to equip itself for leadership in black, independent, house and cell church groups alongside Baptists.

The noticeboard legend seemed to capture the *raison d'être* of theological colleges – the equipping of men and women for effective leadership in the local church. There are some pertinent issues that arise for those whose task it is to provide the education and training necessary to develop leaders for today's and tomorrow's church. For example, how can such a statement be turned into an appropriate curriculum for ministerial leadership training?

Any such curriculum needs to be designed with the clear intention of meeting the requirements of the intended goal. If leaders for churches are to be the outcome, then the content and the process of the training must provide explicitly for that end.

A further question arises about the curriculum content required to facilitate the development of leadership ability, which will enable potential leaders to grow into leadership during their college course and beyond it.

The purpose of this chapter is to examine two models which suggest some necessary and sufficient requirements for the training of leaders for today's and tomorrow's church. The first model, the 'Wheel' diagram, identifies the views of people in churches as to what makes for effective leadership in the Christian ministry. The second, an adaptation of the familiar 'Three-Circles' of John Adair, proposes a new model for the integration of critical components for the development of ministerial leadership.

The first model examines the requirements for Christian leadership in the church from a new perspective, that of the laity, who experience leadership from their clergy, week by week. It does not deal with the weaknesses of ministerial leadership but with the qualities and skills perceived in those who are considered 'good', that is, effective leaders in ministry by the people who took part in the information-gathering process. Hence we are dealing here with perceived standards of excellence in leadership in ministry.

Setting the agenda

Who sets the agenda for ministerial training and education? The syllabus is generally determined by members of a college faculty subject, where necessary, to the scrutiny and approval of the validating body and to denominational demands. One can argue that this is entirely appropriate since, generally, most college tutors have been ministers and have spent time serving as pastors in local churches. The difficulty with this is that a stereotypical agenda can be constructed without reference to, or consultation with, congregations who are served by the ministers produced from the colleges. Year after year, without exception, students leave these colleges to go and serve in churches, taking with them everything that others have decided is necessary for long-term, sustainable ministry. It can be argued that in providing trained ministers in this way, without consultation with the recipient churches, colleges are doing things *to* students and churches, rather than doing things *with* them, thereby neglecting to take the important requirements of the churches seriously.

Such neglect was addressed by the writer during his time as Director of Pastoral Studies at a Baptist theological college. An initiative was introduced by which discussions were entered into with a range of churches and Christian groups in order to discover what perceptions of the qualities and skills of 'good' leadership in the Christian ministry were held by people in congregations.

The underlying premise was that if such qualities and skills could be identified, then it might be possible to shape the training and education so that it would enhance the leadership ability of students and help them cultivate some of the qualities, skills and habits perceived in the 'good' leader during the training. This work recognised that Christians experience leadership from their clergy and that they form impressions of 'good' leadership from these experiences. They look for certain qualities and skills in their leaders, which are a benchmark as to how far they will actually follow the leadership offered.

Leadership is not only about those who lead, but also about those who follow. It is the followers who determine whether someone is a leader or not. What is evident from this research is that, in the local church, followers have very clear views about what they look for in, and from, their leaders when they are given an opportunity to articulate their views. This appears to be a fact that the theological colleges seemed to have ignored.

Gathering the information

Over a period of about two years a series of workshop sessions with a range of Christian groups was held. The purpose of these sessions was to identify the qualities and skills that group members reckoned were present in 'good leaders' in the ministry and to ascertain if there was any commonality of views across the different groups. The process was carried out in such a way as to relate the enquiry to those who were ordained clergy, so the question being asked was, what makes a minister a good leader?

The process

At each session, people were asked to reflect upon the ministers of whom they had had experience. They were asked to note those whom they would classify as 'good' leaders. Participants were left to make up their own minds as to how the adjective 'good' should be interpreted.

Feedback was collected and this identified the qualities, characteristics and activities of those designated 'good' leaders. This was followed by an exercise aimed at ascertaining whether or not there was any commonality in the views expressed and where it occurred among the responses, and whether the participants would choose to rank any of the qualities and characteristics as being more important and necessary for good leadership than others.

Developing the 'Wheel'

Stage 1 – Key indicators

The information gathered revealed that a large number of key attitudes, qualities and skills had been registered by the participants. These are shown in Figure 4.1 and are called, for ease of reference, key indicators.

This suggested that there was a wide range of key indicators and ability to communicate ideas; appreciates others; apt to teach; attention to detail; authority; aware of humanity; aware of world/ theological situations; close to God; communicates effectively; conceptual ability; concern for spiritual development; concern to relate faith to life; courage; creates and takes opportunities; creative thinker; delegator; devoted; discerning; emotional command; encourage/enable; equipper; evident love of God; example; firmness in confronting opposition; flexible; gains credibility; generating vision; generous in spirit; gift discerner; giving/gaining commitment; gracious; humility; humorous; inner strength; integrity; involves others; keeps confidences; listener; loves people; loves to be with people; makes people feel valued; management skills; manages change well; mission conscious; motivator; networking; not drawn into division; not traditionalist; organised; pastor's heart; people person; perceptive; persuader; plans, acts and reviews; prayerful; preaching/teaching skills; promotes growth in people; relates to others well; recognising different perspectives; relevant teacher; respected; risk taker; sense of personal purpose; sensitive to people; servant; sets high personal standards; sounds out others; student of the Word; takes personal interest; teachable; team builder; theological grasp; trainer; trustworthy; understands how people tick; visionary; world conscious

Figure 4.1 Key indicators of 'good' Christian ministers as leaders

there were strong views about what made for the 'good leader' that were registered repeatedly. Figure 4.1 lists each different response recorded. What it does not show is the number of times each indicator was repeated in each of the groups. Where there was similarity among the responses, it suggested a commonality of perception about the qualities and skills of the 'good' Christian minister as a leader.

The core qualities and skills of 'good' Christian ministers

The key indicators were grouped into six *core qualities and skills* areas, shown in Figure 4.2.

Good leaders in the ministry appear to have major strengths in each of the core qualities and skills areas of Figure 4.2. The information shows how followers in the churches assess their leaders. They appear to evaluate them on personality and character traits and their competence in ministry tasks. It is significant to note that three of the core qualities and skills areas, *spirituality*, *personal qualities* and

Figure 4.2 Core qualities and skill areas

inter-personal skills, indicate that Christian followers are intensely impressed by the character and personality of their leader. This suggests that signs of authenticity and integrity, displayed in personal and inter-personal behaviours, are valued highly.

If a church leader is to gain and retain credibility with followers, it needs to be recognised and accepted that consistency in the matching of beliefs and values with personal actions is a crucial component of 'good' Christian leadership.

The three areas, *leadership*, *management* and *communication skills*, indicate that Christian followers are also looking for leaders who demonstrate an ability to undertake the functions and roles assigned to them effectively. Credibility comes not only through the quality of the leader's persona but also through the leader's capability to undertake the ministerial role competently. From this we can deduce that the leader's character, knowledge and skills are critical components which must be addressed in the education and training of Christian leaders for the local church.

'Inventing the Wheel'

The key indicators and the core qualities and skill areas were brought together into a diagnostic tool in the 'Wheel' diagram reproduced in Figure 4.3.

The 'Wheel' was constructed from the information gathered in a way that its hub consists of the core qualities and skill areas which hold together the leader's life and work.

Each segment of the model contains one of the core areas with some examples of the key indicators connected with it. This gives a model

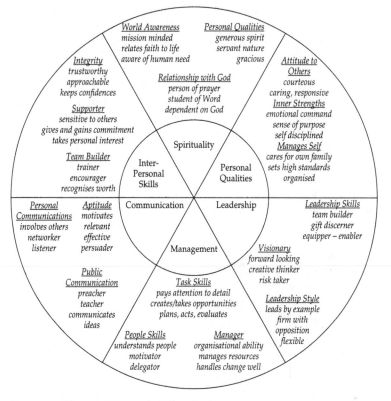

Figure 4.3 The qualities and skills wheel

that reveals the basis on which the Christian minister as a leader is perceived to be good in the role and what that leader does to perform acceptably well in that role.

Figure 4.3 is an edited version of the total information gathered during the workshops and does not contain all the key indicators. It is sufficiently detailed, however, to offer a clear view of the way in which followers perceive the qualities and characteristics of their 'good' ministers, as leaders, in the churches.

If the information contained within the 'Wheel' diagram is taken seriously, it can be incorporated into theological college procedures. For example, it can provide prospective candidates for the ministry with information about the knowledge, qualities and skills required for leadership in the church and in the ordained ministry. Those providing references for prospective students can be supplied with a questionnaire based upon the content of the 'Wheel' and asked to give their perceptions of the student's strengths and weaknesses using the model as a guide. During the college course, an annual appraisal could be developed which, among other things, would help the student to identify progress in the six core areas of the 'Wheel' and enable students to set personal goals for ongoing appraisal in those areas.

The 'Wheel' is also useful in that it gives recognition and value to the perceptions of people within the churches as to what makes for 'good' leadership. It recognises that personal qualities and character are crucial factors in the identification and recognition of good Christian leaders. It indicates that the spirituality of the good minister, as leader, is of high importance. It affirms that the competence of the leader to carry out three strategic areas of ministry, leadership, management and communication, also registers very highly in the minds of followers. It provides a way to ascertain the key qualities and skills required for ministry from the perspective of the churches and it anticipates the development of a curriculum which takes leadership expectations from the church much more seriously than has happened in the past.

The model has its drawbacks, however. It could be open to the criticism that with so many key indicators it is not possible to gain agreement on the accepted traits for leadership in the ministry. A more important issue, perhaps, is the fact that during the collecting of the information one aspect of Christian leadership that was never articulated was that the leader should have had an academic education and possess a recognised educational qualification.

This could be bad news for theological colleges! There appears to be a major dichotomy between the way in which followers in the churches perceive their leaders and the way in which theological colleges prepare people for ministry. It could be argued that Christians in churches are satisfied with ministers who possess integrity, competence and leadership ability but that the personality and the ability of the minister rates more highly to the followers than the possession of a formal, theological qualification. The colleges, in contrast, seem to place a higher value and emphasis upon obtaining satisfactory academic qualifications for ministry. This raises a question about how or whether integrity and competence in academic ability are given value by the laity. Does it matter to what level the leaders are educated theologically if they do not demonstrate integrity or are perceived to be incompetent in the leadership tasks of ministry? Who puts the premium on an academically qualified leadership? From the processes that produced the 'Wheel', it can be argued that, for Christian followers, the personal character of their leaders is more important than their theological education. It is also possible that the reason for the lack of explicit value being placed on the academic ability and achievement of the leader may lie in an assumption, on the part of the followers, that those coming out of the theological colleges into the ministry will possess the requisite academic ability and that somehow it does not figure in the perception of good leadership. From the perspective of the followers, character, integrity and competence were valued most highly. Academic attainment was valued, perhaps, less so. At least, it was not given an explicit value. Whatever value was given to it was never articulated.

A similar assumption appears to be made about the necessity of possessing leadership ability. This again was never mentioned as such, and it may be that this is another instance of the way in which Christian followers make assumptions about their leaders and their attainments during the time spent at theological college. The process of constructing the 'Wheel' exposed real differences in emphasis and importance in the content of training for leadership in the churches and in the colleges. Traditionally, from the perspective of the theological college, it is of first importance to provide a sound academic education to, at least, Diploma level and, hopefully, upwards to an Honours Degree and beyond.

There is less emphasis placed upon the development and formation of Christian character and spirituality, although these are recognised as fundamental requirements of a Christian leader. It has often been left to the students to address these on a self-development basis. Although to be fair to some colleges this is now being rectified through the use of a range of personal development tools.

Leadership competencies for ministry

Another outcome from the 'Wheel' model was the production of a set of competencies for ministry which the denomination could reasonably expect students to have gained when they complete ministerial training.

Using the 'Wheel' as a guide, a set of seven 'Distinguishing Competencies' was constructed to describe the major performance areas of 'good' leaders in ministry. Each of these is based upon one of the six core qualities and skills areas of the 'Wheel' and it can be argued that the effective leader in ministry will operate to a high standard in these seven competencies, and are recognised by their followers to do so. These are set out below:

The distinguishing competencies

1. The ability to engage in theological reflection and application
2. The ability to construct a foundation of spirituality to undergird ministry
3. The ability to carry out mission and ministry with integrity
4. The ability to communicate in public and private settings
5. The ability to lead others
6. The ability to engage in effective pastoral care and support
7. The ability to manage self and workload in a competent way

Functional competencies

These functional competencies are the activities that 'good leaders' engage in, when they are operating in the field of the 'distinguishing' competency.

1 The ability to engage in theological reflection and application

- developing the skills of interpreting and expounding Scripture
- demonstrating an understanding of Christian doctrine and its relevance to life in the world
- investigating the story of the Church (including the Baptist part within that story)
- analysing issues in contemporary society and identifying their implications for mission
- examining the breadth of ministry and mission in the modern world
- participating in the process of theological reflection alone and with others

2 The ability to construct a foundation of spirituality to undergird ministry

- demonstrating appropriate self-awareness and constructing and using helpful patterns of personal spirituality
- developing personal disciplines in the use of time and energy
- exploring the ways mission is built on spiritual foundations
- participating in spiritual retreats and/or other forms of spiritual growth and renewal

3 The ability to carry out mission and ministry with integrity

- determining personal values and beliefs and ascertaining how these influence and shape approaches to mission and ministry
- operating to Christian ethical standards in mission and ministry
- implementing sensitive approaches to different cultures, world-views and theologies
- providing evidence of an ability to adapt mission to the circumstances and situation of the local church

4 The ability to communicate in public and private settings

- developing an effectiveness in preaching, teaching and leading public worship
- improving skills in personal communication within and outside the church context
- working with people, in a way that shows a commitment to and an ability in active listening
- carrying out the communication of ideas in an informative and persuasive way
- reflecting the Baptist distinctive values in all mission and ministry communication

5 The ability to lead others

- applying vision, creativity and risk-taking in leadership, in order to achieve real and intended change
- discerning gifts in others and equipping people to use those gifts in mission and service
- leading by personal example and demonstrating professional competence in ministry and mission
- working with others effectively, building and motivating teams
- leading groups, teams and meetings, including church members' meetings, appropriately

6 The ability to engage in effective pastoral care and support

- delivering appropriate pastoral care for individuals and groups
- showing an acceptance of individuals inside and outside the church
- providing environments that stimulate personal growth in recipients of pastoral care
- identifying the need for counselling and the appropriate agency to provide it
- providing proper pastoral support through the rites of passage, with special reference to the process of Christian initiation and growth, for example, baptism and church membership

7 The ability to manage self and workload in a competent way

- carrying out work in a systematic way, showing an ability to plan, do and evaluate
- showing a grasp of the principles of human relationships and group dynamics, working with others in a leadership style which is appropriate for the circumstances and situation
- handling change effectively and sensitively
- managing a sensitive balance between the mission of the local church and maintaining its inner life

This list enables the creation of a framework for a possible curriculum for leadership training and education for the ministry that is based upon serious consideration of the information from the 'Wheel'.

This would not, of course, be the only input into any proposed curriculum, but such a contribution from within the discipline of Leadership Studies and Pastoral Studies would be innovative, to say the least. The distinguishing and functional competencies offer clues and hints as to the aspects of leadership development that need to be concentrated upon in any curriculum, and reveal something of the uniqueness of Christian leadership in the first four distinguishing competencies.

The functional competencies offer possible areas for the assessment of ministerial ability and skills within a possible new approach to theological education. This could, for example, take the form of a joint Theology and Christian Leadership degree and, following on from that, a Master's degree in Christian Leadership studies on a par with similar secular courses offered, for example, at the Centre for Leadership Studies at Exeter University.

Towards a new model of ministerial formation

The 'Wheel' diagram revealed a gap in the understanding of and approach to education and training for leadership between theological colleges and congregations. Traditionally, colleges have emphasised the priority of attaining appropriate subject knowledge and, since the 1970s, have added the requirement of pastoral skills. This emphasis can lead, however, to the neglect of the equal need for development and growth in the areas of spirituality and self-awareness. Colleges have recognised this need but have tended to treat it as a matter of individual and personal concern. The emphasis from the churches was quite different in that it stressed the need for appropriate character, personality and spirituality whilst appearing to be somewhat indifferent to academic attainment.

This raises the question of what might be the critical components of any education and training syllabus in leadership for the ministry. I suggest that there must be three basic components: the attaining of the appropriate level of knowledge, the acquiring of leadership skills and the development of personal character and spirituality.

The task of the theological curriculum is to bring together these three critical components in an appropriate balance to ensure an integrated course of knowledge-based study, skills enhancement and a deepening personal development that will meet the needs of future leaders in the three areas of knowledge, skills and character. The question is, how can they be brought together?

The second model for training leaders for today's and tomorrow's church goes some way to resolving some of the issues raised. Figure 4.4 represents a coherent and integrated model for training leaders referred to at the beginning of this chapter, which I called the 'Three-Circle' model, following John Adair.

The centre of the model, spirituality, represents the student's relationship with God in Jesus Christ. This is where the call to Christian leadership is located and rooted and it is this call which is at the centre of all the learning experiences and holds everything together. Spirituality is deemed to be the relationship to God in all aspects of life and, in this instance particularly, the outworking of that call to leadership, integral to every other aspect of the content of the model.

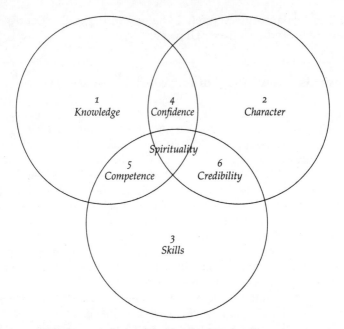

Figure 4.4 The three-circle model of leadership development

The three circles

Circle 1 – Knowledge

In order to lead the people of God, the trainee requires academic knowledge, to an agreed, acceptable level, of the traditional disciplines of theological study, in such subjects as Biblical Studies, Church History, Theology, Ethics and Understanding Modern Society, Mission Studies and cross-cultural studies.

Circle 2 – Character

This represents the need for Christian character in leadership. This would include aspects of personal growth in areas of self-awareness, spiritual discipline and enrichment. It is this area that, I maintain, has been the neglected one in the past and in this model it is given the same significance as is given to the attaining of knowledge and skills.

Circle 3 – Skills

This circle represents the necessary acquisition and improvement of leadership skills for ministry and mission in the multi-cultural world of today.

The overlapping areas

Numbered 4, 5 and 6, these are intended to suggest that when the relationship with God, self and others is in appropriate balance and tension, and when the three major circles are appropriately balanced, there will be growth in the personal confidence, competence and credibility of the potential leader.

Overlap 4 – Confidence

What emerges when knowledge, skills and appropriate Christian character come together in balance is a personal self-confidence within the trainee. This is a legitimate self-confidence, we would argue, for a Christian leader because it is rooted in the faith relationship which the leader has with Christ. Such self-confidence is suggested by St Paul in some of his letters in the New Testament, for example, in Romans 12 and Philippians 4.

Overlap 5 – Competence

This develops when the Christian leader can bring together the acquired knowledge and skills in training and uses them in ways that enable the tasks of ministry, to which the person has been appointed, to be fulfilled, consolidated and supported by the demonstration of Christian character.

Overlap 6 – Credibility

Credibility can only be earned and this happens when the Christian leader brings character, knowledge and skills together in a way that communicates to followers that beliefs, values and actions are consistent with the Christian faith. These connections do not occur spontaneously. The equation seems to be that when the leader demonstrates integrity then credibility is given by followers.

These overlapping pieces of the model show that where there is an appropriate balance of content of skills and knowledge in the curriculum of trainee leaders and where these are supplemented and sustained by a personal development programme, the leader can make progress towards an integrated preparation for leadership in the ordained ministry.

It is no exaggeration to state that the heart of the model is the spirituality that holds the other components of ministerial formation together in tension. Without it, the diagram simply reflects similar constructions for development and training in other domains. Trainers in education and social work, for example, have suggested some similarities in the formation of teachers and social workers. The difference with this approach is that it roots the drive, the energy and the inspiration to become involved in this process of education and training for the ministry to an inner sense of the call of God in a person's life. This call is tested in Baptist ecclesiology by the local church and then by the wider denomination, through the Regional Ministerial Recognition Group, which is intended to confirm that call and the spirituality of the ministerial candidate.

This central core, holding everything together in tension, is not just about sensing and testing the call. It is this spirituality which inspires the discipline required to support the lifelong demands of life in the ministry during the period of education and training and beyond it.

When faced with a 'dark day' when the pressures of the ministry weigh heavy and the temptation is to remain in bed 'under the duvet' and not rise to face the challenges, it is this inner sense of spiritual vocation which generates the motivation to 'get out of the bed' and face all that the world brings onto the minister's agenda. It is another expression of the Martin Luther dictum, 'Here I stand, I can do no other', and has its roots in this inner core of spiritual conviction.

Rightly understood, this spirituality should lead to creativity in every aspect of a minister's life when functioning in the core qualities and skills areas of the 'Wheel' model discussed earlier.

Ministerial formation is not designed nor intended to lead to a rigidity of approach but, rather, should generate the ability to be flexible. This is particularly the case in the exercise of leadership. An integrated programme of education, skills-based training and personal development for leadership in the ministry, during ministerial training, should enable the minister to respond to leadership demands and situations in an appropriate manner for the circumstances and the people rather than in any fixed, conformist style of leading.

The challenge of character formation

Since the inclusion of character and spirituality development is so vital to the leadership training process and since its neglect within the curriculum in the past has led to a lack of integration in that process, we will examine the Character circle (circle 2) of the model further. This illustrates the need for providing potential and future leaders with the opportunities they need to examine their beliefs and values appropriate to and for Christian leadership.

Having a leader who is credible encourages cooperation, commitment and a strong sense of team working within any group. Colleges must seek to train Christian leaders who will be seen as credible as well as competent and who will make a difference by the way in which they bring Christian character to bear on how they lead.

Putting the matter simply, education and training for leadership in the church must offer people the opportunity to engage in a programme of holistic, personal development.

This should include within it the requisite balance of academic knowledge, the necessary skills for leading in the church and the opportunity to practise ministry and test ability by being able to put that learning into practice during the training period. This gives people the chance to prove their calling to the leadership role by engaging in productive assessment and appraisal, thereby developing self-awareness.

The distinguishing and functional competencies that I have formulated indicate the areas that need to be covered in leadership preparation and training for ministry. Further work will need to be undertaken to determine how the curriculum of a theological college would need to be structured to ensure that the model and the competencies are supported by appropriate and integrated content for ministerial and leadership development.

The 'Three-Circle' model offers a coherent, integrated approach to leadership curriculum development. Some of the benefits of the model are that it takes seriously the need for relevant academic courses of study in the education and training for Christian leadership offered. It also provides the environment and opportunities for the development of leadership and ministry skills and it addresses the neglected dimensions of self-awareness, personal growth in spirituality, character and integrity which are requisite for those who believe themselves called to lead the Church of Jesus Christ.

5 Can church leaders learn to be leaders again?

MARTYN PERCY

Leading the Church of England is like trying to herd cats. (Traditional proverb)

Leadership in the Church of England is a complex business. At parochial level, and as a distinct community of practice, churches may contain a range of employees who are 'professionals' of sorts (i.e. trained clergy, etc.), who preside over and work with volunteers who also have significant interests and power within the said ecclesial polity. At a macro-level, bishops may be said to hold some ultimate authority within an ordered hierarchy, but this is still within the context of a largely voluntary organisation. Then there are synods, with their distinctive mission in representation and leadership. And finally there are the accoutrements of power associated with being an established church. The monarch (a layperson) is the Supreme Governor; no ordination or consecration can take place without an oath of allegiance. The Church of England is, in a real sense, the property of the crown, and held in trust for the people. Establishment prevents the church from imagining that it belongs to itself; it is a national treasure rather than a project or product of the Archbishop's Council.

Small wonder, then, that many who hold authority within the church can often be heard to complain that they are hamstrung when it comes to making decisions or offering decisive leadership. The very nature of the organisation – a complex spaghetti of democracy and autocracy, synodical and episcopal, local and national, clerical and lay, voluntary and professional – seems to militate against clarity of purpose and direction. Indeed, the church protects and perhaps honours the tradition of loyal dissent; the church embodies too many views to be too easily led. Leading it is, in common parlance, like trying to herd cats. Little can be driven; much must be coaxed. But given that the nature of the Church of England's ecclesial polity is

48

obvious, we could be forgiven for asking why, exactly, those who find themselves in positions of leadership and authority are so frequently frustrated? Should it not be apparent that the organisation is *not* shaped for easily defined aims, objectives and goals? Indeed, it is not obvious that the Church of England is, in a profound sense, a - community of practice bound together more by manners, habits and outlooks than it is by doctrinal agreement. Indeed, one could argue that Anglicanism, at its best, is a community of civilised disagreement.

In this chapter I want to explore what it might mean to talk about leadership within the church, by focusing on the nature of theological education. I should say at the outset that this is not a theology of leadership per se. It is, rather, a preliminary attempt to sketch just some of the contours that I believe to be characteristic of good theological education and leadership of either a parish or a diocese. Fundamental to my thesis is the assumption that listening and learning from congregations (and I mean deeply here) is an essential prerequisite for any teaching and directing. As James Hopewell writes in his seminal study:

> [A]n analysis of both local congregational idiom and the way the gospel message confronts and yet is conveyed by that language would be a better starting point for efforts to assist the local church. Rather than assume that the primary task of ministry is to alter the congregation, church leaders should make a prior commitment to understand the nature of the object they propose to improve . . . many strategies for operating upon local churches are uninformed about the cultural constitution of the parish . . . (Hopewell, 1987, p. 11)

Hopewell's commonsensical observation is rather understated. Books and programmes that purport to be able to shape and direct the church are a dime a dozen. But guides that educate ministers into a deep engagement with their congregation are few and far between. The assumption is – no doubt generated from the womb of theological college or seminary – that the congregation is an essentially passive body to which the 'professional' Christian leader is called to minister. I hold this to be an impoverished view of churches (operant religion or grounded ecclesiology), which is supported by a flawed educational philosophy, which falsely constructs and then divides the teacher from the learner, and the leader from the led. Correspondingly, a more dynamic and fluid understanding of how congregations are shaped, learn and taught may provide an important key to comprehending how leaders function within a complex ecclesial polity.

Transformation and leadership

Commenting on the fragmentation and concentration of theological training programmes in the USA, Poling and Miller note how ordinands (or seminarians) are pulled deeply into isolated and disconnected wells of expertise, such as biblical studies, church history and various types of (competing) theologies. In contrast, they argue for a process of

> community formation [establishing] critical awareness of the tradition, focused community planning . . . reinterpreting the interplay of covenant and tradition . . . the [Pastor/Priest/Minister] relates so as to stimulate the formation community . . . [standing] between the interpretive and political processes . . . as midwife to community formation . . . (Poling and Miller, 1985, p. 147)

Poling and Miller are conscious that there is a deep problem in theological leadership, education and formation. First, its lack of groundedness in the real or authentic life of the church means that ordinands or seminarians quickly unlearn, forget or distrust all that they have been taught at theological college. Second, this leads to a weakening of their ties with their congregations, because what has been offered (and quickly discarded) was essentially abstract and verbal. Third, the former students learn to distrust not only their teachers but also the idea of teaching: they quickly lapse into 'what works' and, at best, manage a kind of orthopraxy:

> Action and reflection methodologies encourage instant theologising, quick responses to whatever is offered. The disciplines of scholarship are replaced by agility of response. (p. 149)

More likely, however, they will be slightly schizoid in theological orientation: cherished theories seldom match practice. The irony here is that the depth of theological formation has probably not gone deep enough. A crisis in leadership is already being shaped at this point. Interestingly, Poling and Miller suggest that the missing element from many theological programmes is any serious attention to the ways in which a sense of *community* is a major part of the process of formation.[1] Rather, it is as and when the community (of practice) or congregation recognises that the environment and context itself is educative that something deeper can commence. Once students realise that the theological college or seminary itself is merely *part* of the schooling process, they can begin to understand how what they are studying relates to who and where they are, what they are about and about to become.[2] So, inevitably, we are drawn to saying that most theological education rarely reflects on itself (as a dynamic, process, etc.) and is seldom able to evaluate its performance. This is extraordinary when one considers the all-pervasive nature of theological reflection across faith communities, which is by no means restricted to professional clerics or academics. In one of the more influential essays in the field of theological formation, Edward Farley calls for a 'hermeneutic of situations' in which the taught and skilled interpreter will learn to

> uncover the distinctive contents of the situation, will probe its repressed past, will explore its relation to other situations with which it is intertwined, and will also explore the 'demand' of the situation through consideration of corruption and redemption . . . a practical theology of these activities and environments will correct their [i.e. the clergy's] traditional pedagogical isolation through a special hermeneutics of these situations . . . (Farley, 1987, p. 67)

Again, this approach challenges some of the fundamental assertions relating to the nature of theology. In Farley's thinking, the situations are themselves the crucible for learning and teaching, not something other to which theology is 'applied'. In theological education, therefore, stories, world-view and narrative take on a new significance as the *place* of engagement and interpretation. Or, put more theologically, Christian education and the leadership that flows from that becomes an expression of the incarnate dimensions that it ultimately bears witness to.

But in truth, the problem is deeper and more widespread than is at first apparent. The churches, in valuing their tradition, are not only slow to change, they are also often guilty of resisting it. Proper admiration of the past quickly becomes a dialectical mode: modernity versus the sacred, change versus tradition, and more besides. Paradoxically, transformation can be seen as a sign of weakness, and a lack of depth. In such situations, theological leadership can become extremely difficult, and can often lapse into a series of pragmatic negotiations that end up colluding with and protecting existing vested interests.

Reflecting upon this dynamic more personally, two stories come to mind. First, in attempting to investigate the changing patterns of healthcare chaplaincy in England, I was able to secure a generous grant from a prestigious research body to enable the appointment of a research fellow. In the process of designing the research, I naturally approached the Church of England's Hospital Chaplaincy Council to see if they would contribute to or participate in the research. I was surprised to be turned down flat, on the basis that 'we know all there is to know about the field, and we can't really see what you are doing this research for'.[3] The research went ahead anyway, and, unsurprisingly, the research fellow discovered a wide range of practices in hospitals related to the delivery of chaplaincy services. Some NHS Trusts had proper systems of accountability, and worked hard to make (state-funded) chaplaincy religiously inclusive by thoroughly involving non-Christian faiths in the shaping of the service and the profession. In contrast, the research fellow also discovered hospitals where the chaplaincy service was ill defined, poorly managed, lacking in sensitivity to non-Christian faiths, and generally offering a poor service to patients and hospital alike.

One can only guess as to why the Church of England should resist research into its own performance at this level, particularly when hospital chaplaincy is mainly funded by the state. But the educational implications are, arguably, the more serious issue here. Research-led investigations into ministerial performance (evaluation) could feed directly back into the present state of theological education. We might ask, 'How are Anglican chaplains (who constitute almost 70 per cent of the state funding for hospital chaplaincy) supposed to relate to ministers of other faiths, and build religiously-inclusive chaplaincy teams?' It is not as easy as it sounds when we consider that the study of non-Christian faiths (or, even, for that matter, other Christian denominations) is part of the approved curriculum for trainee ministers. Neither does the subject become an issue during Continuing Ministerial Education. In other words, the church is deficient in research-led education to enable processes of transformation. And because of this lack, it resists change, including self-critical reflection that would lead to transformations of its own educational formation.

Second, a similar problem exists when it comes to analysing why clergy leave ordained ministry. Each year, approximately two hundred and twenty clergy leave full-time ordained ministry in the Church of England.[4] The data is collected, but has never been reflected upon. The educational cost alone of this apparent 'wastage' is surely substantial, and yet researching the phenomenon – which might lead to transformations in selection, training, the management of clergy and so forth – is fiercely resisted at almost every level. Again, one can only guess as to why the Church of England would not wish to look at such an obvious area of research. But the lack of critical self-reflection continues to prevent any kind of transformation. So in advocating a matrix of research, critical reflection and evaluation, I am conscious of its limits, especially in relation to theology and the church. Not every-thing can be counted; skills are not easily measured; teaching and learning may resist certain types of commodification. True, theology is an art, not a science, and its appeal and argument are more usually aesthetic than systematic. Nonetheless, I hold that the key to the transformation of the church lies in research, evaluation and critical reflection.

In her ground-breaking *Transforming Practice* (1996), Elaine Graham uses the Aristotelian concept of *phronesis* to identify the type of 'practical wisdom' that ecclesial communities need to seek in order to adapt and transform themselves. Using the work of Don Browning (1991) as an additional foundation, Graham argues that practical theology as transforming practice can come about when it is reconceived as 'the articulation and excavation of sources and norms of Christian practice' (Graham, 2000, p. 104). In other words, theolog-ical education needs to take seriously ecclesial communities as a pri-mary *place* and *focus* of theological education. But how would this become transforming practice? Five points need making here.

First, one understanding of practical theology is to enable churches to 'practise what they preach'. To do this, particular attention needs to be paid to the habits, customs and beliefs of churches, in order to identify what it is they value and espouse. Graham argues that this kind of enquiry requires a 'postmodern' methodology of *bricolage*, one that pieces together fragments of knowledge, aware that disclosure of identity is often ambiguous and incomplete (Graham, 2000, p. 106).

Second, Graham argues that the postmodern is less of a successor to modernity and more of a complementary and critical corrective to it. It is through postmodern templates that the hubris of modernity can be questioned: its optimism, literalism, imperialism, objectivism and totalitarianism can be interrogated, and its limits probed. From here, the *alterity* of communities (including churches) can move from the margins into the mainstream as their voices are heard afresh.

Third, a focus on the entirety of Christian practice allows for a new opening up of the boundaries and horizons of Christian education. Once *praxis* and *context* are seen to be 'hermeneutically primary', Christian experience is properly repositioned as the *origin* of theolog-ical formulation, and not the application of 'learning' upon experience. Correspondingly, ecclesial communities are once again established as the primary ground of theological education; a critical discipline that interrogates the norms and values that shape and guide all corporate activity, through which 'the community enacts its identity' (Graham, 2000, p. 106).

Fourth, practical wisdom, which emerges out of the first three stages, now breaks through the typical theory-practice or abstract-applied dialects, and now sees all writing, speaking, theorising and activity within churches as performative *practices* that bind communities together, enabling them to share commitments and values. Thus, the *phronesis* of an ecclesial community is both inhabited and enacted. Theological education and spiritual formation is an innate part of the *ordinary* life of the church.

Fifth and finally, Graham's attention to *alterity* (otherness) invites churches to reflect on their diversity and inclusiveness. Distinguishing between disclosure and foreclosure, Graham notes how certain groups, practices, needs, insights and agendas are often overlooked or silenced by the churches. True theological education, therefore, in order to fulfil its transformative vocation, must pay constant attention to 'the other'. This requires not only openness (in terms of boundaries and horizons of possibility), but also a hermeneutic of suspicion that will have the capacity to excavate norms and sources with a critical-reflective mind (Graham, 2000, p. 112).

To earth these observations a little more, and to root them in the idea of theological leadership, let us return to an instance that I referred to earlier in this section: clergy leaving full-time ordained ministry. With Graham's insights to hand, we are now in a better position to understand why the agenda (in terms of research, better pastoral care and a review of selection and training methods) is so easily marginalised within the churches. To explore this area would require the registering of pain, the recognition of failure, the hurts and wounds that institutions inflict on individuals, and that individuals inflict on institutions. It is a messy, complex arena to address, and one that could only begin to be approached through narrative *bricolage* (i.e. a sensitivity to people's stories, an acuity for the latent oppression inherent within many practices and organisations, etc.) and method-ological *bricolage* (i.e. ethnography, ecclesiology, pastoral studies, etc.).

Furthermore, it requires the church to explore its own types of marginal alerity, and in so doing, revisit its praxis in the light of its conventional norms and sources, excavating their meaning and application. So, we might ask, what does Christian tradition have to say to people who, for whatever reason, fail in Christian ministry? What do the codes and rules of the church say, and, more importantly, what do they *convey* to those who have departed or been forced to leave? How is the pain and grief of the laity who lose a minister addressed or recognised? How is the hope of redemption manifested in disciplinary procedures (occasionally ecclesiastical trials) and other measures that are sometimes taken against a departing minister? It is in addressing the pain, here, in the body of Christ itself, that transforming practice can begin to emerge and offer the genuine possibility of the renewal of theological education.

In other words, theological leadership in this situation requires individuals and communities that are prepared to work within a matrix of evaluation, critical reflection and research. This is a risky and potentially lonesome task, for true leadership would move quickly from naïve interpretations of the church and its ministry and practice to those that are shrewd (or ironic). But true leadership would have to venture even beyond this into the realm of the revolutionary, since a proper appraisal of the situation requires radical research and a no less radical response.

Education, liberation and theological leadership

These observations take us, quite naturally, back into the field of liberation theology, a term that is loosely used to describe a variety of theologies that makes the specific liberation of a group (marginalised or oppressed by virtue of class, race, gender, sexuality, wealth, ethnicity, etc.) its primary purpose and a theological fundamental. The roots of liberation theology lie principally in Latin American theology and also in the Civil Rights struggles within the USA. But at the very base of these roots lies a theory of education (and therefore transformative leadership and community development) that was first developed by Paulo Freire. For Freire, two approaches to education must be rejected. The first is the traditionalist (or naïve), which '[defends] class interests, to which that faith is subordinated'. Here Freire cites an example of how faith is narrated as something to be 'protected' against the potential ravages of revolution or Marxism. Second, the alternative modernising agenda (or shrewd/ironic) is also opposed, which is deemed to offer reform, but only so as to 'preserve the status quo'. Freire rejects both these options in favour of a prophetic perspective on education that envisages education as 'an instrument of transforming action, as political praxis at the service of human liberation' (Freire, 1973, p. 544, and Astley, 1996, p. 167). For

Freire, that will necessarily involve a further, more radical excavation of norms and sources. Thus:

> They [i.e. the churches] discover through praxis that their 'innocent' period was not the least impartial . . . [when others] insist on the 'neutrality' of the church . . . they castrate the prophetic dimension . . . (Freire, 1973, pp. 544–45)

Freire's agenda has been taken forward by a variety of scholars. For example, Thomas Groome (1980) argues (rather as we have been) that Christian praxis is the normative form of theological education. This contribution, from a more mainstream (Western) theologian, opens up the possibility of theology beginning with the praxis of the poor. But at the same time the more radical edge of liberation theology should not be lost in the milieu of praxis-centred theology, for the *desiderata* of liberation theology remains liberation, not development. There is a perpetual rawness to liberation theology that refuses to be consolidated and consoled by accommodationist strategies that do not fully embrace a radical revolutionary revision of structures and contexts.

Again, this type of assertion about the nature and purpose of theological education takes us back to a fundamental question: the nature of theology itself. What, or perhaps who, is it for? There are several different answers to this question, but our purpose in opening up this brief section on liberation with the attacks on neutrality is to show that there is no point on the theological compass, or in Christian leadership, that is non-directive. In other words, an enquiry into the *nature* and *purpose* of theology is an inherently political question that challenges the shaping and ordering of the discipline itself, long before anything is ever 'taught' by anyone, or any church is 'led' by an individual.

That said, liberation theology still stands within a broader tradition of theology: that of the hope of transformation. As Richard Grigg (1990) perceptively argues, religion itself can be defined as 'a means toward ultimate transformation' (Grigg, 1990, p. 8).[5] But although one might try and distinguish between theology and religion – theology being the 'intellectual approach to the infinite' – the distinction barely works in practice, since

> [T]he infinite that theology attempts to understand is just that infinite which can aid us in dealing with fundamental practical dilemmas connected to our finitude . . . theological reflection tends always to point to religious practice. (Grigg, 1990, p. 8)

Grigg extends his theorising to reflect on the particularity of liberation theology, and what is methodologically distinctive about its prog-ramme for the field of theological education. Drawing on the work of Robert Long,[6] Grigg identifies six characteristics of liberating hermeneutics.

The first is 'a different starting point'. Instead of beginning with abstract theories, liberation theology commences with the 'experience of being marginalised or excluded'. Second, there is a different inter-locutor. Liberation theology does not seek to persuade non-believers with intellectual or philosophical doubts; rather, it works with the people who are oppressed. Third, liberation theology uses different tools. It sets aside metaphysical speculation, and opts for the insights of sociologists, political theorists (often Marxist) and historians. Fourth, liberation theology offers a different analysis. Instead of assuming a harmony between peoples and a degree of neutrality in methodology, liberation theology presumes that injustice is already inbuilt. Fifth, there is a different tone to the engagement. Instead of assuming that there will be a definitive Truth or principle to be arrived at, liberation theology maintains that the struggle for justice and truth will be ongoing, and be known only in perpetual praxis. Sixth, and finally, liberation theology proposes a different kind of theology. Instead of truth 'from above' (that is often then imposed on the world), liberation theology seeks to discover liberating truth in praxis, through a process of critical reflection. It is these six charac-teristics that, together, will begin the process of transformation that may actually and ultimately enable liberation (Grigg, 1990, pp. 75–6).

Having briefly discussed liberation theology and education, it is important to state that the promulgation of formation, transformation and liberation as essential characteristics of theological education are by no means confined to the field of liberation theology. Post-modern writers have been quick to identify the agenda as one that is consonant with their own hermeneutics of suspicion in relation to modernity. Consider, for example, the African-American literary scholar, bell hooks:

> To educate as the practice of freedom is a way of teaching that anyone can learn. That learning process comes easiest to those of us who teach who also believe that there is an aspect to our vocation that is sacred; who believe that our work is not merely to share information but to share in the intellectual and spiritual growth of our students. To teach in a manner that respects and cares for the souls of our students is essential if we are to provide the necessary conditions where learning can most deeply and intimately begin . . . (hooks, 1994, p. 13)

As Hodgson (1999, p. 4) notes, hooks sees that teaching 'touches, evokes, energises the very depths of the human, liberates peoples to realise their potential and transform the world'. He links hooks's work to that of John Dewey (1916), who maintained that teaching and education have a sacral dimension precisely because they are the means by which human beings maintain themselves through renewal. But how exactly is such education the 'practice of freedom'?

Peter Hodgson (1999, pp. 71–80) argues that the tradition is an ancient one, although more implicit than explicit in early theological writings. Gregory of Nyssa, for example, saw Christian *paedia* as renewal, liberation and transformation through individuals imitating Christ. It is here, claims Hodgson, that we first encounter a language of transformative pedagogy. The theme of freedom and education also emerges in the work of Herder and Hegel, with the latter showing particular concern for families and the state and the education of children. Where poor children were put to work at an early age, lack of education meant lack of freedom, and a form of economic slavery. Here, the practice of freedom took priority over the consciousness of freedom: Hegel's work is unavoidably political.

Hodgson develops his thesis by suggesting three discrete areas where theological education and liberation combine to make a richer theology. To some extent these points already echo points we have made earlier, but they merit some further elucidation here, as we seek to establish the meaning of theological education. First, Hodgson agrees with Freire's assertion that liberation is not a deposit made in humans. Rather, it is a form of praxis: 'the action and reflection of human beings upon their world in order to transform it' (Hodgson, 1999, p. 75). As Freire notes,

> The teacher is no longer merely the-one-who-teaches, but one who is himself taught in dialogue with the students, who in turn while being taught also teach. They become jointly responsible for a process in which all grow . . . (Freire, 1972, pp. 66–7)

What Freire is saying here is that the subject matter *gives* itself (especially in theology), and that teachers and students are caught up in the dynamic of this gift, which in turn creates, sustains and then transforms their relationships. To be taught, then, means not to be taught *things*, but *how* to think, which alone can then enable transformation and liberation.

Second, education as the practice of freedom is about radical democracy and social transformation. However, this transformation may not only be about resisting and challenging established social norms – it may also involve enabling society to live more peaceably with its many differences and diversities. One of the higher vocations of education is to enable 'the celebration of difference . . . [but] persons must learn how to play the politics of difference' (Hodgson, 1999, p. 77).

Third, education as the practice of freedom is potentially conflictual and painful. Education presupposes transformation, and this will necessarily involve clashes with prejudices, habits and 'acceptable' forms of behaviour. In other words, it is only when truth is disputed that truth can emerge. And it is only by entering the debate that a dispute can take place. This takes us back, again, to the character and shape of theology. It is not something settled, signed, sealed and delivered. It is, rather, a way of educating: forming, transforming and liberating. Freedom, then, is not easily attained. The road to liberation (through the practice/praxis of education) is full of traffic with competing interests and going in different directions. The would-be traveller is not guaranteed a safe and smooth passage. The would-be leader is assured of an uncomfortable journey.

Summary

This chapter has sought to show how theological education might be reconceived as a process of transformation and liberation in relation to notions of leadership. I have offered an overview of how this might work, recognising that application of the essentials discussed will take on markedly different characters in various types of ecclesial communities. However, I have also sought to show how theological education is a corporate, dynamic and collaborative exercise, rather than something that is done to or for individuals. Inevitably, the debate and discussion is political in character, since the excavation of the meaning of theological education takes us back to challenging the nature and purpose of the discipline itself. However, we cannot leave the debate at this point, poised as it were, for an endless number of ongoing political disputes.

Hodgson suggests that the way forward for transformative pedagogy is to recognise that it has a dual responsibility quite apart from its vocation to challenge and liberate. The first is to offer 'connected teaching'. Hodgson reverts to the Socratic midwife analogy. Teachers draw out truth from their students, and enable the dialogical processes of education. The creation of this 'space' also enables spiritual formation, and resists the 'banking' model of education in favour of nurturing, encouragement and trust. 'Connected teaching', in other words, assumes a level of cooperation with the student; it requires grace, communion, reserve, inspiration and inclusion.

Second, learning is seen as cooperative. Hodgson asserts that teaching and learning are at their best when the role of the teacher shifts from 'expert/authority figure to facilitator/coach' – one who 'observes, monitors and answers questions'. Again, recognition of the shared nature of learning is at the heart of a transformative pedagogy, and this, in turn, questions many of the prevailing assumptions about the nature of theological education and leadership that are often present in most churches. To be sure, the recipe advocated here is one fraught with risk, but it issues a simple invitation. Can church leaders learn to be learners again? And can its leaders learn to truly teach, rather than simply indoctrinate?

Bibliography

Astley, J. (ed. with L. Francis and C. Crowder) (1996), *Theological Perspectives on Christian Formation*, Grand Rapids, Eerdmans.

Browning, D. (1991), *A Fundamental Practical Theology: Descriptive and Strategic Proposals*, Philadelphia, Westminster.

Dewey, J. (1966 [1916]), *Democracy and Education: An Introduction to the Philosophy of Education*, New York, Free Press.

Farley, E. (1982), *Ecclesial Reflection*, Philadelphia, Fortress.

Farley, E. (1988), *The Fragility of Knowledge*, Philadelphia, Fortress.

Farley, E. (1987), 'Interpreting Situations', in L. Mudge and J. Poling (eds), *Formation and Reflection: The Promise of Practical Theology*, Philadelphia, Fortress Press.

Freire, P. (1972), *The Pedagogy of the Oppressed*, London, Penguin.

Graham, E. (1996), *Transforming Practice*, London, Mowbray.

Graham, E. (2000), 'Transforming Practice', in S. Pattison and J. Woodward (eds), *The Blackwell Reader in Pastoral and Practical Theology*, Oxford, Blackwell, pp. 99–106.

Grigg, R. (1990), *Theology as a Way of Thinking*, Atlanta, Scholars Press.

Groome, T. (1980), *Christian Religious Education*, San Francisco, Harper & Row.

Hodgson, P. (1999), *God's Wisdom: Toward a Theology of Education*, Louisville, Kentucky, Westminster John Knox Press.

hooks, b. (1994), *Teaching to Transgress: Education as the Practice of Freedom*, New York, Routledge.

Hopewell, J. (1987), *Congregation: Stories and Structures*, London, SCM.

Mudge, L. and J. Poling (eds) (1987), *Formation and Reflection: The Promise of Practical Theology*, Philadelphia, Fortress Press.

Pattison, S. and J. Woodward (eds) (2000), *The Blackwell Reader in Pastoral and Practical Theology*, Oxford, Blackwell.

Poling, J. and D. Miller (1985), *Foundations for a Practical Theology of Ministry*, Nashville, Abingdon.

Notes

1. Poling and Miller also criticise theological colleges for being 'in bondage to upper middle-class interest[s]' and male interests: 'the concerns of blacks, Hispanics . . . native Americans, Asian and African Christians are seldom represented . . .' (p. 149).
2. For an alternative vision, see J. Pobee (ed.), *Towards Viable Theological Education: Ecumenical Imperative, Catalyst of Renewal*, Geneva, WCC, 1997, and R. Ferris, *Renewal in Theological Education: Strategies for Change*, Wheaton, IL, Billy Graham Center, 1990.
3. See H. Orchard, *Hospital Chaplaincy: Modern, Dependable?*, Sheffield, Sheffield Academic Press, 2000 (series editors M. Percy and H. Orchard).
4. Substantial studies do exist in the USA. The Hartford Center for Religion Research has conducted a number of surveys for different denominations that examine why clergy leave full-time ministry.
5. Cf. F. Streng, C. Lloyd and J. Allen, *Ways of Being Religious*, Englewood Cliffs, NJ, Prentice Hall, 1973, p. 6.
6. R. Long, *Theology in a New Key*, Philadelphia, Westminster, 1978.
7. See J. Dewey, *Democracy and Education: An Introduction to the Philosophy of Education*, New York, Free Press, 1966.

6 Strategic church leadership

ROBIN GILL AND DEREK BURKE

When we first met ten years ago we found that we had shared concerns about leadership within the Church of England in a context of institutional decline. Derek, with a long engagement as a lay Anglican, also had nine years of experience as a Vice-Chancellor at the University of East Anglia, while Robin, an ordained Anglican, also had experience as an academic theologian and sociologist. We soon realised that both of us were convinced that leaders within the Church of England could learn much from the concept of strategic leadership that was being developed within other voluntary organisations. As a result of many conversations we eventually decided to write our book *Strategic Church Leadership* (1996). It is now a good time to take stock.

Some church leaders were enthusiastic about our book while others were more critical. Frankly we would both rather be criticised than ignored. Of course we have been grateful for the enthusiasm, but it is important that we take account of some of the criticisms that are referred to later.

Empirical concerns

It might be helpful if we return to the concerns that we expressed in our original Preface to *Strategic Church Leadership*. We argued as follows:

> British churches – and especially the Church of England – are currently facing acute anxieties about leadership. The world seems to be changing fast and yet church leaders often seem perplexed and paralysed by change.
>
> Churchgoing continues to decline in Britain. Yet church leaders are often reluctant even to admit this decline. There is a growing problem of authority and establishment. As an established church the Church of England faces many of the widespread criticisms that are made of other institutions, such as the monarchy, parliament

and the police, in Britain today. Yet church leaders are often at a loss to know how best to respond to this criticism. They face a paradoxical mixture of a growing secularism, of resurgent forms of fundamentalism, and of increasing religious pluralism.

Secure jobs are becoming for many laypeople a distant memory. Yet senior and junior clergy alike frequently insist that their jobs must remain secure, even whilst the very economic base of these jobs is becoming less and less secure. The Church Commissioners' investment debacle of the 1980s is likely to affect the Church of England for many years to come. Resentment is growing amongst congregations about the new financial burden arising from clergy stipends and pensions being increasingly placed upon them.

In short, church leaders in Britain at the moment are facing major problems.[1]

There are two major empirical items at stake here, the first concerned with churchgoing decline and the second with financial management within the Church of England. Alongside this we expressed a more generalised concern about authority and establishment within the Church of England. It is worth addressing the two empirical items first. Has anything changed in the last decade in relation either to churchgoing decline or to financial management?

The short answer is probably not. If anything, churchgoing statistics and finances within the Church of England are sadly more precarious than they were ten years ago. Despite a courageous and determined effort led by Archbishop George Carey to establish structures that would promote church growth and greater financial stability, the results have been disappointing.

Robin's own empirical research has largely been on churchgoing statistics[2] rather than finances. However, as active church people, we are both very conscious of the deep financial concerns that are troubling Anglican parishes in many parts of the country. Central quotas and clergy costs are now increasing at levels several times that of general inflation. Congregations today must pay through the parish share towards the pension contributions of active clergy and can expect little or no subsidy from the Church Commissioners. As congregations become thinner and more elderly, they are now expected to fund both the full cost of their clergy (for the first time in living Anglican history, though this has always been a responsibility of Free Church congregations) as well as maintaining church buildings that are often subject to heavy demands from being listed as historic buildings. Whatever judgment is finally reached about the investment policy of the Church Commissioners over the last two decades, there is very widespread concern at parish level.

We also believe that there is widespread grass-roots concern about churchgoing decline. Yet official reactions to this within the Church of England have at best been ambiguous. Two recent Church of England reports, *Statistics: A Tool for Mission* and *Hope for the Church: Contemporary Strategies for Growth*, provide sharply contrasting approaches. The first of these was written after a period of anxiety about the reliability of 'usual Sunday attendances' within the Church of England (an anxiety, as Robin has argued elsewhere,[3] that may owe more to a desire to disguise decline than to assess trends impartially). The second report, despite its optimistic title, offers a frank, even bleak, analysis of long-term institutional decline within the same Church. What divides the two reports is whether or not they use adequate longitudinal statistics (i.e. statistics gathered on exactly the same basis at separate points in time) in assessing trends.

Statistics: A Tool for Mission, which reported after a wide-ranging review and consultation, gave a number of different reasons for the decision to disregard 'usual Sunday attendances': those under 16 had not previously been included in such a count; 'there is anecdotal evidence that week-on-week attendances are more variable now than in past years, and a simple average across all the weeks in the year, excluding festivals and holidays, may not adequately represent the overall attendance figures'; congregations at occasional offices had not been included; variability within and between dioceses in methods of calculation existed; links with financial calculations could act as a disincentive to count attendances accurately. Most of these would be reasons for adjusting procedures rather than for discontinuing the collection of these statistics. From the subsequent commentary it is clear that the reason which we quote below and which came from a diocesan survey, was considered to be the most important:

> Research in the Diocese of Wakefield provided a snapshot of the broader picture of numbers of attenders and patterns of church-going. A register of every person who attended a church service was taken over an 8-week period from October to December 1997 in 17 parishes . . . It was observed that 3,432 individuals attended a church service at some time during that period; this is 41 per cent higher than the usual Sunday attendance figure. In contrast, only 144 people (4 per cent) attended on all eight Sundays. (There were also 51 people who attended a midweek service, but not a Sunday service.)[4]

On the basis of this and two other similar local surveys, the report concluded that 'as a sole measure of church attendance, adult usual Sunday attendance no longer seems appropriate'. The problem with this conclusion is, however, that it introduced the comparative phrase 'no longer' when it cited only single-point rather than longitudinal data.

Bob Jackson, the author of the more recent report *Hope for the Church*, soon spots this error. He argues that the fact that electoral rolls have tended to decline faster than 'usual Sunday attendances' suggests a very different picture:

> Many clergy have the sense that their people are coming to church less frequently than in the past. This can only be true globally if membership is falling less rapidly than attendance. But it is not – comparing the national statistics of membership and average attendance suggests that there has been no reduction in the average frequency of church attendance. This theory of declining frequency has arisen partly as a result of certain deaneries and churches taking a register for a period of a couple of months or so and finding that more individuals were coming less often than they had imagined. From this important finding some people have made the erroneous assumption that attendance frequency must have dropped because in the golden age of the past we know that everyone came every week. But we don't know that. Only a repeat survey can establish whether there is a trend or 'it was ever thus'.[5]

In contrast to *Statistics: A Tool for Mission*, Jackson argues that the official longitudinal statistics of the Church of England for baptisms, confirmations, marriages, stipendiary clergy, churches open, electoral rolls, Easter and Christmas communicants, and usual Sunday adult and child attendances, all show a significant decline in the 1980s and an even faster decline in the 1990s. He bluntly dismisses single-point evidence to the contrary: 'For one year only, the Church of England is able to say: "Good news, there are more of us on the *Titanic* than we thought" – but the *Titanic* may still be going down.'[6]

We believe that it is essential that church leaders within the Church of England take evidence of churchgoing decline, alongside evidence about precarious finances, very seriously indeed. Of course there is abundant evidence that other denominations in Britain (and more widely in many parts of Europe, but not always in the USA) are facing serious problems as well, but the Church of England as an established and historically well-endowed church has often been able to ignore them. We are still convinced that, faced with such evidence, church leaders should be encouraged to think more clearly in terms of strategic leadership and attempt to deal with these issues.

In *Strategic Church Leadership* we set out four key areas of strategic leadership and attempted to relate them to the Church of England as it is and as it could be. The four were: setting priorities; determining objectives; strategic planning; and strategic ownership and accountability. We propose to do the same again now, albeit of course much more briefly.

Setting priorities

In our book we argued that strategic church leaders should set priorities in order to meet the needs of a changing society. Even this modest statement raised concerns: setting priorities is 'management', itself seen as a dirty word, the reverse of Christian leadership, unspiritual and judgmental. Academic critics such as Stephen Pattison and Richard Roberts argued passionately that such an approach deeply distorts the nature of the church. For Roberts, in particular, such 'managerial enforcement involves a highly differentiated process of de-skilling and the gradual stripping away of professional autonomy from middle-ranking employees'.[7] In contrast, for us 'setting priorities' is an indispensable technique (it is emphatically not a creed) for intelligent and effective leadership, whether in the church or any other large organisation; it is no more than a structured way of making choices. If there is no discussion of priorities, then a choice has de facto been made already, that is not to disturb the status quo. There is no way of avoiding making decisions. We argued that unless church leaders have a clear set of priorities, they cannot deal with rapid change effectively and creatively. Sadly we still believe that too many church leaders have failed to come to terms with the implications of this area of strategic leadership; for example, by answering the rather obvious questions as to how priorities should be set, and who should set them. In addition, too many church leaders have failed to address the question adequately about how priorities can be monitored and reviewed in view of changing circumstances.

More specifically we argued for a clear theological basis to 'setting priorities' for the church focused upon worship:

> Such worship constitutes the core of our mission statement. This is, so to speak, the vertical feature. A horizontal feature is important too, since most churches also believe that they are committed to teaching and changing individuals as well as moulding social structures through Christian faith, morality and worship. This horizontal feature is double-edged: it is concerned with both

outreach and with social action. Outreach is the attempt to draw outsiders into the church, whereas social action is the attempt to engage the church with the needs of the outside world . . . Our suggestion for a mission statement is as follows: *The central aim of churches in modern Britain is the communal worship of God in Christ through the Spirit, teaching and moulding as many lives and structures as deeply as possible through this worship.* Christian worship, outreach and social action – or worship, witness and service if you prefer – are all fundamental to this mission statement. It also assumes that worship is **communal** and involves **teaching** and **moulding** – both the lives of individuals and the social structures within which they live.[8]

What is our impression of the changes since we first wrote? Manifestly, despite the hard work of many, and with some splendid exceptions, church attendance has not risen, numbers of baptisms, confirmations and church weddings have continued to fall and, above all, our society appears to be increasingly estranged from the churches. It is obvious everywhere; the stream of cars coming to shop every Sunday while a very modest number make their way to church, the contents of an average evening of television viewing, and above all the tone in which much political and moral discussion is set. In the face of this we give thanks to God that the decline has not been steeper, but we all want to do better and so we have to ask how good have church leaders been in finding new challenges that people will pick up, in giving congregations a new vision, while maintaining the best of the past? Not very well, we are afraid. The Decade of Evangelism has been quietly forgotten, there have been some successful new initiatives, but then some of us wonder if what we are discarding is more valuable than what we are picking up. There are tensions within congregations between traditionalists and non-traditionalists, between charismatics and non-charismatics, between growing and declining congregations, and between financially self-supporting and 'subsidised' congregations. Change has been hard for everyone: bishops, archdeacons, parish priests and congregations, and everyone is busy, with little time for extra effort. 'How can we do more?' they say. We suggest that there has been too little discussion of what are the most important things for us both to do and to monitor carefully. And that is what setting priorities is all about.

One special tension is between the young and the old, the young naturally wanting to express their own faith in their own cultural terms, with their own music, their own informality, their own approach to spirituality. But those changes, in turn, make church life difficult and often uncongenial for those who are in the last decade of their lives, have been faithful Christians and churchgoers throughout, valuing the traditions and language inherited from the past, and looking to their parish priest for support in their last few years. Many priests are doing that splendidly, but others cannot help but give the impression that if only these older folk could start acting as if they were 40 or 50 years younger, enjoy the modern music, abandon the Prayer Book, then all would be well.

As well as the successes, there have been some disasters, often because of inexperienced leadership. We suggest that one of the problems lies in a failure to understand what modern management is about; for it is not about exerting power, nor about being tough with difficult people, nor about asserting authority (showing them who is the boss). It is about releasing energy, creating a vision for the future, ensuring ownership of any new project, and crucially building trust. Trust is hard to win and easily lost. The heart of management skills is the motivation of the people. 'Where there is no vision, the people perish' is as true now as it ever was. Indeed priests who say they distrust management are perhaps only saying that they distrust the arbitrary use of power, and often they may be effective managers of change – because they love their people, have a vision for the future for the church, and crucially are able to share that with their congregation in such a way that it becomes their own, and decisions are made, rather than suffer the endless procrastination which often seems so characteristic of the church.

Determining objectives: opportunities and threats

This chapter in *Strategic Church Leadership* opened with an explanation of SWOT (strengths, weaknesses, opportunities and threats) analysis as applied to the Church of England. A number of questions were identified in that analysis which is still very relevant. For example:

* Declining congregations. Who is growing? Just the charismatic congregations? How important have the Alpha/Emmaus courses been? How effective was the Decade of Evangelism? Do we know how to evangelise in multicultural Britain? How can we bridge the barrier between the church and the unchallenged?
* Inclusiveness. Always a strength of the Anglican Church but how possible is it in a society that is fragmenting? Is the concept of inclusiveness still appropriate?
* Amorphous. The Anglican Church has kept together by deciding to

be a broad church and amorphous in character. Is this a strength or a weakness? There are new threats to the broad nature of the Church of England from ongoing debates over sexuality, women bishops and disestablishment. These are real challenges to leadership, especially for a new Archbishop of Canterbury.

• Declining resources. Most of the resources that are generated by income from investments are now being used for existing clergy pensions, leaving the dioceses to be almost self-sufficient. Can they cope?

The proper use of such questions should leave us with decisions to be made; some things that are going well will need strengthening; some things which are not going well will need to be discontinued; and of course new initiatives will be needed. So 'What has worked well and where?' is an important question to answer, but there is also a second question: how can innovation take place if the current members of the congregation resist change? The temptation for some priests is simply to abandon services which are largely populated by the over-sixties, and to start again with young people's services, use more contemporary music, explore the use of modern spirituality, in fact do almost anything that is different. In contrast, a both/and policy, running both conventional services and novel ones, at different times and sometimes not on a Sunday, might work better.

Strategic planning

In *Strategic Church Leadership* we asked whether strategic planning was appropriate for the churches and wondered whether the style of leadership within the business world was in any way appropriate to the churches. Alternatively should the style of leadership be more like that of a servant or a shepherd of a flock? We discussed the insights that have come from modern management about the importance of motivation and asked whether that style was characteristic of the church.

We asked about financial delegation and raised the issue of the parish share, which is now a major item of many church budgets and is often seen as a central tax, when it is no more than a way of spreading salary costs across the dioceses in a reasonably fair way. We also raised the issue of the central costs, and wondered how deeply resented they are. We suggested that there is a need to account carefully for central costs, and asked how we can encourage a sense of greater financial self-sufficiency in local churches.

Then we raised the question of career development for the clergy, and asked whether there should be any regular appraisal of incumbents? Does anyone, we wondered, ask them how they think they are doing?

There have been some successful and encouraging developments here in the last few years: Alpha and Emmaus courses[9] still have an important role within many local churches (possibly because they meet the deep loneliness in our fractured society), clergy appraisals are happening more widely, the contribution of women priests has been very widely welcomed, as has the appointment of Rowan Williams as Archbishop of Canterbury, churches continue to repair and build in an impressive way, and on national occasions, such as the death of the late Queen Mother, a deep religious vein within the British people shows itself. But this does not result in rising church attendances or in an influx of the young and newly-married into the churches.

But we also know that some parish priests are still very lonely. One, Derek, expects to see his archdeacon once every three years on a routine basis, and there does not seem to be any suggestion of personal feedback, no suggestion of appraisal, no indication of new ways forward for the very good reason that the archdeacon has not got the time. So what happens in these circumstances? Sometimes priests have a spiritual adviser, sometimes a colleague in a similar situation; others talk to their churchwardens, and that is often a very sensible thing to do, for they often have wide experience of the secular world, possess management skills and above all wisdom and judgment. But when Derek last went to a churchwardens' training course, the talk was on how to clear the gutters and move the chairs! We suggest we need to raise our sights for these splendid churchwardens up and down the country, enable them to do better and provide the training to make it possible.

How can loneliness be lessened and priests encouraged in a time of decreasing resources? Team ministries are one important solution widely adopted in rural parishes and they certainly help solve the problem of the loneliness of the parish priest. But how well are they working? It is true, as in every other sphere, that leading a team needs special skills and gifts, but are we training team-leaders? Are women priests often better than men at working in teams, as some suggest?

Meantime Derek cannot help noticing that in the centre of a city like Cambridge there is a church every fifty yards along Kings High with little coordination and considerable overlap in their natural congregations. There seems to be no strategic planning – possibly the churches are averse to planning, seeing it as the harbinger of threatening change, and the opposite of being 'spiritual'. But can no one in such a city actually sit down and think out how different churches, by mutual consent, could go in complementary directions? Depressingly it does not seem to be possible. Often it seems that neither the archdeacon nor the bishop have the authority, and both are too busy with other things. Endless business with less important issues is a characteristic of poor management and we are afraid that the church is full of it.

Ownership and accountability

In *Strategic Church Leadership* we asked how we could gain a greater sense of ownership and accountability in the local church. We asked how we could remain as an inclusive church with congregations of widely differing levels of commitment, and how to persuade them to take on the responsibility for the local church and its work.

We made a sharp contrast between consensus management (which we judged still to be the dominant style of leadership in the Church of England) and strategic ownership. We described the latter as follows:

> This process can be described by the phrase 'top-down, bottom-up, top-down'. The top must initiate. It is the task of strategic leadership to set the challenge, to refuse to let the institution fudge the issue, to ensure that the real questions are dealt with and, over and over again, to bring the debate back to central issues. Then all those deeply involved must respond: question, argue, and propose alternatives 'bottom-up'. Finally, the leadership must take the best proposals through for final approval. These proposals might not be universally agreed. Consensus is not always possible, but there comes a point when nearly everyone realises that the current proposals are the best that can be obtained and, then, leaders must act. Strategic leaders must, of course, take the criticism and perhaps even the opprobrium for the final decisions – after all, that is what they are paid to do – to lead. There has to be a desk where 'the buck stops'.[10]

We think that there is still too much evidence of consensus management rather than strategic ownership within the Church of England. Nevertheless there is beginning to be awareness in some dioceses that local financial ownership and accountability is possible and important. Specifically in relation to finance we argued at the time that a greater sense of ownership (including local budget-holding) and accountability are essential if congregations are to flourish:

There is extensive research showing that self-funding churches are much more likely to flourish and grow than subsidised churches. Subsidised churches have a tendency to lack motivation to change, to lose any impetus towards evangelism, and to show signs of dependency. In contrast, self-funding churches have to change if they are to survive, tend to be much keener on evangelism, and often show signs of independence. Precisely because of this spirit of independence, they may appear troublesome to some church leaders. They may be more likely than other churches to challenge central church policies and to question the use made of their contributions to central funds. In addition, they may well wish to have more say over their own clergy appointments and expect their clergy, once appointed, to live up to their own ideals. A wise church leadership should look at all of these tendencies of self-funding churches as opportunities rather than as threats. Without such features it is difficult to see how churches as a whole might once again grow. Local budget-holding gives congregations, or clusters of congregations, an important measure of ownership. Once members of a congregation know that it is their resources alone which will pay for their ordained ministry, then they cannot but be challenged.[11]

But when we look at the financial changes of the last few years, little seems to have happened strategically; for the most part there has simply been slow attrition. We are still cutting back, but who is monitoring the effects of these changes? Who has the power or the interest to reverse the bad decisions? And what about the parish share? Many rural and inner-city churches we know of simply cannot afford to pay. Has the church any response to this or is it all in the 'too difficult' tray? The parish share is not owned by the parishes; perhaps it would help if it were broken down into different sections – so much to pay for your own clergy, your rectory, support of your incumbent, so much to pay for running the diocese, so much to pay for your bishops and archdeacons. Then we would know what was being done with our money.

And how can we change our giving habits? They are changing – the ability to reclaim income tax on a weekly offering, no matter how small, as long as you pay standard rate income tax, is helping. But how do we move to the self-sufficiency of, say, the Baptists in Britain, let alone the generous giving of the North American churches? There is a real need to kindle what is sometimes termed 'biblical generosity' among churchgoers within the Church of England.

Some dioceses are indeed beginning to make local deaneries

budget-holders. We believe that this is an important step towards ownership and greater local accountability. Yet there are still many problems to be faced, not least about how central costs can be made more accountable, for as mentioned earlier these are increasing well beyond inflation (in some dioceses, at three times the rate of inflation). Before the spectacular financial losses caused by the Church Commissioners' property investments in the 1980s, central costs could largely be absorbed by the Church of England's inherited wealth. Today (especially after further recent losses, this time caused by moving investments into a bear Stock Market) central costs must be raised instead through parish shares. Yet the Church of England still behaves as if it is a rather badly run 1960s company. For instance, why does it still retain such buildings for its central bureaucracy as Church House or the Church Commissioners' immensely valuable building at Millbank, both at Westminster? ICI abandoned its expensive Millbank offices years ago, delegated and dispersed responsibilities and thrived. Even after the Turnbull Report, it is astonishing that three separate expensive central bureaucracies still exist side-by-side in Church House, Millbank and Lambeth Palace. Again, no (unsubsidised) commercial organisation would have expensive regional offices and staff in their equivalent of every diocese around the country. Indeed, as the Church of England has continued to decline numerically, it has actually increased the number of stipendiary but non-parochial clergy and almost doubled the number of bishops (themselves considerably more expensive to pay and support than parochial clergy). In short, deep concerns remain about how effectively changes (or lack of changes) are being monitored within the Church of England and about who has the power to reverse decisions even when they are acknowledged to be wrong.

In terms of strategic leadership within the Church of England the question remains about who has the final authority, the responsibility, and the ability, to drive through change. No one, apparently – not the average churchgoer, not the PCC; while parish priests have a particular care, archdeacons are too busy with personal problems and the quinquennial visitations, and bishops have very limited power, it seems. We do have central bodies that have some power: the Archbishop's Council, the House of Bishops, the General Synod and the Church Commissioners. Yet no one seems to know where the power really lies.

Of course the concept of strategic church leadership is not a panacea for long-term churchgoing decline and financial precariousness within the Church of England. We are not claiming that. Nor are we claiming that it is a substitute for prayer and theological reflection.

We do believe, however, that it is a style of leadership, developed in other large organisations, which might well bring benefits to the Church of England. It is a way for the Church to set priorities carefully and then to follow them through effectively. We believe that it is strongly needed in the Church of England today.

Notes

1. Robin Gill and Derek Burke, *Strategic Church Leadership*, London, SPCK, 1996, p. 1.
2. See Robin Gill, *The 'Empty' Church Revisited*, Hants, Ashgate, 2003.
3. See Robin Gill, *Changing Worlds*, London, Continuum, 2002.
4. *Statistics: A Tool for Mission*, London, Church House Publishing, pp. 18–19.
5. Bob Jackson, *Hope for the Church: Contemporary Strategies for Growth*, London, Church House Publishing, 2002, pp. 6–7.
6. Jackson, *Hope for the Church*, p. 10.
7. Richard Roberts, 'New Directions', General Synod, January 1996, p. 5, and his *Religion, Theology and the Human Sciences*, Cambridge, Cambridge University Press, 2001. See also Stephen Pattison, *The Faith of the Managers*, London, Cassell, 1997, p. 185.
8. *Strategic Church Leadership*, pp. 48–9.
9. Although see Stephen Lane, *Anyone for Alpha?*, London, DLT, 2001.
10. *Strategic Church Leadership*, pp. 73–4.
11. *Strategic Church Leadership*, pp. 76–7.

7 Leading without leadership: managing without management

WESLEY CARR

In this chapter I wish to reflect upon the impact of management studies in Continuing Ministerial Education and why it proved more difficult than anticipated, even at a low level of sophistication.

The background

Complaints from lay people about their vicars were increasing in the period around 1970/1980. The modern church had more bureaucracy than most of the clergy in parishes could cope with – or better perhaps, would cope with: for most the interminable filling in of forms and returns was scarcely central to their or the church's task. They were increasingly required to manage affairs in parishes (which were often now multi-beneficed posts calling for extra management skills) and were unable to understand what was expected of them. Soon the standard panacea for all such ills was being touted – add a module to the pre-ordination syllabus, and send the newly ordained out with some sort of management skill, not perhaps an MBA, but something. I was involved with ACCM[1] at the time and we were able to point out that such issues were better addressed with representative clergy from most of the dioceses, who knew a little of life as a vicar. The topic was ideally a theme for those in their first incumbency. Charles Handy and others, with staff from ACCM and myself, ran two pilot courses on management for experienced clergy. They included some theory but were mostly exercises, role play and practical activities. I recall much humour and quite a bit of learning as participants were given exercises in priority setting and time management, as well as earnest discussion about the nature of the 'real' church as opposed to the theoretical ones that were the core of several exercises. These pilot courses led to a report which in turn was to encourage dioceses and regional training schemes to incorporate aspects of management into

their own in-service training courses. The dioceses and regional training schemes were also encouraged to make use of any local management training courses. Some did and some did not.

The minister as manager

The participants were ambivalent. They recognised that in today's
churches administrative matters called for more managing than they
might have wished. They therefore sometimes joined wholeheartedly
with one another and sometimes withdrew into the security of the
familiar by invoking vocation and priesthood. It is that nervousness
that lies behind the title of this essay. There seems to be a reasonable
wish to manage the church at many levels without, as many see it,
selling out to the secular themes of management techniques. This
is matched by a longing to lead without adopting contemporary
approaches to leadership. Although the theoretical basis may be
unknown, there is among the clergy often an instinctive grasp of what
is primary, while they recognise that there is a distinctive pattern to
priesthood and ministry. This has its own integrity when questions of
management and leadership are raised.[2]

The second point was the novelty of looking at management issues
and discovering that the core themes are the same for churches as
for other organisations. For some, however, the unfamiliar setting
alone was enough. This was a theological problem, since they were
suspicious of anything that could not be drawn directly from
Scripture.

Thirdly, there seemed to be very little written material (or rather
material that was written and to which there was access). The seminal
text was still Rudge.[3] To an extent that has changed, although there is
still a paucity of books.[4]

But one thing became very clear: the clergy were interested in
managing themselves and the internal life of the parish better but they
had insufficient understanding of the dynamics of the church –
parish, archdeacon, bishop, priest and so on – to be able to apply and
use their learning. Consequently they were (and this is a generalisa-
tion) happier with diary management, assessing priorities and so on.
But in terms of systems and their place within them these representatives were largely ignorant and happy to remain so. Yet, as some
found, many of the issues that they thought they had to manage were
in fact products of a fault in the system, which, when they were
identified and addressed, removed the apparent need for new staff or
staff training.

The minister as leader

A parallel development was occurring at the same time, at least in the Church of England. A particular understanding of the ordained minister was quietly emerging. It owed something to technology and something to theology, and, I suspect, something to social change. The technology was, of course, the personal computer. At the early stages merely an advanced form of typewriter, the PC represented a generational change. The picture of the vicar out and about was replaced to an extent by the priest in his (and later her) study sending and receiving messages.

The accompanying theology of ministry was based on leadership. There was, and is, much talk of the minister as either the leader or the one who authorises local lay leadership. There was a steady stream of candidates for ordination who lacked much understanding and experience of the Church of England. They also had little, if any, grasp or awareness of priesthood (for all its complexities) and who saw themselves merely as 'salaried Christians' working full time alongside voluntary part-time lay colleagues.

This led to and was confirmed by a number of pointers. Ordinands arrived in a parish with a 'two-session' approach. They reasoned that the day fell into three parts – morning, afternoon and evening. To be effective the minister (leader) should work only two of these three.[5] They also brought an avowed collaborative model of ministry. Although the precise meaning varied, it seems chiefly to mean reducing any sense of difference between, for example, lay and ordained. Within the church's activity the differences are minimised. For example, some advocate (and illicitly practise) abandoning clerical dress and from some directions an increasingly strident call comes for lay celebration of the eucharist. Such stances, together with the notion of 'enabling', became prominent. The consequent image was of the minister/leader sitting at home at the computer sending messages to his/her collaborators for implementation by ministry groups led by other ministers/leaders.

It is difficult to be sure to what extent such developments were also the product of general social change. But the decline in status of many professions, including that of the clergy, may have been a factor. The notion of 'enabling' was also popular, although few seemed to perceive how patronising this (together with 'empowering') could be.[6]

Leadership and management

Such an approach to ministry brings firmly together the twin themes of leadership and management.[7] In the churches it is easy to mock management, while at the same time embracing a model of leadership as an appropriate style for a curate. But what in such a context would leadership be?

> Like beauty, or love, we know it when we see it but cannot easily define or produce it on demand . . . So what is this mysterious thing and how does one acquire it? The studies agree on very little, but what they do agree on is probably at the heart of things. It is this: 'A leader shapes and shares a vision which gives point to the work of others'.[8]

Charles Handy was writing about running organisations. And this is a very good definition. The difficulty for churches lies in 'a leader shapes and shares a vision which gives point to the work of others'.

Perceptions, of course, vary. As I draft this essay there are two reports in the papers. One concerns Westminster Abbey, where with the Queen and members of the royal family, diplomats and religious and secular leaders, Commonwealth Day was celebrated with hundreds of children. The second concerns the increasing number of attacks on clergy and churches. In Bradford one church is a focus of aggression. Youths break in and try to burn it; the vicar is attacked with bricks; windows are smashed; and after 20 years the Brownie pack has had to leave after parents and helpers were abused by groups of Muslim youths.[9] The priest understood, however, that the underlying issue was the problem that these youths had with authority in any guise, and for these people the clergy and the churches have become an easy target. The impressive incumbent is reported as saying that young people of all faith communities 'have a serious problem with authority and for these people the clergy and the churches have become an easy target. Our task is to work within these communities and earn their respect.' What was so unusual about this was not the saintly forbearance of the vicar, but the way he seems instinctively to have perceived that the problem was not inter-religious but one about how the church was perceived and the illusion that it constituted. To discern appropriate leadership and promote better management, we need some clarification about the church and how it is perceived.

Managing the church as an institution

A more detailed example of how by missing the institutional dimension even the best intentioned may drift into error is found in
probably the most recently significant report to the Church of England:
*Working as One Body: The Report of the Archbishops' Commission on the
Organisation of the Church of England*.[10] The principle of subsidiarity
has been invoked alongside a presumed, but not argued, hierarchy. In
principle the idea sounds fine. The concept has a theological side and
was formally expounded by Pope Pius XI as long ago as 1931:

> Just as in respect of those things which can be carried out by
> individuals through their own exertion and industry, it is unlawful
> to seize them and hand them over to the community, so also in
> respect of those which can be effected and undertaken by smaller
> and lower-level communities (*inferioribus communitatibus*), it is
> unjust to divert them to a greater and higher association (*altiorem
> societatem*). It is similarly a serious wrong and overturns due order.
> For any social activity by its strength ought to afford support
> (*subsidium*) to the members of the social body and certainly never
> destroy them or take them over.[11]

This idea does not, as is popularly supposed, describe levels in a
structural hierarchy, up and down which information flows and tasks
are delegated. It is a theological concept about a system undergirded
by grace and justice. Subsidiarity, therefore, is to do with tasks and
where they are appropriately located and not with a structure of
levels of activity. If such levels are given undue prominence, the
tendency will always be to seek structural parallels between them
rather than to create an effectively interactive organisation. This
seems to have happened with the Church of England, for example,
where the adoption of Turnbull and the creation of the Archbishops'
Council has not removed any of the existing structures.[12]

Institution and organisation

The terms 'institution' and 'organisation' are often used interchange-
ably. But they can draw attention to a useful distinction. The former
requires leadership; the latter, management. An institution is largely
a picture held in our minds, where what is inside and what is outside
come together to produce the 'institution-in-the-mind'. Specifically
this is a mix of the projections and fantasies of all concerned. That can
be a very wide range of people, far beyond church membership.[13]

These become negotiation points as people deal with each other and create the notion of an institution with which they work and around which they join. This is a matter of belief. Churches, with their symbols, buildings, traditions (always a mixture of local myth – 'We *always* do such and such' – and the Christian tradition which they carry) are rich and complex institutions negotiated in the minds of many more than the congregation.[14]

But everyone working within such an institution will also be aware of its organisation. This, too, is composed of a series of mental images of how it works. But these diverse ideas are not always consciously negotiated: there seems to be a greater awareness of this dimension as the symbolic nature of institutions recedes. For example, a meeting of the Church Council needs to be aware of the church as institution, but will be more organisationally aware if it is planning, say, new lavatories.

There is, then, on the one hand, the institution, which is ultimately a complicated set of unconscious constructs in the mind. And, on the other, there is the organisation, that aspect of the institution that invites conscious reflection and handling. The two themes are not separable. It is difficult to conceive of an institution that does not require some organisation.

The connection is also illuminating for the twin themes of leadership and management which have become confused. We might make the following distinction. An institution, being largely an unconscious construct, requires leadership. This calls for the capacity to be sensitive to how powerfully oneself and others function in the area of fantasy and, particularly, projection. Without some awareness of these dimensions to life, both of individuals (including oneself) and of groups and corporate bodies, the attachment that people feel to one another and to their institutions will be undervalued. The result can be an increasing, but usually not articulated, sense of discomfort with the institution and even dissociation from it. Sometimes, therefore, the pressure to manage affairs better is not a useful response.

By contrast, the organisation does require management. It is the area where remedies for problems can be supplied – a change in the system, an external consultancy or new technology. These are not to be discounted, but they prove illusory as solutions to dynamic issues that reside in the mind. We might register, therefore, that one of the skills of the genuine leader is to be able to hold these two facets of institution and organisation together without abandoning one or the other.

There is obviously a danger in so simple a classification and any such dichotomy is suspect: what is being split off and off what? But as a working definition it has value. It also illuminates some of the problems that we see in institutions today. For the demands of the organisation call for people who will get things done and, on the whole, disregard or discount the unconscious. By contrast the concept of institution calls for leadership, a more nebulous idea, but one that invites a leadership that is essentially an interpretative function. This may today be regarded as too conceptualised and complicating the practice of good management.

Leader and led

However, let me now turn briefly to some consequences. There can be no leader unless there are also the led or, at least, those willing to be led. Yet two aspects of contemporary life make this relationship suspect. First, as we have seen, the social context puts a premium on autonomy. To describe oneself as a follower or, even worse, as 'led', carries overtones of failure. So to follow is not an obviously 'good thing'. But followership may give us more of a clue as to why there may be felt to be a crisis in leadership at present.

In an organisation, tasks are usually broken down into sub-tasks and management systems developed to perform them. But in the institution-in-the-mind the task moves the other way: it becomes larger as the wider boundaries and implications are discerned. Leadership, therefore, has to generate a shared vision that can relate to and sustain this large task. Some charisma is required, so that, as leaders and followers together subscribe to this shared vision, the followers can identify with the leader. They do so in a variety of ways. The link between leader and disciple is the learning, and the prevailing dynamic is necessarily dependent. When they are fellow workers, then this is a form of interdependence. Collaborative working, shared interpretation and mature use of dependence combine in the joint recognition that the leader can neither achieve nor sustain anything alone. The task of institutional leadership must always be to work with other institutions to create what we might call 'opportunities for negotiated meaning' which will occur where worlds of moral discourse meet.

Management and task

All churches are caught up in management and its dilemmas. What is more, it is important that they remain alert, if only as a matter of professionalism and businesslike practice. The church has survived failures in this field as much as in others. Managing is today a point of contact, and therefore of engagement (some might even call it 'mission'), between the church and society.

The Church's primary business is concerned with God and with people. That much is agreed. But church people are, therefore, prone to slip easily, but erroneously, into making two assumptions about management – usually a bit of each. First, mere human beings should not presume to manage God. We should, therefore, do our best and leave the rest to him. One problem here is that because it is unconsciously believed that God has infinite resources, then somehow these might eventually become available to us.[15] Planning is avoided in the interests of muddle, and those who suggest another way are accused of being less than faithful. Second, there is the belief that management is about people and that how you manage them is the crucial issue.

But we do not and cannot manage people. Whatever his or her managerial responsibility, a manager manages tasks. So the questions which always have to be asked are as follows. What is the task of this institution? What is it about? What is it for? What must it do to continue as it is? To develop? And where does the organisational question emerge? The trouble is, hearts sink. Which of us has not been involved in interminable debates about these topics? But the issue is inescapable: the first area of scrutiny should not be the internal life of the church or organisation or its administration. It should be the contexts (for there will be several) in which it works and from which expectations come. And one task that will emerge in some form is that churches are there to be used.

I am not, of course, referring to the practical use of buildings for various purposes but of something more profound. Institutions do not exist in isolation. What they are varies according to who is involved. This is emphatically not a casual surrender to laissez-faire within the status quo, although some might escape from difficulties that way. It is rather a recognition that what we are managing may in many ways be all too real – money, buildings, tax, etc. – but basically it is continually being created in people's minds. The idea of being used is a way of inviting interpretation of those expectations, negotiation (or as we might say, dialogue) about what they mean and consequently change for all involved.[16]

This is a huge subject, but without a grasp of it we shall go in the wrong direction in all our attempts and efforts at administration, communication and enterprise. One of the things that interests me most when I work at consultancy outside the church is the way that people see that the church actually has quite good systems for this task, even though we often fail to recognise this and tamper with them.

There, of course, explicitly theological language is not used. But in fact they are making a simple management point with theological overtones: the management structure of any organisation must be congruent with its task. In the case of churches, the task of being used is itself congruent with the model of Jesus' ministry. As the stories go, he was willing to be used; he became whatever people wished him to be – Rabbi, teacher, healer, man from Nazareth – in order to engage with them and change their assumptions about themselves, him and God.

Task, structure and context

The concept of 'task' directs our attention always to our context and the interaction of a church with it. That will, of course, affect both the church and the context. There can be no sense that we do things to that context: on the whole we do things with and sometimes for it. This is important for our administration because we have in this generation been discovering that what is happening inside a cathedral chapter, a parish staff or any sub-group is evidence about what may be happening between those or other configurations and its environment or between different parts of the system.

This is one reason why churches are hotbeds of feelings. Of course they are – and always have been. Why should this be? There are two main reasons: our structure and our context.

Today's churches are enthusiastic for all things to do with joining and 'collaborative ministry'. 'Team', therefore, and 'collaborative' and 'healthy' are currently politically correct. A team is usually brought together fairly randomly and is full of enthusiasts. While striving for an immediate objective, the members are willing to subsume differences and do so. But this style of activity is not so good for consolidation. In that phase the differences which have been submerged as the energy has been expended on the project now surface. Myths and memories prevail and strife occurs.

As I have already pointed out, much inarticulate religion is focused in churches. A few reasons why things are acute just now may be adduced. The decline, which is more than we care to admit self-induced, is of parish churches as places for all people and not just the believers or 'members'. That form of managed attendance is shown in what seems to have been a discernible shift towards cathedrals as large-scale parish churches. People who might have dropped into their local church dare not do so and travel occasionally to what they hope will be a more reliable church – the cathedral.

For these reasons – and no doubt more – feelings are likely to run high and occasionally burst out. What should be the manager's response? An article in *The Harvard Business Review* explores (in a wholly secular approach to management) the place of feelings as data:

> Such feelings are not just the inevitable emotional residue of human work relationships. They are *data*, valuable clues to the dynamics of boundary relationships. In this respect feelings are an aid to thinking and to managing; they are a real part of real work.[17]

Some final thoughts on managing

Now I turn explicitly to management. My own checklist of good practice does not mean that I always achieve these. But the list is something that I aim at, though have not achieved.

To devolve responsibility

This seems in principle good practice and it probably is. But it depends on what the real meaning of devolve is and where subsidiarity comes in: it is not passing a responsibility downwards. The aim is to put the resource for the task where it is appropriate. For the professional in the organisation (almost always the incumbent), devolution can easily become self-justification for getting others to do the work which is measurable (or so it is thought), leaving the 'spiritual' activity to himself. That is poor theology, weak psychology, unclear sociology and, more often than not, abdication.

Budget control by budget spenders

This seems obvious, but all church finance is fraught with hard decisions and demands a wide view of the needs of churches, other than your own. Tight budgetary control of those holding money needs to be exercised. Again this is not very usual in churches, but it can be useful and effective, even in small ones. Not only does it introduce more people to the realities of finance but it also puts all major expenditure in the public arena.

An evolving structure

This is essential for a growing institution, the organisation of which develops, too. It might be thought that something based on such a history as the church and with its 'output' largely (though not completely) beyond this life, is not likely to go further.[18] However there are types of development, and good management is alert to these. Usually in such an organisation the development is less by violent adjustments than through long and extensive debate.

Staff development

Clergy today do far more training after ordination than did their predecessors, and that is largely for the good of church, people and clergy. In a job which may be considered and felt to be a vocation there is little room for material reward, either of a pecuniary nature or in terms of promotion. The personal reward, therefore, has to be in terms of the satisfaction of professional competence.

Clear aims and objectives and Communication

These two issues go together. When people begin to talk about communication alone, it is often a sign that something task-oriented has been lost; if they speak of change of any sort without the dimension of communication, then it is likely that they have lost sight of the original task.

Some final thoughts on leadership

Apart from the confusion to which I have already referred, the major problems of leadership in churches are to do with the lack of space within the institution. The business model is not really parallel. But we might note that the two most commonly emulated ideas from the business world are the two which are under severe scrutiny in that environment.

The first is the alignment of the roles of chief executive and that of chairman. The combination of presiding over both policy-making and being the chief executive who carries out those policies concentrates power. In the churches it is very difficult to create much space between the two roles and the resulting concentration of power can be formidable. But at the same time the church is a voluntary association and it does not have to make a business model work but to devise a structure that is commensurate with service leadership.

The second dangerous model is that of non-executive directors. In a series of financial scandals[19] this has been shown to be a role in which we should not repose confidence. Far from being an independent scrutineer of an organisation, such people emerge as only as effective as the executive allows them to be. In the Church of England this approach is, for example, espoused in the new Cathedrals' Measure based on *Heritage and Renewal*.[20]

Leadership involves sensitivity to the feelings and attitudes of others, ability to understand what is happening in a group at the unconscious as well as the conscious level and skill in acting in ways that contribute to, rather than hinder, task performance. But increased sensitivity and understanding are means, not ends: the end is service of the church as servant of the Kingdom of God. That institution needs leading, but not the paraphernalia of leadership; and it needs managing, not the seductions of management.

Notes

1. The Advisory Council for the Church's Ministry, later ABM (Advisory Board of Ministry), the predecessor of the Division of Ministry. The changes reflect shifts in thinking about it and consequential restructuring.

2. There is also the obvious point that Jesus lacked any institution to which to belong and therefore had no organisation to manage, whereas he could always be considered a leader.

3. Peter F. Rudge, *Ministry and Management*, London, Tavistock, 1968.

4. Among them we may note R. Gill and D. Burke, *Strategic Church Leadership*, London, SPCK, 1996; G. R. Evans and M. Percy (eds), *Managing the Church?*, Sheffield, Sheffield Academic Press, 2000 – a range of essays, not all germane to the subject; M. Harris, *Organizing God's Work: Challenges for Churches and Synagogues*, Basingstoke, Macmillan, 1998; S. Pattison, *The Faith of the Managers: When Management Becomes Religion*, London, Cassell, 1997 – something of a diatribe against contemporary managerial culture.

5. It was often claimed that the idea came from David Sheppard when he was Warden of the Mayflower Centre in South London. In *Built as a City*, London, Hodder, 1974, p. 259, he implies that this approach was essential given the hours that he was working. These new ministers were doing nothing like those.

6. For a useful explanation about the dangers of such language see E. J. Miller, *From Dependency to Autonomy*, London, Free Association Press, 1993, p. xvi.

7. Parts of this section were given as the keynote address at the Twelfth Scientific Meeting of the A. K. Rice Institute in Washington in May 1995 and published in *The Leadership and Organization Development Journal*, 17.6 (1996), pp. 46ff.

8. C. Handy, *The Age of Unreason*, London, Hutchinson, 1989, pp. 105ff.

9. *The Times* (11 March 2003).

10. *Working as One Body: The Report of the Archbishops' Commission on the Organisation of the Church of England*, London, Church House Publishing, 1995. It is widely known as The Turnbull Report after its Chairman, Michael Turnbull, Bishop of Durham. For more detail, see my chapter in R. Hannaford (ed.), *A Church for the Twenty-First Century*, London, Gracewing, 1998.

11. Pius XI, 'Quadragesimo anno', in H. Denzinger, *Enchiridion Symbolorum. Definitinum et declarationum de rebus fidei et morum* (Editio xxxiv), Freiburg, Herder, 1966, p. 732. My translation with the assistance of Canon P. F. Johnson.

12. It was noticeable at the enthronement of the Archbishop of Canterbury (27 February 2003) that the longest procession was that of assistant and suffragan bishops and that members of the Archbishops' Council processed with the officers of the Convocations. The first group consists of those who, although bishops by virtue of their orders, ultimately have little or no authority – the buck does not stop with them. The Council was intended to be a working body and the Convocations were to have sunk into desuetude, if indeed not disbanded. To see them side by side at Canterbury was a visible reminder of the organisational problems that the church creates for itself.

13. See my *The Priestlike Task*, London, SPCK, 1985.

14. For a convenient collection of stories and argument see, e.g., G. Ecclestone (ed.), *The Parish Church?*, Oxford, Mowbrays, 1988.

15. This is an instance of that dependency that constitutes the basic stance of people towards God and in religion generally. There is a large literature, but see, e.g., A. W. Carr, 'The Exercise of Authority in a Dependent Context', in L. Gould, L. F. Stapley and M. Stein, *The System Psychodynamics of Organizations*, New York and London, Karnac, 2001, pp. 45ff.

16. I once asked a group who used their church – one of the great churches of England. After a lively discussion I pointed out that the chief 'user' was in fact God. The resultant work and activity was remarkable.

17. L. Hirschorn and T. Gilmore, 'The New Boundaries of the "Boundary-less" Company', *Harvard Business Review* (May–June 1992), pp. 38ff.

18. Miller and Rice in their seminal book made this assumption at first, but later modified it. See E. J. Miller and A. K. Rice, *Systems of Organization*, London, Tavistock, 1967, p. 255; A. W. Carr, *A Handbook of Pastoral Studies*, London, SPCK, 1997.

19. In the UK, Independent Insurance and Equitable Life Assurance; in the USA, World.com and Enron.

20. *Heritage and Renewal: The Report of the Archbishops' Commission on Cathedrals*, London, Church House Publishing, 1995. This is widely known as 'The Howe Report' after its Chairman, Lady Howe.

8 Believing in leadership

PHILIP MAWER

I have been asked to address the theme 'Believing in leadership'. Before I do so, I want to pay two tributes. The first is to MODEM for the way in which it has carried the torch for the importance of considering issues of leadership and management in relation to those of ministry over the years. This is never a popular theme in churches, which often wrongly assume a separation between the theological and pastoral on the one hand and the worldly and managerial on the other, but it is a vital one. Those who so conscientiously and energetically serve on MODEM's organising Committee deserve our warmest thanks.

The second tribute is to John Adair, co-editor of this book, for his path-finding, one might say missionary work, on leadership, and his unselfish giving of himself to the task of making converts to its significance. He has been and remains a significant influence on all of us, and I in particular have good cause to be thankful to him for his help in the early stages of the formation of the Archbishops' Council.

Which brings me to 'Believing in leadership'. This is a theme which can be examined at several different levels and in a moment I will suggest four of them:

- belief in the leader
- belief in the led
- the leader's self-belief
- the leader's belief in something beyond themselves, which for Christians of course means essentially a focus on God.

But first a few thoughts about belief itself.

Belief can be entirely inward-looking: self-belief. But I suspect that if it seeks to be entirely self-sustaining it will not last long. Even those with the most towering egos require occasional reassurance and encouragement. Indeed, in my experience, the more overwhelming the apparent self-confidence, the more likely it is to be brittle and require regular maintenance and support in private.

Belief is essentially about relationship – between the believer and the object of their belief. It implies the allocation of trust and confidence: it is about mutuality. It cannot always be rationally explained, though we may be able to identify some conditions which encourage it. And it is dynamic, constantly shifting both as the relationship between the believer and the object of their belief alters and as it is impacted by external events.

I want us to hold these brief points about the nature of belief in mind as we turn to consider 'believing in leadership'. As we do so, I simply observe that the key qualities or characteristics of belief which I have identified – mutuality, trust, dynamic development – are, for Christians, at the heart of their understanding both of the relationship within the Trinity and of their own relationship with God.

I write of four levels or aspects of 'believing in leadership'. The most evident is *belief in the leader*. In order to effect leadership successfully, the leader needs to generate a sufficient degree of belief among the led in his or her right and ability to lead. Initially, the leader may be accorded the right to lead because of the office or rank they hold. But if that remains the sole ground of their claim to leadership status, that claim will be thinly rooted and acquiescence in it grudging and surly.

How does the leader develop not merely acquiescence but a genuine belief among the led in their right to lead, with all the supportive energy that goes with that? Part of the answer is by developing and convincing others of their vision for the organisation or cause which they aspire to lead. But I emphasise the word 'part'. Whilst it is certainly desirable to develop and promulgate a clear and convincing vision of where you want to go – consulting others of course, in the course of formulating it – in some types of situation and organisation it may be neither possible nor desirable to do so. I have in mind, for example, those continuing organisations which are essentially coalitions of partners, and those situations in which change is protracted and what people want is not a fresh vision but 'a bit of peace and stability, please'. In such circumstances, what people may need is not so much a vision of the way forward but of who and where they are. So I accept that part of the challenge of leadership is to develop and offer a clear vision, but it is by no means the whole of it.

A second way in which belief in the leader is developed is through their actions. There may be key occasions on which they demonstrate leadership for all to see and are rewarded with respect in consequence. More often it is the demonstration of continued competence which matters, or at least of competence in those things which the led judge to matter. The 'authority of competence' is a less dashing but a necessary part of developing belief in the leader.

Thirdly, there is an 'authority of being', the authority, even the affection which comes from who the leader is rather than what they do. This is not simply a matter of personality but of the values, attitudes and beliefs which they model and are seen to embody. In all truly great leaders, there is a quality which is more than the sum of their parts and which inspires confidence, respect and trust. Having said that, great leaders are not super-human: they are flawed like the rest of us. It is simply that we can see that their particular combination of gifts is exceptional and is right for this particular moment.

The second aspect of believing in leadership which I identified above was *belief in the led*. This is the reciprocal aspect of belief in the leader and it is crucial to underpinning the mutuality of the relationship between leader and led. Showing confidence in those who work for and with you is essential to building their self-esteem and ability to achieve shared goals. In today's open, democratic and accountable society in particular, the style of leadership which works best in many (although not necessarily all) situations is likely to be one based on mutual respect, valuing each individual, enabling each individual to develop and achieve their full potential within the team. Effective leadership is not just, therefore, about 'hard' skills – such as envisioning, planning, marshalling resources – but 'soft' ones too, such as showing respect for others and their particular skills, motivating people by example, etc. Unless this is done, objectives will not be realised, the vision not achieved, the organisation not flourish.

As an African proverb says, 'He who touches the clouds stands on the shoulders of others'. Effective leaders must constantly show their belief in the led, even when the led fail to meet their best expectations.

The third aspect of 'believing in leadership' which I want to examine briefly is *the leader's self-belief*. The effective leader has to have confidence in the goals they are trying to achieve (their 'vision') and in their own ability, with the help of others, to achieve them. That self-belief must, however, be based on a true self-understanding, one which acknowledges – to oneself at least – areas of weakness (and realises the need to offset or compensate for them) as well as areas of strength. Many failures of leadership seem to me to be due to our obsession with the macho style of leadership model – the mistaken belief that the leader has to be out front all the time, be all-competent and all knowledgeable. This obsession is manifest in the relationship between modern politicians and the media – the former unable to admit when they don't have the answer, the latter ready to pounce on any supposed sign of weakness. Much modern government is about the management of uncertainty rather than certainty, but we seem incapable of recognising this and its implications for our proper expectations of our political leaders.

The wise leader recognises their own limits – and the need to set limits for themselves – if they are to do their job well. One of the most significant causes of stress and failure in clerical ministry in my experience is the model of the all-competent parish priest or bishop. It is a model which the unreal expectations of the laity have created as much as any work myths among the clergy. Whilst this model is gradually fading and being replaced with a more modest and balanced set of expectations and understandings, it is still too much in evidence. Learning that although they themselves may be able to do the job better than anyone else, they would be wise not to attempt it but to focus on the things which are critical to their role and which only they can do, is one of the hardest and most difficult of the lessons effective leaders must learn.

As developing leaders move through their organisation into positions of greater leadership, they have to acknowledge that leadership involves working through others, not doing it alone. To accept this requires not just a belief in themselves but a high degree of personal maturity and, above all, of humility.

The fourth and final aspect of 'believing in leadership' which I want to explore is *the leader's belief in something beyond themselves*. I am not here talking of their belief in their vision or in those they are privileged to lead, but of those external sources from which they draw support, confidence and strength. For all of us those sources may include the example of others we know or have known; the love of family or partner; the sense of vocation or calling we have to a particular role; the basic values which are the bedrock of our understanding of the world, of what we want it to be and of our part in realising that understanding.

I begin to touch here, of course, on some of the themes explored in MODEM's fascinating research project, 'The Hope of the Manager'. If I find the analysis in the project report incomplete in any respect it is in relation to the notion that 'spiritual energy' (whose definition I still find myself grasping after) is released only in circumstances in which one has an inspiring purpose, functions in a liberating and empowering context, and is full of an attitude of hope, confidence and commitment. I have encountered such occasions, but more often have had to function in those where you may be inspired by your purpose but others are not, the context is anything but positive, and your attitude could better be described as one of battling through. Yet it is precisely in the midst of such difficulties that I have been most conscious of drawing on a source of sustaining support which one might characterise as embodying spiritual energy.

The Christian leader should not, of course, find it difficult to say what the source of that energy might be. The more experience I have, the greater the belief I have in Providence, in the hand of God at work in the affairs of humanity. We, of course, show an amazing ability to snatch disaster from the jaws of success. It is the grace of God at work in and through us that enables disaster to be avoided, human weakness to bring forth strength and progress to be made.

The Christian leader must believe that all they do is dedicated to God, is committed to him. In return, his power will sustain them even in the darkest of times. In this context, ensuring space for reflection, for prayer, for waiting on God in the midst of a busy life are essential if they are to do his will.

So we see that, like much else in life, 'believing in leadership' involves grappling successfully with paradox. The effective leader must foster belief in their right to lead but not at the expense of the leadership role of the led. They must be ready to lead but also to give place to others. They must be capable but aware of their own limitations, confident yet humble. They must both act and know when to be still.

Many of these paradoxes are embodied in Christ's model of the servant leader. It is a model of leadership out of tune with the macho image of the leader which dominates current popular perceptions of the nature of leadership, but more in tune than that dominant model with the reality of the complex demands of leadership in our own time. It is a model which is potentially liberating for both leader and led. It emphasises the relational and dynamic nature of the task of leadership. And – as portrayed by Jesus – it is a source of continued inspiration to all of us, at whatever level, who are faced with the challenge of 'believing in leadership'.

9 Come and see

NORMAN TODD

'My Job,' said the designated Church Leader (DCL), 'is to keep the show on the road.' Whether he was also a creative Church Leader (CCL) I am not sure. He may have been right; he was experienced in his job, popular and well thought of, but questions come to mind. What is being shown for people to come and see? What attracts them? Are those who come expected to join the show? Where is the road, and hence the show, going? Somewhere special, nowhere particular, or on some kind of a circuit?

The Church Leader as a circus owner and ringmaster brings other questions to mind, particularly regarding leadership. Is there something called leadership, neutral in itself, which can be applied to any occupation: business, sports team, circus, church? Or does the purpose of the organisation (what is being shown, and the objective, or at least direction, of progress towards it) determine what is required in its leaders?

Apart from the simple notion of leading as being out in front with others following (or vice versa if it's the Duke of Plazatoro) might it be that very different qualities are required for leading a global capitalist business, a communist five-year plan, a protest march and a church. The bottom lines on the balance sheets are certainly different ('you cannot serve God and Mammon') and this may mean that leading one is very different from leading another. Even if there is some overlap it may mask a pull in opposite directions.

Creative leadership introduces a further question. Is the creativity of a Christian martyr similar in any way to that of the circus proprietor of the Colosseum in Rome designing a new spectacle of entertainment for the crowds who come to see the martyrdom?

For example, the principles of time management and diary-keeping as taught by secular experts could be adopted by CCLs. Or they could start by heeding the advice of the medieval Christian mystic, 'All the time that is given to thee, it shall be asked of thee how thou hast spent it. And it is quite right that you should have to give an account of it . . . So be very careful how you spend time. There is nothing more precious. In the twinkling of an eye heaven may be won or lost.'[1] This could lead to prayerful self-examination, penitence, thanksgiving and amendment of life.

Or another example. A group of DCLs had listened to a careful and systematic presentation in Leadership and Management by a senior officer from the Military Staff College. They thought it had no relevance to them because, as they said, they were leading a church, not an army fighting a war.

Most DCLs, whether also CCLs or not, are strongly opposed to management. A recent advert for a clergy training course emphasised that it was about leadership not management and referred to the church as 'over-managed and underfed'. I wonder how many lay people would agree. One said to me recently that his church was without a vicar, but was being managed much better by the church-wardens than it had been by the last vicar. There have been many initiatives in the Church over the last 50 years or so (from Towards the Conversion of England to the Decade of Evangelism) but little has come of them, probably because there was no management of the follow up. There have been plenty of trumpet blasts. As Ian Ramsey (then Bishop of Durham), in a document to be quoted more fully later, remarked in 1972,

> As for the trumpet, let us recall that St Paul in this metaphor was protesting against unintelligibility not diversity: whereas our main trouble today is that trumpets are sounded on all sides all too clearly and all too readily. The moral, however, is not that we exclude some rather strident and ear-splitting notes but trace all the notes back to their blowers to see whether with patience and wisdom a new and altogether unexpected harmony may be created.[2]

The mention in the quotation from the *Cloud of Unknowing* that heaven may be won or lost in the twinkling of an eye gives a clue to the reason for caution in examining these questions. If the goal of the church is heaven then the way to follow, in some sense, leads out of the world (age, aeon, epoch, state of affairs, life) as we know it and humans have always known it, into something new. The old way of living is left behind or is so transformed as to be hardly recognised. Words like 'reborn' and 'regenerated' leave an awareness of minuscule continuity between the old and the new; the adjective 'new' with various nouns emphasises the radical break with the old. It is a change of direction that everyone yearns for and yet in which all are frustrated. So-called civilisation is mere coercion by common cupidity, physical and mental.

This change is what the disciples of Jesus believed he had claimed to be demonstrating and teaching. It is what they claimed to be experiencing as a result of his coming, crucifixion, resurrection and ascension, and sending another Paraclete.

The immediate effect of Jesus was the formation of the Church, not as a deliberate act on the part of the disciples but as an exploration of the results of having the same Jesus with them, but in a new way, more or less as remembered in the Acts of the Apostles. As if they are saying,

'This is how we, as a community and as a community of communities, discovered a new way of living. This becoming conscious for the first time, and bit by bit, that Jesus has led us into a new way of life that meets, and explodes in fulfilment, all our yearnings, fostered and guided by the partial insights of the prophets.'

The letters of the New Testament can be read as advice from guides ahead of us on how to die to the old life that crucified Christ and live the new life in the presence and power of Christ raised to life by the God of Abraham, Isaac and Jacob.

Earth has been connected to heaven via the personality and work of Jesus. Messengers are ascending and descending on him as a living Jacob's ladder. Whatever it is that separated our world from its source and perfection has been pierced, torn asunder, and Jesus is on both sides of the veil of separation. A rope ladder hangs for us to climb, anchored firmly within the eternal Holy of Holies. The heavens have been wrenched open by the descent from glory and ascent to glory of the person we had known or our trusted friends had known. He went to prepare a place for us. We are born again from above. The communication from beyond our normal experience dwells in our hearts and minds. Our inner eyes (the eyes of our heart) are opened. Ears are unblocked. Personal relationships are transformed.

It is as if every category of thought available is used to point to where Jesus has gone and can lead us. And the evidence for all this? Come and see. We have changed direction and are on the way. Things are different.

The disciples remember the words and actions of Jesus, ponder them in their various communities, and begin forming them into tales and narratives of how he lived, taught, challenged, encouraged, understood the Scriptures; how he promised that where he was going they would be able to follow, in a new power poured out from the mystery met in the holy name, though not pronounced except in awe and wonder and with bended knee.

The Lord's Prayer had been answered in the Lord and is being answered in us now as we learn how to receive the power to change, which includes the eyes to see something of the further change still required. Again every metaphor is exploited to describe the indescribable. And again, the evidence? Come and see.

When St Paul, going on his way to imprison members of the church in Damascus, was blinded by an unworldly light, the voice he heard identified Jesus with the Church Paul was persecuting. He had to wait for a DCL, who was also a CCL, overcoming his understandable fears of a trap, to come and accept him. 'Brother Saul, receive your sight.' Even if a trap had been sprung it would have been right for Ananias to go. He would have witnessed through his suffering and death; another martyr like St Stephen. Both Stephen and Ananias played their part in the recreation of Saul as the apostle to the gentiles.

The question asked by Thomas, according to the Fourth Gospel, 'Lord, we don't know where you are going, so how can we know the way?' was answered, 'I am the way, the truth and the life.' 'It is the Father living in me, who is doing his work . . . at least believe on the evidence of the miracles themselves.'[3] These quotations are intended not as proof texts but as examples of how the Church understood what they were experiencing.

The New Testament, in the context of the Old Testament as understood by the first churches, is normative for the continuing Church because it describes the first direct result on human life and culture, and the beginning of the first transfer from one culture to another. The experience was transferred from the original Semitic, Aramaic-speaking culture, via the Jewish dispersion, to the Greek-speaking cultures of the Roman Empire. Here, in the New Testament, are the being-changed men and women struggling to describe to one another, and to understand, what has happened and is happening. An integral part of the new life is the discovery that it is for all people and affects everything. Jesus continues his campaign within and through the community of his disciples. The weapons are those of Jesus. The temptation to cast off the new armour (helmet of salvation, sword of the Spirit, etc.) and don again the worldly armour of coercion is not always resisted. The authority of the leaders can slip back from that of those who accept the full authority of Jesus as author of eternal salvation to that of the rulers of the old world.

In other words, the CCLs are those recognised as saints, whether designated as such or not (St Stephen and St Ananias). Some are recognised immediately; others, perhaps most like the Old Testament prophets, are at first rejected because they challenge, explicitly or implicitly, the Church for having lost its way. St John of the Cross was kidnapped and imprisoned by the unreformed members of his own Carmelite order. His teachings were denounced to the Spanish Inquisition. A learned defender of St John referred to the facts that:

> St Jerome was attacked for his translation of the Bible from Hebrew into Latin; St Augustine for his teaching about grace and freewill. The works of St Gregory the Great were burned at Rome; those of St Thomas Aquinas at Paris. Most medieval and modern mystics have been victims of persecution – Ruysbroeck, Tauler and even St Teresa.[4]

Rehabilitation can sometimes take a long time. Condemned in 1329, Meister Eckhart has only recently been accepted and defended by scholars of his own Dominican order. John Bunyan and F. D. Maurice now appear in the Church of England lectionary.

Of course not everybody rejected by the DCLs is later acknowledged as a CCL. Such examples do, however, illustrate the difficulty contemporaries have in recognising the genuine CCLs. Usually, as with the Hebrew prophets, their teachings are preserved by a small band of disciples, until they are accepted by the DCLs and made available to the general membership of the Church.

There have been massive changes in the last 150 years, and particularly in the last 50, in the ways the Christian traditions are understood. The changes are caused by the application to human affairs of the scientific method of enquiry – the human sciences. They came in the teeth of opposition from the Church, the DCLs conceding bit by bit what for a long time had been accepted by the scholars and visionaries.

The great Victorian scholar and spiritual guide F. von Hugel was saved from excommunication only by being a layman and hence not a DCL in his church. The furore over *Honest to God* was caused not by its ideas but by their being advocated by a DCL. John Robinson, a Cambridge don, became a suffragan (i.e. assistant) bishop. In 1963 he wrote (while he was recovering from a back illness) a short book for the Book Club of the Student Christian Movement, about developments in scholarly theological thinking. It contained nothing that a student would not be familiar with. Popularised by a summary in a national Sunday newspaper, the book came as a welcome release for many people whose consciences were burdened by what had become meaningless religious traditions. It came as a threat to the traditional faithful, especially if they had fundamentalist leanings. There were a number of published responses. Perhaps the most gently reasoned was from the Archbishop of Canterbury, Michael Ramsey, a former

Regius Professor of Divinity. In his summing up of the 15-page booklet the Archbishop wrote,

> As a Church we need to be grappling with the questions and trials of belief in the modern world.
>
> It was possible to learn from the Darwinian revolution in the last century a greater understanding of the process of Creation without becoming dominated by a dogma of automatic progress. It was possible earlier in this century to learn from the rigours of New Testament criticism without submitting to the liberal theory of Harnack or the scepticism of Bultmann. So too some of us have faced the message of a Kirkegaard or a Karl Barth and through the deep darkness have learned more fully of the greatness of God and the nothingness of man, and have emerged not disciples of Barth's system but people who see their old faith in a new light. So today it is for us to be ready to find God not within the cosiness of our own piety but within the agony of the world and the meeting of person with person every day. But wherever we find him he is still the God who created us in his own image, and sent his Son to be our Saviour and to bring us to the vision of God in heaven.[5]

The grappling continued. In 1972 the situation was described as 'The Crisis of Faith' by the then Bishop of Durham, Ian Ramsey, speaking at the Church Leaders Conference at Selly Oak Colleges. A soundbite presentation of his argument would be, 'we must change from prescriptive theology [telling people what to believe] to exploratory theology [helping them explore their faith]'. Of authority he said,

> Our problem today – whether in theology or morality, whether in making personal or social or political judgments – is how do we embody in our judgments, our organization, our planning and our structures, the authority which fulfils and releases and speaks of freedom rather than the authoritarianism which oppresses and restricts and speaks of tyranny: realizing that part of the devilish attraction of authoritarianism is to be clear and forceful in its views and to yield striking success by criteria as immediate as they are superficial, in other words, that is matched by the long-term disas-ters which it brings in its train. We may also recognize that nothing is likely to make men (*sic*) authoritarian more than the idea that they are uttering a God-given language: in these circumstances, men not only forget that they are men, not God – they also forget that their God is not a god who makes them mere larynxes and

vocal cords for the production of divine noises. God's grace in Jesus Christ is a relationship which makes that supposition a blasphemous travesty of the facts. But here again we see how inter-connected and criss-crossed our present problems are: for it is all too easy to misread the Bible in such a way as to conclude that God uses men as mere mouthpieces. Unless we are either very unsophisticated or very sophisticated, passages in the Bible which use the word 'God' as the subject of a sentence are hazardous in the extreme: for they read as if God had been observed to say and to do precisely what is there described. They conceal the fact that the words are the writer's interpretation of a situation, not his reporting of observable features as news of the world and God. If all this seems by this time trite and obvious, I can only say that unfortu-nately much of our reasoning about God, man and the world proceeds on the assumption that far from being obvious, it is plainly false. This is another measure of the Herculean task which confronts us.

Of leadership Ian Ramsey said,

[W]hat is needed is a new concept and pattern of leadership. Leadership must no longer profess to give ready-made answers to all questions of importance. What is important is to ensure that in every problem the points at issue are made plain, a radical treat-ment is given, the roots displayed, that we are articulate about the gospel in such a way as to give an authoritative, but not an author-itarian grounding to the principles which are used, and all this in the hope that a creative decision will emerge whose light is that which glorifies the Father and alone gives a clear lead. We do not give a lead, although those who ask us for one often suppose we do, by reiterating conclusions which those around us wish to hear or wish to have without the trouble of reaching them. We give a lead only by displaying in our utterances or otherwise, that which inspires us. 'The power of God is the worship he inspires', said Whitehead. Christian power, we may infer, is the inspiration of God's love in Christ: Christian leadership must display this which leads us – the light of Christ – and this can be more evident from the quality of our struggles and our co-operative endeavours than it is from any claim to have already arrived where we are sitting at ease in Zion dispensing packaged answers. As pilgrims and pioneers . . . our eyes must be fixed on Jesus, on whom faith depends from start to finish, and that faith can be evident from the way we run, and the way we struggle together, if only we do.

He concluded,

> So crisis though it is, I see no cause for depression and despair, still less for nervousness and fright, neurotic and reactionary responses such as were evident in the 19th century. Today I see the possibility of advancing with all the vision of the pioneer, the pilgrim, the man of faith, who endeavours to talk as best he can, and in his practice to display as best he can, that which inspires him, that which called forth and constantly renews his commitment, and points him forward to fulfilment. It is a critical time, but for that very reason it is a time in which we should be glad to be alive. 'This is the day that the Lord hath made; let us rejoice and be glad in it.'

What Ian Ramsey referred to as a decisive time between two eras has since been called a 'paradigm shift'. It derives from T. S. Kuhn's now famous theory of the development of science, which, as well as the gradual build-up of hypotheses, data and theories, periodically undergoes much more fundamental or revolutionary changes in its pattern of basic assumptions. The analogy from science to theology was made quite quickly by I. G. Barbour in 1974 and worked out more fully in a discussion between a physicist and two Roman Catholic theologians in 1992.[6] Writing, of course, after the Second Vatican Council, they find parallels between their two disciplines. Here is my précis of their summary of the paradigm shift in theology.

The new paradigm in theology, instead of believing that the sum total of dogmas added up to revealed truth, sees revelation as a process of one piece with individual dogmas focusing on particular moments in God's self-manifestation in nature, history and human experience. Instead of thinking that there is a set of supernatural truths which God intends to reveal to us, the history of salvation is itself the great truth of God's self-manifestation. Instead of assuming that theological statements are objective (independent of the believing person), subjective and non-conceptual ways of knowing (intuitive, affective, mystical) are valued. The metaphor of reality as a building of fundamental principles is replaced by that of a network of relationships, and theological statements as an interconnected network of different perspectives on transcendent reality. The new paradigm, by greater emphasis on mystery, acknowledges the limited approximate character of every theological statement. Ultimate truth lies not in the theological statement, but in the reality to which this statement gives a certain true, but limited, expression.[7]

This paradigm shift is almost a rediscovery of the raw materials of religious faith. With it comes a rediscovery of the mystical tradition of the Church but no longer with the suspicion that it is for the elite few alone but available at least in some degree to all, rediscovered almost as a scientific exploration of the interaction of the spirit or soul of a person with the Spirit of God. The Christian classics are available as never before, and being used as guides. Mental prayer, meditation, contemplative prayer, are being taught in retreats and courses. Church music is being composed and performed.

A friendly sociologist[8] commented on these challenges to the Church by describing three possible reactions. The Church could retreat into fundamentalism, we could dilute into a vague liberalism, or we could choose the hard way of rediscovering our traditional faith in the new culture based on the new understandings of human nature and human society. He also suggested that the sociology of knowledge could help us understand what was happening if we chose the third way. Here were the beginnings of deconstruction and postmodernism.

Theologians have responded to this opportunity. Some of them are still banned or frowned on by the DCLs of their own churches. Either way they have had little effect on the Church as an organisation. One of the most challenging of them admits this.

> Today, theology is tragically too important. For all the talk of a theology that would reflect on practice, the truth is that we remain uncertain as to where today to locate true Christian practice. This would be, as it has always been, a repetition differently, but authentically, of what has always been done. In his or her uncertainty as to where to find this, the theologian feels almost that the entire ecclesial task falls on his own head: in the meagre mode of reflective words he must seek to imagine what a true practical repetition would be like. Or at least he must hope that his merely theoretical continuation of the tradition will open up space for a wider transformation.[9]

Milbank (a disciple of St Augustine firmly within the contemporary world) argues forcefully that the Church must be 'rigorously concerned with the actual genesis of real historical churches, not simply with the imagination of an ecclesial ideal', but unless this is done by DCLs who are concerned with creating a church in which the way of life of Jesus, different from that of the rest of the world, is being realised there will be nothing to be seen by those who come to see, nor indeed by those who remain within such an insubstantial church. This is always the crucial task of the leaders of the Church.

Organisation, the working of a corporate body, people in relationship cooperating to achieve a common goal, this human phenomenon has been the subject of an enormous amount of empirical study over the last few decades. Helping a business succeed in making a profit has become a successful business. It has often been assumed that the methods of the market in the private sector can be simply transferred to the public sector where the goal is not financial profit but service to the community, helping it work for the common good. Whether this is so is not our concern here. We are asking if the methods can be simply transferred to the Church, whose goal we have been remembering.

The Church has always had, for its individual members, a discipline of self-examination followed, as is appropriate, by thanksgiving or by penitence, confession, penance, forgiveness and amendment of life. It has not applied the discipline to its corporate life. The secular disciplines have both improved the methods (though not for confession and forgiveness) and applied them primarily to organisations as a whole. The methods can be used, with very little adaptation, by the Church. Investors in People, Force-field Analysis,[10] the system described by the late John Walker in the first MODEM book, various consultancies and audits are available. But there is strong resistance from most DCLs, who feel criticised, and by lay people who have had a bad experience of such methods being used at work. They can be used to control, manipulate or to put on an outward show.

Such careful attention to the effective working of an organisation is particularly important in our society with the shift from personal to corporate service. How can a primary care unit have a bedside manner, a comprehensive school know the names and circumstances of all the pupils, a chain of supermarkets provide genuine personal service? How can what was valued personally in the old be produced in its new corporate form? The challenge is everywhere and particularly acute in the Church. How does the local DCL transfer his/her personal ministry through the whole congregation, or a senior DCL care as a parent or shepherd who knows every member by name within a complex and changing organisation? The new can be better than the old if the ministry is shared by the whole body, but we have to explore how it can be done.

Although I do not have space to present it in detail, the research and its development by Christian A. Schwarz is of very great interest. It concerns growth in church quality usually followed by quantity. One of the eight areas of concern, Functional Structures, is that in which church structures are evaluated on whether they serve the growth of the church or not.

One of the biggest barriers to recognising the significance of structures for church development is the widespread view that structure and life are opposites. Interestingly enough, biological research reveals that dead matter and living organisms are not distinguished by their substance, as some people might think, but by the specific *structure* of the relationship of the individual parts to each other. In other words, in God's creation the living and the non-living, the biotic and abiotic, are formed from identical material substances and are distinguished only by their structure.[11]

Exploration is a time-and-word consuming activity. Even in heaven something like it will continue, or just be present, to which perhaps the words 'wonder and worship of unknowing loving' may point. I wonder how heaven is organised; anything like the vision of Dante, or C. S. Lewis, or Julian Barnes, or St John the Divine?[12]

There are four main areas to which I think DCLs who aspire to be CCLs should direct our attention and more of our resources.

1. The practical denial of the Church as the Body of Christ by its divisions. How can explanation proceed across the schisms? In what way can we turn them into opportunities for mutual growth? If you visit the HQs of various churches and compare all that is invested there with the investment in the HQ of Churches Together[13] you will see where our priorities lie. The disparity is just as glaring at the local level.

   This peace-making activity must also be encouraged between the various traditions of describing and entering into the mystery of our awareness of transcendental mystery. Inter-faith dialogue (including the faith of those who deny the objective reality of transcendent being) is increasingly recognised as of great urgency but we are not exploring it with great urgency.

2. The nature of hierarchy in organisations. Recently a former junior or officer in a crack regiment of the British Army was extolling to me the effective way his CO was always asking those under him what they thought. 'He really wanted us not to be shy but to tell him what we thought and if we thought the regiment were getting things right. He really did listen and did not put you down.' My friend, who belongs to a church other than my own, though he knows mine well, continued. 'My CO had a very different idea of leadership from the clergy. Clergy want me to listen and obey. I don't want to be controlled by them and join the life of the Church. What life? One always dominated by the clergy directly or indirectly.' There is a kind of institutional pride that successfully tempts most leaders even if they are humble in private and it is

more apparent in the Church because it is a scandalous denial of the Way.

3. The spontaneous growth of Christian groups outside the traditional church structures. Communities, house churches of various kinds, missions, institutes, pressure groups, such movements are like green shoots suddenly appearing. This has always happened – it was how religious orders and missionary societies of various kinds originated. Then there is 'the spirituality of people who do not go to church', being researched by David Hay.[14] We need to understand and to learn and accept. The Spirit blows where he pleases, not where we tell him to.

4. The nature and practice of 'exploration'. It involves moving out of the security of our own beliefs and towards those of another traditions. We suspend our own certainties, especially our metaphysical certainties, and play with the experience of sharing those of the other. It is serious play, a form of temporary culture shock. A number of words have been used for it: conversation (Theodore Zeldin, Rowan Williams), corresponding (Gillian Stamp), dialogue (Hans Küng), dissolving the wall of partition (St Paul), corporate discernment of spirits (Jesuits), lateral thinking (de Bono), deliberation (Michael Ignatieff).[15] Most interesting is the New Testament word transliterated *paraclete*. The verb describes putting yourself closely alongside someone else and courteously calling forth from each of you a potential for trusting relationship. So 2 Corinthians 1.1–4 becomes: 'the God of all paracleting who paracletes us in all our tribulations that we may be able to paraclete them which are in any trouble by the paracleting wherewith we ourselves are paracleted by God.' It connects with the Beatitudes (Matthew 5.3–10), the fruits of the Spirit (Galatians 5.22–3) and the hymn to love in 1 Corinthians 13.

Where do we begin to make these changes? As we acknowledge the need for purposeful change, we recognise that there are already signs of change. There are green shoots. We can foster them and learn how to propagate them. We find others who are yearning for creative development. We network across the boundaries of denomination and faith. It takes time, effort and courage to explore our own yearnings with the help of others and to engage in experiment to learn what works and what does not. We discover, recover, a vitality that is in continuity with that of the saints.

We are all called to be CCLs. The calling involves not letting DCLs get away with anything less than their calling to be CCLs. We must not make excuses for them or for ourselves lest all of us should be so concerned to keep our show on the road as to forget where we are going, how we should be travelling and with whom we are travelling.

Notes

1. *The Cloud of Unknowing and Other Works*, Harmondsworth, Penguin Books, 1978, pp. 62, 63–4.
2. 'The Crisis of Faith', Church Leaders' Conference, Selly Oak Colleges, Birmingham, 1972.
3. John 14.5–7, 11.
4. E. Allison Peers, *St. John of the Cross*, Burns Oates & Washbourne, 1935, vol. 1, p. lxiii.
5. Michael Ramsey, *Image Old and New*, London, SPCK, 1963, pp. 14, 15.
6. F. Capra and D. Steindl-Bast with T. Matus, *Belonging to the Universe*, Harmondsworth, Penguin Books, 1992.
7. Ibid., pp. xi–xv.
8. P. Berger, *The Heretical Imperative*, London, Collins, 1980.
9. John Milbank, *The Word Made Strange*, London, Blackwell, 1997, p. 1.
10. Kurt Lewin's field theory has proved its effectiveness over time as a way of determining what action should be taken to achieve a desired change.

    In brief, having determined both the current state of affairs and the desired state, a change programme will list the restraining forces, and their magnitude, that are preventing the desired change and those forces, and their magnitude, that are driving change towards the desired state.

    It will then take action in the first instance to weaken or remove the restraining forces and then, if necessary, to strengthen or add to the driving forces that will move the individual or organisation towards the desired state.

    See Kurt Lewin, *Field Theory in Social Science: Selected Theoretical Papers*, ed. Dorwin Cartwright, New York, Harper, 1951.

    (Note provided by MODEM member Revd John Rice. John successfully introduced this analysis at Rolls Royce, Derby, where he was a senior manager, and is now applying it to his church in Derby.)
11. *Natural Church Development*, p. 29. This book and *Paradigm Shift in the Church*, also by Schwarz, are extremely interesting (available from British Church Growth Association, The Park, Moggerhanger, Beds MK44 3RW; bcga@the-park.u-net. com.
12. See: Dante Alighieri, *The Divine Comedy*, 3 vols, Harmondsworth, Penguin, 1962; C. S. Lewis, *The Great Divorce*, Fount, 1997; Julian Barnes, *History of the World in 10½ Chapters*, London, Cape, 1989, last half chapter.
13. Churches Together in Britain and Ireland is a fellowship of churches

renamed from the previous Council of Churches. It provides a forum for joint decision-making and enables the churches to take action together.

14. David Hay, 'Understanding the Spirituality of People Who Do Not Go to Church', research paper, Nottingham University, n.d.

15. See: Theodore Zeldin, *An Intimate History of Humanity*, Vintage, 1998, ch. 2; Rowan Williams, *Lost Icons*, Edinburgh, T&T Clark, 2003, pp. 92–4, 105, 113–15; Gillian Stamp, 'Pastoral Theology Redefined', in John Nelson (ed.), *Management and Ministry*, Norwich, Canterbury Press, 1996, pp. 37–58; Hans Küng, *Global Responsibility*, London: SCM Press, 1991, pp. 135–8; Jesuits, *Applying the Discernment of Spirits to Corporate Decision-making*, no details; Edward de Bono, *Text Book of Wisdom*, London, Penguin, 1997, pp. 238–78; and Michael Ignatieff, *Human Rights*, Princeton University Press, 2001, pp. xxvi, xxvii, 120.

10 Lessons from the secular world

PAULINE PERRY

In the long years of its history, the Church of England has faced, and overcome, many crises. Born of the twin elements of conflict and conviction, it has had to reconcile these themes over the centuries and has triumphed, with God's grace, to survive into the twenty-first century, still the established church of our nation.

The challenges today are, however, of a new and more difficult kind. Our church is no longer recognised as the natural authority on those moral and ethical matters which so trouble us, whether of just war or personal relationships, where people turn to media reporters, pop stars or academics to guide their views; nor is its position as the established church any longer taken as a given in national debate. The admirable wish to recognise the multi-faith character of our society affects legislation and the decisions of government as much as the day-to-day decisions made by individual schools, local authorities and businesses about the way in which they should conduct themselves. Equally, falling numbers in Sunday worship, and the increasing secularisation of Sundays and Holy Days all demonstrate that the delicate balance of our society between the religious and the secular has, in the space of a generation, tilted sharply in favour of the secular.

None of these challenges look to diminish in the years ahead. Perhaps never in its history has the church so acutely needed leadership at all levels. Instead, 'by schisms rent asunder' over issues such as homosexual priests, the marriage of divorced persons and the promotion of women bishops, it has failed to give a clear voice to those who so urgently wish to hear it. From the leadership of the archbishops at national level, through the bishops, to the leadership offered by the priests at parish level, a clear voice is urgently desired by the people of the church, and by the many who still see themselves as in some way followers of the Christian Church, even if they seldom occupy its pews.

In the secular world, it is no surprise that in times of rapid change and fragmentation, where the old certainties are gone, and the traditions of centuries are put aside in favour of iconoclastic 'modernising', people are seeking leadership in all walks of life. The media and the public constantly call for better and stronger leaders in business, politics and the public sector.

We are right to call for strong leaders in these times. The evidence from both public and private sectors is that the quality of the leader, chairman, chief executive, head teacher, vice-chancellor or chief medical officer, is decisive in achieving success in the organisation, as well as satisfaction for staff and clients. Anyone who watches the Stock Exchange knows how share prices rise and fall according to the movements of the CEO or chairman of a plc. Those of us who have seen a school turned from failure to success by the appointment of a new head can testify to the importance of the right kind of leadership. As one wise and experienced head once said to me, 'A good head can carry a weak staff to success, but even a strong staff cannot for long carry a weak head.'

Yet the current perception is that good leadership is in short supply. Business leaders, we are told, 'don't listen to their customers'; schools 'forget pupil outcomes'; politicians 'are too occupied with spin, offer no vision'; hospitals are 'putting targets before patients'; and so on. Examine these criticisms – legitimate whether or not justified – and they convey a simple message: people want leaders who have vision, and that vision should be one which centres on the needs of the community and every individual within it. All of us want to feel that we matter to our leaders, to know that they are not remote and inwardly directed, but looking out to their constituencies – clients, customers, parishioners or stakeholders – to hear their voices and respond to their needs.

In 2001, The Institute of Management (now the Chartered Management Institute) published the results of a project to examine what leadership means to those who follow.[1] Asked what characteristics they believed were most important in a leader, respondents from a wide variety of walks of life named as the five they believed were most important: 'inspiring', 'strategic thinker', 'forward-looking', 'honest' and 'fair-minded'. The characteristic of inspiration was far and away the most important. However, when asked what their own experience was of the leadership in their own organisations, only 11 per cent felt that they had an inspirational leader, and only 6 per cent felt that they enjoyed leadership with all the characteristics they believed were most important.

No such survey has been undertaken for the Church of England, but it is interesting to note that St Paul's list of the characteristics desirable for a bishop or elder is not so different from the list given by the secular middle-management employees. In his letter to Titus he says that a bishop should be 'of unimpeachable character ("honest"), right-minded, just ("fair-minded"), able to move his hearers ("inspiring")'. I would even suggest that 'adhering to the true doctrine' and 'devout' are the apostle's words for what we might today call strategic thinking!

Far be it from me to examine whether the leaders of our church fulfil these expectations, but it would be a brave person to claim that all was well in the church. The longing for inspirational leadership, for a leader with the power to 'move his hearers' as St Paul said, is certainly strong. At national level the voices of all the leading figures of the church, and the voices of the clergy in the pulpits up and down the land, have for many years not been as loud and clear, and therefore not as influential or decisive, as many of the followers of the church would have wished. Perhaps the time to play it safe, and avoid giving offence to governments of whatever colour, has passed. Those who lead at national or parish level must address the issues which concern the people they serve, not bury themselves in the arcane internal debates within the church. Inspirational leadership requires courage, but such courage would be rewarded by the delight of those who have yearned to hear the voice of their church spelling out the beliefs on which it stands. Such courage too might bring back to the empty pews those who have long felt alienated from the church to which they once adhered.

Those of us who are members of the Ecclesiastical Committee in Parliament have been told by the recently formed Parishioners' Society that some of the laity, the members of some congregations, feel a 'degree of apathy and helplessness' when their feelings and their voluntary contribution of time and effort are ignored by their parish priest. They claim to have experienced a 'domineering' style of leadership, instead of mutual cooperation, and leadership 'by vocational example'. This is a story sadly not so very different from that heard in the secular organisations studied by the Institute of Management.

If good leadership is so precious, and not as common as is needed, perhaps we should look more closely at what good leaders do and are. In this context, it is salutary to reflect that not so many years ago, people talked about 'management' rather than leadership. The language reflected the reality of management style generally accepted before the 1980s. A manager was expected to 'manage', both people and processes, to be something of a benevolent dictator, perhaps, decisive and firm, but with strong discipline and order in his (rarely her) organisation. In all too many examples he would be distant and aloof, ruling with a rod of iron, dealing 'tough' with the unions, and taking home salary and share-options often ten times greater than the junior staff on whom he depended for the firm's success.

It was only in the early 1980s that influential thinkers like Tom Peters and Nancy Austen began to draw our attention to the finding that while this management style could just about get by in good times, it was not successful in hard times. Companies which survived the days of recession were managed in a different way – a way which had more to do with inspirational leadership, listening to clients and above all care and consideration for staff. Management was necessary – but was more to do with the detail, getting everything exactly right, and this was the responsibility, but not the job, of the most senior leaders. Ensuring that something is done well, and inspiring those who have to do it, is very different from trying to do everything oneself. As one senior and established leader in the Institute of Management study put it: 'I associate leadership with clarity of thinking; clarity of communication, being able to articulate a direction and then asking people and trusting people to find the ways to deliver that direction.'

This is why it is in my view wrong to set up in opposition the 'technical' style of leadership to the 'adaptive' style. Both, as one of America's leading women bishops said recently, are necessary, and good leaders use each as appropriate, often looking to those whose strength is different from their own to ensure that both the technical and the adaptive styles are brought to bear in any project. Detail must be right, for the good of the organisation, and people must be moved to want to change, to see the broader picture, and be ready to adapt as the environment changes. Nature has given this lesson in evolution; our ancestors adapted, generation after generation, to their environment, moving with the grain of nature and yet being ready to innovate, to follow their God-given curiosity, and so to progress beyond what had been previously thought possible.

Some of the most important research into effective leadership has focused on emotional intelligence. One of the 'multiple intelligences' which go together to make up the effective leadership of any organisation, emotional intelligence, is increasingly recognised as the key factor. Howard Gardener, Professor of Neurosciences at Harvard University, speaks of interpersonal intelligence – the ability to see how others are feeling, and to respond to their innermost needs and aspirations, an essential ingredient of the inspirational leader, who seeks to motivate others.[2] This, however, should be coupled with intra-personal intelligence, that is the ability to know oneself. 'Remember', he says, 'when you look in the mirror you are looking at the problem; but you are also looking at the solution.'

This message is not the sole property of the modern secular management world. There is an interesting example of a Christian message about good leadership style being passed on to the secular world. Father Dermot Tredget of the Benedictine Order runs highly successful management courses at Douai Abbey, in which he teaches about emotional intelligence based on the twelve-hundred-year-old Rule of St Benedict. That ninth-century Rule, just like the contemporary psychologists' findings about emotional intelligence, emphasises the importance of leaders creating a motivated and contented environment in which people can 'grow in virtue', integrating their work into a broader sense of purpose and meaning. All those who lead, in Church or State or corporation or small school, could benefit from such reflection.

One sensitive businessman, Harry Newman jr, recognising the danger of what has happened to him as he became a tough manager, reflects this well in a poignantly sad poem about self-knowledge which comes too late:

> Again I search the mirror's darkening eye
> I see an image passing by
> Of a kind and gentle mien
> Seeking courage to be seen.
> Love yourself, it says, for what you are
> Ere time snuffs out your life's own star[3]

Leaders with emotional intelligence see teamwork as the key to their model of good management, recognised as the most effective model since it enables a multiplicity of skills, and multiple forms of intelligence to be brought to bear on the organisation. Such leaders recognise, identify and use all the available skills within a balanced team. They resist the temptation to appoint 'clones' of themselves, knowing that this will limit their leadership to one narrow band of all the kinds of intelligence needed. A balanced team might, according to the nature of the task, include some with linguistic intelligence (like T. S. Eliot, writing world-class poetry at the age of ten), others with kinaesthetic intelligence (like David Beckham or Rudolph Nureyev), some with logical or mathematical intelligence (like Stephen Hawking) and others with spatial or musical intelligence. All of these characteristics can together offer imaginative and relevant solutions to problems. Even more, though, they will contribute the leap of faith and vision to see the next move to be made, and the way ahead for the company or organisation.

This style of leadership is a far cry from the linear 'boss' style still all too common both in the secular world and, as I am told, in many parts of the Church. It engenders low morale amongst those who are led, and all too often, for those at the bottom of the hierarchy, a choice between being a compliant courtier to win the favours of those above, or losing motivation through disenchantment, feeling unrecognised and undervalued in the work they do.

Leading people with a strong sense of vocation requires special skills, and a deep commitment to the inspirational, team style of leadership. Professionals, doctors, teachers, lawyers and academics, are motivated largely by their relationship with their clients – patients, students or defendants. This is a professional relationship, unmonitored in most cases from outside, since the doctor with his/her patient or the teacher and lecturer with their students interact with each other directly and in private. The relationships such professionals form with their clients are immensely important, as well as personally rewarding, to the professional concerned. She or he will often see those above them in the organisation as at best irrelevant, and at worst an irritating hindrance to getting on with the tasks they consider important. I speak with some experience, since in my career I have spent 14 years in a leadership role with academics as well as 12 years in such a role with members of the nationally dispersed and highly professional force of Her Majesty's Inspectors of Schools.

Clergy are, it seems to me, the quintessential case of such professionals, whose relationship with their flock is of overriding importance to them, and whose contacts with those above them in the hierarchy of the diocese or wider church can be both distant and infrequent. While autonomy in their daily work has been shown to be the most desired condition sought by professionals, this does not mean that they lack ambition, or can operate without recognition. It is a foolish leader who takes professionals' commitment to their clients as an excuse to leave them alone. Leadership may need to be more lightly exercised, and recognition of professionals' need for freedom in their relationships with clients should be paramount, but it is wrong to assume that no encouragement from those above them is needed. The very nature of the professional role means that many carry a lonely burden, and their need for reassurance and a listening ear can be more acute than that of the office worker in a structured environment, with both close colleagues and line manager present on a day-to-day basis.

It is common 'management speak' to praise devolved decision-making and 'de-layering' of structures, but many leaders in the secular world are better at paying lip service to these concepts than to carrying them out in practice. It is difficult to loosen the reins of an organisation for which one holds the ultimate responsibility, and natural to feel that, if a job is important, 'I'd better do it myself'. It is even worse to delegate a job and then hover anxiously over the person to whom the task has been delegated, offering spurious and unwelcome advice! This is why I add humility to the necessary characteristics of leadership. Genuinely to accept that someone else can do something better than oneself is a necessary part of delegation, and therefore of any truly and successfully devolved organisation. This does not mean that the leader devolves responsibility. If people are to make the right decisions at the grass-roots level, and if they are to be enabled to perform well, they need training and tools for the job, they need adequate support both material and spiritual, and they need to have been well chosen as the right person for the job they are given.

The issue of selecting the right person for the job is, in my experience, the single most important task of any leader. 'Picking winners' at every level ensures the total success of the organisation. Almost every senior leader in the secular world, at least, can tell of spectacular successes when the right person was appointed – and ghastly mistakes in appointment, which resulted in both costly and painful disasters for their company. I once spoke to a woman who headed the Human Resource department of one of the world's leading IT companies. Her colleagues at the most senior level in the firm had told me that she was a legend in the company for her ability to pick the winning candidate for any post, including the most sensitive research posts where scientific ability had often to be combined with leadership of a highly creative and 'unmanageable' research team of professionals. I asked her how did she do this? How did she spot the person who was just right for the job, time after time? She told me that she saw in her mind the team with whom this person would work as 'a jigsaw with one piece missing'. The specification for the post was, therefore, not just the technical details of qualifications and experience, but the much more difficult area of personality and skills which would fit the jigsaw exactly, and make up the perfect team.

Picking the winners when it comes to the most senior leaders is of course the most important task of all. Companies in the private sector have always expended huge resources in head-hunting just the right person to lead the company, as well as expecting her or him to be highly skilled in picking the senior team to provide the back-up in leadership. In recent years, organisations in the public sector have also turned to expert head-hunters and human resource professionals to find their most senior team members, believing that the money expended was well worth the result, given the senior leaders' key role in the organisation's success.

Since the publication of the first Report of the Committee on Standards in Public Life (chaired then by Lord Nolan), which laid down guidelines for the way in which public bodies should make appointments at both governance and management level, public bodies and organisations have begun to be much more open and transparent in the way in which appointments are made. National advertising with openly declared criteria for the appointment, interviewers who understand the requirements for equal opportunity, time-limited appointments for governors and board members, all these have begun to change a culture of 'old-boy networks' and entrenched oligarchies which could hinder the progress of a school, a university or hospital. Private companies have increasingly followed the lead of the public sector in this regard, and it is not uncommon to see open competition for posts which once would have been simply in the gift of the chairman or the senior management.

The Church was not at first ready to join in this culture of openness, but, in 1998, the General Synod voted to set up a group to review the processes of the Crown Appointments Commission which is responsible for the appointment of diocesan bishops and the archbishops. That group, which I was privileged to chair, found much that was good in the system, but also found too many areas where a lack of openness could lead to poor practice and incorrect information, possibly missing the best candidates for any vacancy simply because they were not sufficiently known to the small group involved in preparing the short-list. All members of the working group were delighted when General Synod overwhelmingly backed our report in 2001, and equally delighted when Professor Clarke, who with great skill chaired the group set up to implement our recommendations, received similar support in 2002 and 2003.

The new processes go a long way to bring the church's appointments process for these most senior posts into line with best practice in the public sector, and with the recommendations of the Nolan Report. It will be open to individuals to put their names forward for any particular vacancy, and they will be given an opportunity to correct the information made available to the members of the appointing commission. Only the written information which they have seen and corrected and the letters of reference from those whom they choose and from their current diocesan bishop will be available to the members, so there should be no more unattributed and anecdotal evidence submitted in the privacy of the commission's meeting.

However, the strength of the system will depend on the care and fairness of the regular system of ministerial review, to which in theory all clergy are entitled. This will be used to provide the evidence of an individual performance and vocation over the whole of her or his ministry. It is therefore essential that it should be consistent in form and subject to regular updating and recording. It should also allow individuals to contribute their own judgements of their strengths and weaknesses, their sense of their vocation for the future, and the details of what they have accomplished, perhaps well below the eye-level of their immediate superiors. The evidence suggests, however, that practice varies widely between dioceses, and that the open and frank exchange necessary to ensure a fair record happens to some but not to others across the church in England as a whole. There is still much to be done, if we are to be sure we have the leadership we so urgently need.

Here again, there are lessons to be learned from the secular world. Appraisal as a management tool began in the private sector, but has become a widely accepted tool for developing and placing staff across most of the academic world, and is increasingly required by legislation for schools and the Health Service. Although it cannot replace the need for day-to-day contact and exchange between staff and manager, at its best, appraisal is a means of ensuring that staff sit down at regular intervals – every year or every other year – with their immediate superior to discuss fully and openly their performance and their future plans and prospects. It should be a two-way exchange, with each able to contribute their perception of how successful the past year or so has been, the reasons for things going wrong or right, and to set targets for the period ahead. All these devices, from the formal appointments system to the annual appraisal, are ways of trying to ensure that we really do have 'winners' at every point in the organisation. Fitting the person to the job that is right for them can make an apparent failure into a happy success. Making the right use of each person in the organisation, playing to their strengths, finding their motivations and meeting those with their placement, can transform a failing organisation into one where the whole team works to a common and shared purpose. In my own exercise of leadership, I have maintained the faith that every human being wants to do well, wants the satisfaction of a job well done; none is a 'loser' unless made so by mismanagement. There is no greater satisfaction than that of finding and releasing the energy which lies beneath what are sometimes years of disenchantment with a system which gave no recognition, or years of being forced into the wrong mould.

There is of course one area where the church falls far behind the best of secular practice, and indeed behind what is now accepted in legislation as well as in practice, as part of the human rights of individuals. This is in its treatment of women in Ministry. Our beloved church gives to the secular world a poor example, in my view, of its stand on human rights and on the value of each individual whom God has made, in leaving its ordained women in a second-class status within the church. For me, it makes meaningless the celebration of ordination when one priest who happens to be male is given a different mission from another priest who happens to be female. The fact that this difference is then reflected in the church's continued exemption from the law against sex discrimination, to which the rest of our society is bound, seems to me to convey all the wrong messages about what our church should stand for in the world. Worse, it gives licence to those of the minority who oppose the ordination of women to insult and belittle them in a hundred different ways.

This is not a problem with which the women of our ministry should have to deal themselves; they have done all that is necessary. Where their ministry is fully accepted and used, they have proved themselves more than fitted to be God's representatives in parish and diocese. It is now a problem for the church, and an opportunity to convey a positive message to the world and to the lay members of the church, most especially the women lay members who feel themselves belittled by their women priests' second-class status. Many of us feel that the time has now come to do away once and for all with the General Act of Synod which allows behaviour which in the secular world is both old-fashioned and illegal. We long to see the appointment of the first woman bishop from amongst the outstanding senior women who now serve in senior posts and are more than ready to take on the tasks which the mitre conveys.

In my discussions with people within the church, often at quite a senior level, I have been surprised and concerned to find how resistance to the concept of learning from the secular world still lingers. This is often presented as a conviction that the church is so different that no parallels apply, and no examples are useful. On examination, this seems to be because, first, the clergy are so scattered geographically that no similar practices from the world outside are applicable. The secular world, of course, has many such parallels; sales people often travel the country and indeed the world, well away from any direct supervision; many companies now place their middle managers around the world with very little immediate support in their location; general practitioners now have to be managed as part of the NHS system, even though many are in small or single practices, far away from their regional managers; in my time as a Chief Inspector with the Department of Education, I led a team which was located across the entire country, who met me or their direct managers on relatively rare occasions, and yet I was responsible for many decisions about their lives, including where they lived, or whether they were promoted.

The second reason put forward as to why clergy are 'so different' is that they are in a job for life – they cannot just go off to apply for some different job. This of course applies to a huge number of professionals. The longer and more advanced the skills and training, the fewer the range of options available to the individual. Civil servants rarely leave the service, and military women and men seldom leave before their agreed retirement date; the service they join is responsible for their career and welfare with very few alternative routes for them, unless they leave and try to start another career, an option available of course to any deeply unhappy member of the clergy.

So I find it hard to see why the practices of the secular world are so inappropriate to the church, although I recognise of course that the vocation of the Ministry is like no other. The reality for the individual priest is that their leader is ultimately he who is not of any earthly hierarchy. With a lay person's deep humility, however, I would ask the church to reflect on those things which are of this world in their work structures, and look to see where their holy calling would be enhanced by a willingness to learn from the best of the world. With equal humility but with some urgency I would ask the church also to reflect how its practices and preoccupations look to the world outside, and the message they convey about their Christian values. The church is the Church Incarnate, just as our Lord was God Incarnate, and those of us who speak, however quietly, from the pews, wish for our church to speak to us in ways which have meaning in the world in which we live, and by word and by example, to help us 'to live and work to God's praise and glory'.

Note

1. Report, 'Leadership: The Challenge for All', December 2001.
2. Howard Gardener, *Multiple Intelligences*, New York
, Basic Books, 1993.
3. Harry Newman jr, 'Ageing Jet-Setter' in Ralph Windle (ed.), *The Poetry of Business Life*, San Francisco, USA, Berrett-Koehler, 1994, p. 134.

11 But me no buts

GILLIAN STAMP

A leader is a person who has an unusual degree of power to project on other people his or her shadow, his or her light. A leader is a person who has an unusual degree of power to create the conditions under which other people must live and move and have their being . . . A leader is a person who must take special responsibility for what's going on inside him or herself . . . lest the act of leadership create more harm than good.[1]

There are three essentials to leadership: humanity, clarity and courage . . . Humanity without clarity is like having a field but not ploughing it. Clarity without courage is like having sprouts without weeding. Courage without humanity is like knowing how to reap but not how to sow.[2]

What I am *for* you terrifies me; what I am *with* you consoles me. *For* you I am a bishop; but *with* you I am a Christian. The former is a danger, the latter salvation.[3]

Creative leadership is making sure you end up somewhere other than you would have done anyway.[4]

As I thought about ancient understandings of leadership, how it is both the same and changing and about my work as a sounding board with leaders in different institutions and different parts of the world, it seemed to me that leaders in churches have a 'head start'. As leadership begins to shift from control to creativity, the emphasis falls on understanding people, understanding the self, the need for meaning, the value of forgiveness. In all these areas churches have long and deep experience on which to draw.

Many examples could be used to illustrate, but two run through so many of my conversations that I have chosen to focus on them: the leadership work of providing conditions in which creativity can emerge, and the creative leadership needed to hold together apparently disparate activities, to provide a way in which it is always possible simply to say 'and' rather than 'but'.

In essence, creative leadership is about doing things differently to make the most of opportunities in the environment. As such it requires courage – to release other people's creativity, to face their anxieties about change, to learn from what is working and what is not, and to live with the loneliness of moving people and an organisation forward at a pace that will by definition be too fast for some, too slow for some, and the wrong direction for others. Creative leadership requires clarity – about direction, expectations, resources and completion so that there can be review and learning. And it requires humanity – to imagine how it is for others. Genuinely to be with them in their world, appreciate that while some are impatient for change, others fear it, others can be encouraged towards it, some will resist openly, some covertly. It is hard, but essential to provide the space in which all involved can make sense of what is happening, and be helped to find meaning in what they are currently doing and in what they are being asked to do differently.

Providing conditions

Leadership that provides conditions is very different from a 'top-down' approach or 'command and control'. The latter may be appropriate when there is little change and the institution is able to set the agenda or at least substantial parts of it. To make the most of change – of what has been called 'permanent white water' – an institution must not be static for it will be engulfed; equally it must not diffuse into the environment or its distinctive competence will be lost. It must be poised, ready to reach out, to respond, to be lively and creative.

Three conditions that make for this poise are coherence, judgement and review. Coherence ensures that there is a shared understanding of purpose and direction as a touchstone for each person to use his or her own initiative, their own judgement as they make decisions. Because it is a touchstone, coherence strengthens the capacity to make the most of possibilities as they emerge, focusing people's energies on the shared direction. If coherence becomes rigidity, it encourages dependency; if it is vague, energy is dissipated.

Coherence allows people to make sense, to build and if necessary rebuild the structures of meaning[5] we all use to interpret and assimilate our world. Leaders in religious organisations have long understood the need for people to be able to give meaning to their work and specifically to their own contribution. In organisations seeking ways to engage and retain people's creative energies there is a call for a new understanding of leadership that allows everyone to 'make sense of their experience'.[6] Some authors suggest that a leader creates meaning, others that leadership connects people to work and to one another at work, and in so doing creates meaning.[7] As Adair points out, 'Effective leadership is a relationship rooted in community'.[8]

The second condition is judgement – each person feeling trusted to use his or her own judgement about how to do their work. Each of us longs to be told the purpose of our work, to understand the boundaries and then to be left alone 'to get on with it', to bring something of ourselves to bear, something only we can bring as we reach out to read a situation and judge the appropriate course of action. Humanity in leadership understands and makes the most of this deep longing. The practice of 'discernment' – being 'patient with uncertainty' – has been used for centuries for spiritual matters and is now increasingly used to describe reaching out to pick up on intricate patterns, on the 'regular irregularities' that thread through complex circumstances. A retired Christian banker[9] writes of discernment as 'another way of defining intuition and creativity. We live in a changing environment and discernment of change . . . is really a basic and universal characteristic . . . it allows us to see what might not be there'.

In the sixth century Gregory the Great emphasised discernment as he sought a way to lead the church in turbulent social circumstances. In his *Liber pastoralis* he suggested that rather than imposing a vision, the leader must seek to discover 'what is really going on' by listening to deeper patterns in the community; helping the community to discover its absolute core values and then finding ways to nurture them even in a time of disorienting change.

The third condition is review – to understand, not to blame, to learn from what is working and what is not, to become a 'learning' organisation. Review requires courage to face the possibility that a course of action one felt deeply about is not achieving what was hoped, courage to persuade others to do things differently, and release from blame in order that there can be learning. That release depends on forgiveness – 'the constant mutual release' from the consequences of action as the exact opposite of vengeance.

> Forgiving is the only reaction which does not merely re-act but acts anew and unexpectedly . . . therefore freeing from its consequences both the one who forgives and the one who is forgiven . . . the discoverer of the role of forgiveness in the realm of human affairs was Jesus of Nazareth.[10]

'Anding' – holding together apparently disparate activities

Drawing again on my work as a sounding board, here are just three examples of the hard work of holding together, of making it easier to say 'and' rather than 'but' or 'either/or'. The first example experienced in all institutions is the dilemma of money and relationships; the second is holding initiatives together where there is 'distributed leadership'; the third brief example is taking account of all aspects of people's lives as they are asked to do things differently.

A book about long-established businesses shows that they do not 'brutalise themselves with the tyranny of "OR", they embrace the genius of the "AND"'.[11] As anyone who does it daily knows, 'anding' is never-ending work. The temptation is great to allow one side to take precedence – the numbers because they are 'objective', 'straightforward', the people because 'they are all that really matters'.

Money and relationships

A business can find itself having to restore creativity in its leadership if cost, revenue and profits become the primary preoccupation and people – customers, employees, 'stakeholders' – and the relationships with them are forgotten. A church can find itself working hard – and in unfamiliar territory – to hold together decisions about resources and policies, costs, people and relationships, at any level, and can all too easily slip into 'either/or' – costs or quality, today or tomorrow, efficiency or purpose, costs or people. Either/or seems to be the default state for human nature – 'This is urgent/appealing, that's where I'll put my energies for the moment. That's less urgent/attractive, I'll put it aside for now.' Sustaining 'and' in the face of these strong tendencies depends on providing conditions so that each person is trusted to use his or her best judgement in the light of their coherent understanding of purpose.

Unexpected as it may seem, a church has an advantage in holding together money and relationships. This advantage lies in its deep understanding of two fundamental motivations of human life – the quest for transcendence and the need to function well in everyday life – and of the importance of holding them together as sources of meaning. Many scholars suggest that the first form of money was shared food representing both a longing for something 'higher' and people's responsibility to each other and to their community. At that stage the spiritual and the material were close complements of each other and money was created to help people provide for each other in the material realm – love thy neighbour. In many settings the two are now far apart so that 'render unto Caesar that which is Caesar's, and unto God that which is God's' tends to carry with it a connotation that the former is not simply secondary but necessarily wrong, even evil. It has been argued that 'the entire problem of the meaning of life in contemporary culture can be defined as the challenge to understanding that saying of Jesus'.[12]

Perhaps one of the hardest aspects of creative leadership in a church is to accept the proper place of money, not to set it aside, or to see it (consciously or unconsciously) as work for lay but not for ordained people, or at worst as somehow regrettable. Awareness of the quest for transcendence and the responsibility for neighbour, is a strength for creative church leaders as they give proper attention to money without being consumed by it or running from it into abstractions 'free from the pulls and bites of money'.[13] If they stay too close to the detail, there is a temptation to solve a particular problem without standing back to see the whole. If they stand too far back, it may at first appear more comfortable but they can lose touch with the sharp realities in communities 'on the ground'.

In working this way creative church leadership has much to offer to commercial organisations where there is always a risk that people and relationships can be sacrificed to immediate cost concerns with inevitable risks to reputation and shareholder value in the longer term. Creative leadership in either kind of institution stays with the hard, endless work of 'anding'.

Distributed leadership

Many organisations are beginning to change the pattern of their leadership in order to be more poised and thus more agile in rapidly changing circumstances. Poise depends on being able to sense changes in the environment, reach out and make the most of them. Reading what is happening in rapidly changing local environments is best done by people who live in them. Decisions about ways forward are best taken in the light of a blend of local knowing and understanding of the wider picture – much easier said than done and especially delicate where resources are scarce and/or are needed to sustain the whole, as in the parish share. But where the local environment is read by those who know it and decisions are made where they 'belong', 'nodes of wisdom'[14] distributed throughout increase poise and agility.

The theological principle of subsidiarity is a valuable framework for helping to understand where decisions 'belong'. The principle is that whatever each individual can do with his or her own power should not be done by the community; whatever the smaller community and authority can do, should not be done by the wider community. Subsidiarity allows 'as much liberty as possible and as much association as necessary . . . subsidiarity carries with it an obligation to solidarity'.[15] That solidarity is for the life of the whole and the parts.

At heart subsidiarity is about imagination – putting oneself in others' shoes in order to understand what they do best and how to provide the conditions for them to thrive.

In any organisation subsidiarity means that each level of leadership has a responsibility to ask those questions no one else can ask, to do only what others cannot do and to provide the conditions in which others can act wisely in doing what they do best – this could include removing 'road blocks', helping to set thinking in a wider context. At its strongest subsidiarity ensures that the whole is always greater than the sum of the parts through holding together different strands, different interpretations of history, of texts and of 'ways of being church'. This is 'anding' at its best, very difficult to sustain, especially in the face of resource constraint and/or different traditions. It seems likely that as parishes in the Church of England become more and more the source of resource for running the Church, the call for subsidiarity will become stronger. Creative leadership will be essential to provide the coherence necessary to counter fragmentation and 'congregationalism' and preserve all strands of tradition.

Holding together elements of people's lives

In many organisations people can be asked to move and/or to take on wider or different responsibilities, perhaps simply to do things differently, and this can sometimes happen with short notice. In a business where money takes primacy, an individual may simply be told to move. In a business where there is creative leadership, time and care is taken to be with the person as he or she works through the implications of change for their own life, for that of their partner, children, family, friends and for their own sense of where their working life is heading. This acknowledges the wholeness of the individual – that as a person he or she is a *maker* of meaning, a maker[16] of decisions; a *member* of a family, a community, perhaps a professional association; an irreducible *mystery*, and a fourth 'M' from a creative leader – 'treating people as people is *messy*'.

Developing leaders

Current and historical thinking and writing about leadership is a
bridge to thinking about how leaders can strengthen their capacity to
provide conditions and to sustain 'and'.

Reflectiveness

One of the key findings in research on leadership is the need for
reflectiveness, and the current growth of interest in and demand for
'mentoring' substantiates this. This seems to suggest that as people
try to provide creative leadership, even those for whom reflection is
not 'natural' find themselves looking for ways to 'think things
through', to 'pause before leaping in and consider a bit'. In my experience this is about having a sounding board, a listener who will be
quietly there as the person hears for themselves what they know,
what they think, how they are going to move forward. As E. M.
Forster said, 'How will I know what I think until I hear what I say?'
Being with someone while they listen to themselves means saying
very little, not rephrasing their words but providing space for 'reverie'
so that they can suspend pursuit of any particular purpose and thus
let their gaze cover the whole.[17]

While vulnerable to pressure of time, reflectiveness is key to the life
of both lay and ordained leaders in churches. There is a wide and deep
background of writing and practice to draw upon, an appreciation of
the value and strength to be gained from pause and quiet, and the
encouragement of daily discipline. The skill and art of reflectiveness is
much harder to acquire for people without a background in belief.
One approach now widely used is to keep a journal as an encouragement to pausing and considering events and reactions. Sometimes
this is with a view to discerning patterns in reactions or in the moments
where the person feels most 'in flow' – confident, competent, enthusiastic and able to use their judgement to effect.

Understanding the self

This links back to the image of casting 'shadow and light' and the
need for the leader to know him or herself, to understand their impact
on other people and how most wisely to persuade and influence
them. As just one current example among many, the man who
founded the Visa organisation writes that the first and paramount
responsibility of anyone who purports to lead is to understand the

self and describes this as 'a complex, unending and incredibly difficult, oft-shunned task'. He suggests that it should occupy 50 per cent of the leader's time and when that is the case 'the ethical, moral and spiritual elements of [leadership] are inescapable'.[18] Another example is Goleman's work on 'emotional intelligence' that has drawn the attention of the business community in particular to the essential role in leadership of understanding and handling the self and others.[19]

Collins's research into leaders who transformed their companies 'from good to great' is in line with a long history of thinking about leadership. His key finding is that these leaders built 'enduring greatness through a paradoxical blend of personal humility[20] and professional will'.[21] In a powerful image he says that these leaders 'look out of the window to apportion credit to factors outside themselves when things go well and they look in the mirror to apportion responsibility'.[22]

As the author of *The Servant Leader* points out,[23] church leaders can draw on a long history of disciplines for deepening understanding of the self and for setting aside a personal agenda for the sake of a wider purpose. These disciplines recognise the courage needed to start on the journey of understanding the self and the need for guidance as vulnerabilities as well as strengths unfold. Many secular organisations use appraisal of individuals and often include in that a gathering of views about the individual from those with whom and to whom they work. In responsible organisations the feedback from these exercises is handled very professionally. Churches have an inbuilt advantage in helping leaders understand themselves but do not always draw on it.

Many leaders find it both necessary and very difficult to discipline their attention. As one put it – 'I need to pause and see what in this moment is devouring my attention, taking more of me than I need to give it'.[24] The outcome of the devouring of attention can all too easily be the weakening of the will and capacity to 'and'.

Awareness of the power of 'attention', of its tendency to wander, of its tendency to fixate and yet also of the gift it can be for the recipient, is intrinsic to religious teaching and so in an important way more readily available to leaders with that background. This is not to minimise the pressures on time for reflectiveness, understanding the self, or directing attention, but to suggest that awareness of the value of all three of these ways of being lies deep within belief.

Four journeys

The more leadership is seen as providing conditions and holding together apparently disparate activities, the greater the need for a framework to keep together the 'being' and the 'doing' of leadership.

The four journeys described provide one such framework. It emerged from many years of listening to leaders as they paused to reflect about their aspirations, their vulnerabilities, the path of their leadership, where they had succeeded, where failed. It seemed helpful to suggest that each of us is on four journeys through our lives and that people with responsibility for leadership need to be particularly aware of each journey and of the work of holding them together.

The underlying journey

The underlying journey is the journey of the self – what unfolds, the events through which we insert ourselves into the world; where we are born, grow up, study, work, the people with whom we live in childhood and adulthood. Reflecting on the journey of the self helps each of us to hear our own story, to see things differently from the way they seemed at the time – to understand more of the experience and see what we have learned. The particular responsibility for leaders is to deepen their understanding of their own strengths and vulnerabilities and to become more aware of the stories of those they lead.

An important element in the journey of the self is our 'capability' as it unfolds over time. Capability is the judgement we use when we do not and cannot *know* what to do. The prerequisite for sound judgement is being able to 'get one's head around' the complexities and volatilities of a challenge. A match between capability and challenge gives the individual a sense of being 'in flow' – confident, competent, enthusiastic. From that the institution gains the poise and agility that come with coordinated, robust decisions.

Capability grows over time. As individuals we all do our best to 'go with the grain' of that growth, to find challenges that stretch but do not over- or underwhelm us, are just right for us at each stage of our growth. A leader is responsible for combining and pacing those individual patterns of growth for the good of the whole.

A leader also has a special responsibility to reflect on the growth of his or her capability because it is the key element in readiness for the complexities and uncertainties of his or her leadership role. The role may have come a little too early and so he or she feels overwhelmed, or perhaps he or she has been waiting for it for a while and feels underwhelmed when the responsibility actually comes. Everyone will have experiences of being over- or understretched by the challenges of their roles and the effect on their feelings and their decision-making. A leader may have considerable experience early in his or her working life of longing for more challenge, for more complexities and interconnections through which to navigate his or her way. Some people faced with this become impatient and try to rush changes; others seek ways to offer their capacity to see a wider and more nuanced picture in support of those with whom they work.

If a leader is overwhelmed by complexities, he or she will not be able to make sense of the ambiguities, interconnections and unpredictabilities of his or her work, so will struggle to make robust decisions. And he or she will be far less able to provide the conditions in which others can use their judgement wisely or to do the delicate work of holding together different and sometimes disparate elements of the work. If a leader is underwhelmed by the challenges of a role, he or she may choose to use 'spare' capability to provide conditions and to 'and'. But some people in this situation can feel aggrieved, ill-used by the institution, not able to use 'spare' capability to serve it and may undermine the efforts of others.

The second journey

The second journey is the public journey at work in which our capability is expressed and affirmed – or not. In times of rapid change the public journey makes heavy demands on everyone. Leaders often find that the demands on time, responsiveness and presence can overwhelm to the point where this journey can seem as if it is the only one. It is in precisely those circumstances that leaders need to be mindful of the importance of the other three journeys for themselves and for those they lead.

In this public journey the leader must do all he or she can to show courage, clarity and humanity, to provide conditions that encourage creativity, and to hold together money and relationships, nodes of leadership and other elements that by their very nature can pull apart.

As any leader knows, the conditions of coherence, judgement (discernment) and review do not sustain themselves and are subject to constant slippage, confusion and weakening. To sustain them requires yet more work – providing clarity, the courage to trust other people to use their judgement and the humanity of giving continuous attention to the alignment of people, purpose and processes through time.

We describe the work of providing clarity about expectations as 'tasking'. People experience this clarity as respect, and our experience is that volunteers seek this respect just as much as those who are paid. A book about the rule of St Benedict explains that the root meaning of the Latin and Greek words usually translated as 'rule' is trellis – 'Saint Benedict was not promulgating rules . . . he was establishing a framework on which a life can grow'.[25] A creative leader sets the boundaries of people's work not as rules but as a frame to shape individual initiative and creativity.

Trusting *en*trusts each person with purpose and trusts them to discern and to use their judgement about how they will do the work for which they are responsible. Trusting is not easy even when an individual is known and understood; far more difficult when they are new, reticent, different, questioning; and this is where the courage comes in – not to trust blindly but to be vigilant, so that trust builds not as dependency but as mutual respect.

Tending is continual mindfulness, the work that keeps things working, that infuses the 'minute particulars' with meaning – as one leader put it, 'you tend because stuff happens'. In order to tend the leader sets aside his or her own agenda for the sake of the whole – a key quality for creative leadership. Tending sustains friendships, gardens, households and institutions and throughout history it has been the work of slaves, women and creative leaders. Because it has no end and no obvious 'achievement', it is unseen and unsung work. In Christian language it is the work of the servant leader, not sufficient in itself but essential as the complement of tasking and trusting. As one bishop once said, 'The weakness comes when tending becomes the task.'

Trusting and tending ensure the coherence that people need to sustain their belief that the work is important. Trusting entrusts people with core purpose, tending keeps that understanding alive through communication. The outcome is a shared, coherent understanding of purpose so that every detail and decision is an expression of it. Tasking and trusting allow judgement to be exercised: tasking sets the limits, trusting encourages each person to use their judgement. Tasking and tending ensure review: tasking prepares for review by establishing completion times; tending prepares for review by keeping systems, practices and people heading in the right direction at the right pace and setting the tone for learning. (See Figure 11.1, p. 129.)

The personal journey

This is the journey through which we do or do not care for ourselves and weave together the other journeys. It is about finding the 'grain' of the self and learning how to go with it. For a leader this journey is a

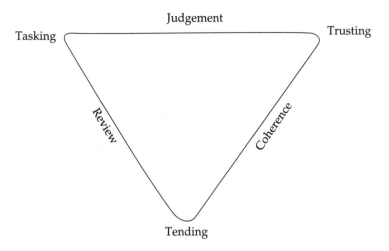

Figure 11.1 Creative leadership

'duty of care' – for the light and shadows of the self, for the conditions provided and to sustain courage, clarity and humanity. This journey may be expressed in prayer, listening to music, gardening. The essence is time and space for the self and for reflection – this may be momentary or more focused. Some people are not aware of and give very little time or attention to their personal journeys until they face a crisis. As someone put it, this is the journey to ensure that your self does not disappear.

In following this journey church leaders have the advantage of belief in the importance of disciplines for understanding and caring for the self – to love thy neighbour *as thyself*. This is not to say that it is any easier to find the time for this journey or to see it as a 'duty of care', but it is a reminder that for people with belief there is a trellis to support and shape growth.

The personal journey puts us in touch with our inner resources – the judgement that allows us to make a wise decision when we do not and cannot know what to do. It may do that fleetingly or we may choose to become more aware of that 'answering activity' that 'knowing that can see forwards and backwards and in a flash give form to the confusions and chaos of everyday living'.[26]

Just as tasking, trusting and tending are the underpinnings for providing conditions in the public journey of the leader, so they can serve as a framework for the personal journey. Tasking the self is an important discipline, an expression of the ancient wisdom 'know thyself' – strengths, vulnerabilities, graces and thirsts. And as

Schumacher[27] showed, there is an essential complement in knowing how others see us so that we can couple awareness of self with insight about the connection between our attributes and behaviour and the reaction of others – we can learn much from the fact that we judge ourselves by our intentions and others by their actions, and recognising that other people do the same.

Trusting one's inner resources is at the heart of being 'in flow' and is at the core of discerning and using one's own judgement. Each of us is deeply sensitive to being in or out of flow: when we are 'in flow', discerning is spontaneous, judgements just come and we feel confident and not self-conscious; 'out of flow' our inner resources slip from our grasp, seem flimsy, even absent or tantalising in that one moment they are there, the next gone. One person described it well – 'when you are in flow, intuition is leading you. When you are out of flow, you become a searcher. You search everywhere and you cannot trust what comes to you. So you try to delay and avoid decisions.'

Tending – continual mindfulness of the self – lies at the heart of living with uncertainty. Tending could be prayer, meditation, reading, running, any time that is for the self. But, as soon as there are demands, we are likely not to find the time for those activities that sustain us, and/or to find ourselves dwelling in the past, leaping to or fearing the future rather than 'being here now', living in the 'dimension of the present moment',[28] accepting its transience.

The Neoplatonic philosopher Plotinus described the duty of care to tend the self:

> Withdraw into yourself and look. And if you do not find yourself beautiful yet, act as does the creator of a statue that is to be made beautiful; he cuts away here, he smoothes there, he makes this line lighter, this other purer until a lovely face has grown upon his work. So do you also . . . never cease chiselling your statue.[29]

For the leader there are three key elements of the personal journey:

- Developing and deepening reflectiveness – pausing to consider the way he or she approaches things; thinking about the way he or she thinks; about the way he or she responds to change; how he or she gives meaning to things, decides what is a challenge, what an impossible demand, which game is worth the candle?
- Ensuring that understanding of the self through reflection is complemented by how he or she is seen by others – 'oh, would the Lord the giftie gie us to see ourselves as others see us'.
- Making sure there is some one person or some people who will tell

it to the leader like it is. Leaders can all too easily become cut off from honest feedback free of agendas. The greater the power and uncertainty, the more critical is this responsibility.

The private journey

And the fourth private journey is shared with family, friends, a community and in it we are very close to others' journeys. In many marriages and partnerships both have public journeys with all that means for expressing and affirming capability, for pressure on time, for managing two careers – and a household! And it seems often to happen that one partner may take on a more senior leadership role around the time when adolescent children need more time and understanding. Or when parents become frail and require more care.

There has been a significant change in the nature of this journey in recent years. For many years it has been common for one partner to have a 'more important' public journey – a leadership role – and the other to see their role as in part providing support for it. So the first partner would not have been expected to buy milk on the way home, make the supper or put children to bed. For leaders this adds to the expectations on them – and to the depth of their relationships with their children – and requires an additional understanding of the balancing of journeys of the people they lead.

The private journey is our 'habitat' – all that belongs to the place we leave and return to as we set out on our public journey. Pressure on this journey comes from a demanding public journey, from growth in capability not yet appreciated by those we work with, from knowing that we are 'out of our depth' but have not yet been able to acknowledge it. And it is easy to feel burdened by and/or a burden to those with whom we share this journey – it can seem as if there is no place in our life where nothing is expected of us. When we feel guilty about neglecting the private journey we often retreat from it rather than trying to weave it into the other journeys. There may still be a sense that this is acceptable for leaders and to an extent that has to be true. But even if the leader and his or her partner make that choice, many of those led will choose not to neglect the private journey. The leader has to carry the responsibility for resourcing, carrying projects forward, meeting emergency demands, while being understanding and patient about 'life-style choices'.

A way of reflecting on the balance between the private and public journeys is to pause and learn from where one has chosen *not* to be.

In this chapter I have tried to show that many of the understandings and disciplines intrinsic to churches offer a special reservoir for leadership that encourages and releases creative leadership. There is much to learn and much to offer from this reservoir.

Notes

1. Parker J. Palmer, *Leading from Within*, Indiana Office for Campus Ministry, 1990.
2. Fushan Yuan, tenth-century Chinese philosopher, quoted in T. Cleary, *The Art of Leadership*, Shambala, 1989.
3. St Augustine, quoted by A. Jones in 'New Vision for the Episcopate?', *Theology* (1978).
4. President of a global company.
5. P. Marris, *Loss and Change*, London, Routledge and Kegan Paul, 1974, p. 8.
6. W. Drath and C. Palus, *Making Common Sense: Leadership as Meaning-making in a Community of Practice*, Greensboro, NC, Centre for Creative Leadership, 1994, p. 17.
7. Ibid., p. 93.
8. J. Adair, *The Leadership of Jesus*, Norwich, Canterbury Press, 2001, p. 118.
9. P. Caron, 'Discernment beyond the Church', *The Way Supplement*, 85 (1996), pp. 107–16 (109).
10. H. Arendt, *The Human Condition*, University of Chicago Press, 1958, p. 246.
11. J. Collins and J. Porras, *Built to Last*, Century Business, 1996, p. 44.
12. J. Needleman, *Money and the Meaning of Life*, Doubleday, 1991, p. 55.
13. Ibid., p. 155.
14. T. O. Jacobs, *Developing Information Age Leaders*, Washington, DC, National Defence University, 2002, p. 7.
15. H. Küng, *Why Priests?*, Collins, 1972, p. 77.
16. 'Maker' in the Scottish sense of a 'poet'.
17. M. Milner, *A Life of One's Own*, London, Virago, 1986 (1934), p. 198.
18. D. Hock, *Birth of the Chaordic Age*, Berrett-Koehler, 1999, p. 8.
19. D. Goleman, *Working with Emotional Intelligence*, London, Bloomsbury, 1999.
20. See Adair, *Leadership of Jesus*, for many historical examples of humility in leadership.
21. Another significant 'and'.
22. J. Collins, *Good to Great*, Random House, 2001, p. 27 (although this work was done in the private sector in the US, it has implications for leadership in all organisations).
23. R. Greenleaf, *The Servant Leader*, Jossey Bass, Indianapolis, IN, 1970.
24. Needleman, *Money and the Meaning of Life*, p. 291.

25. P. Henry (ed.), *Benedict's Dharma*, London and New York, Continuum, 2001, p. 1.
26. Milner, *Life of One's Own*, 189.
27. E. Schumacher, *A Guide for the Perplexed*, London, Jonathan Cape, 1977.
28. M. Holub, *The Dimension of the Present Moment*, London, Faber and Faber, 1990.
29. *Plotinus*, translated by A. H. Armstrong, Harvard University Press, 1966, p. 117.

12 Leadership with vision: a challenge for the churches?

ELIZABETH WELCH

We live in an age when it can seem that creativity and the church are at two opposite ends of the spectrum. The church is caricatured as being about rules and limitations, about burdening people rather than freeing people, about being irrelevant to the world in which we are now set and, at its worst, about being just plain boring. All of these aspects of the church are not conducive to creativity.

Part of this understanding comes from those who would rather not see the church there in the first place. But another part comes from those within the church who feel that the church has become an organisation that has taken itself for granted and settled down in ways that are stultifying rather than in ways that are freeing. The church is not necessarily seen as an organisation which is being continually renewed in each succeeding generation for the work to which God calls it.

There are pressing practical issues in front of the church in the United Kingdom: the decline in the numbers of people going to church, and the imbalance in age profile of those who do go; the challenge of maintaining historic buildings on a decreasing income; the lack of ordained people to undertake the 'basic' work; the need to have a rigorous intellectual engagement with the variety of competing philosophies that make up the mix of life in Britain today.

In the midst of these issues, there can be a temptation to despair, to become more inward-looking and to wait helplessly for an uncertain future.

At a time such as this, a book on creative church leadership helps to paint a different picture. It rightly pulls together creativity and the church and emphasises the need for positive leadership in these changing times.

I want to begin by placing thinking about creative church leadership in a theological perspective. I do so, believing that the church is in God's hands and that the renewal of the church flows out of the life that is God's gift. Leadership in the church has its foundation in our understanding and interpretation of God and God's purposes for the world. The most creative church leadership is that which is deeply rooted within the life of God.

The creativity of God

At the heart of the Christian faith lies the Trinitarian God, Father, Son and Holy Spirit – creator, redeemer and sustainer.

We believe in God the Father and creator.

We look in wonder at the gifts of the natural world – the diversity of flowers and trees; the variety of animal and insect life; the enormity of ocean and mountain; the fire of the sun and the light of the moon; and men and women, reflecting the image of God. As Christians, we look and see the creativity of the creator at work in the world. This is not a world that is limited by rules, but one that is abundant in fruitfulness. This is not a world where everything is the same, but one in which there is a richness of difference. We believe in a God who has been active since before the beginning of time and whose ongoing work sustains creation – a God whose nature it is to be creative, who brings into being new and diverse forms of life.

Our understanding about God shapes our understanding about creation. Creation itself is a gift to be nurtured rather than a commodity to be exploited. Humankind is given the work of sharing in the care of creation.

We believe in God the Son and redeemer.

In Jesus, we see the human face of God – the God who loves the world and desires the fullness of life for all people. In Jesus' ministry he proclaims good news, heals the sick and feeds the hungry. In his death and Resurrection he sets people free and opens up the door to life. The Resurrection points to the conquering of death and all that leads to death. In Christ, people are released from their guilt and burdens and become who they are meant to be. In Christ there is a new creation, setting aside all that had gone astray in the old order and opening up an abundant new life.

Jesus challenged the old order where it had become moribund and placed the needs of people above the rituals which restricted. Because of his impact a new movement came into being, 'the followers of the Way'. People gathered together in groups small and large and were scattered, as individuals and as groups, throughout the world. So the church grew, not so much a well-knit organisation as a body of people, who individually and together with each other experienced the new life of Christ in their midst and who were called to share that new life with others.

We believe in God the Holy Spirit and sustainer.

The Spirit breathed life into creation at the beginning of time. The Spirit alighted upon Jesus at his baptism. This same Spirit gave power to the people of God at Pentecost and gifts for the nurturing of their ongoing life. The story of the early church tells of an abundance of gifts being poured out on the people. The Holy Spirit rested both upon individuals and upon the gathered community. The Spirit came both with particular gifts such as healing and prophecy and also in the setting aside of people in leadership roles such as elders and bishops.

The work of the Spirit was seen in the fruit of people's lives, in such areas as the growth of love and joy and patience. But the Holy Spirit could not be pinned down or contained. The Spirit came in unexpected ways, like the wind, blowing where it wills.

The three Persons of the Trinity are bound together in a bond of love. This love is not kept within the life of the Trinity, but flows out into the world. The creativity of God arises out of the mutual love of the Holy Trinity, love that is ceaselessly poured out for creation.

Creative church leadership is caught up in the action of God for the world. It is leadership that seeks to fulfil God's purposes.

Leadership in the church has both similarities and dissimilarities from leadership in other areas of corporate life. Each is concerned with vision, purpose and effectiveness. But leadership in the church reflects the nature and purpose of the church and therefore has a particular orientation in its style.

I want to continue by looking at some aspects of creative church leadership as they flow out of the life of the Trinity.

Leadership rooted in love

Leadership that flows out of the life of God participates in the love of God for the world.

There are many different views about leadership and many different styles of leadership that can be exercised. Within the church there are both those who call for stronger leadership and those who question the role of individual leaders as being too authoritarian. The model of leadership that flows out of the Trinity is one that is rooted in love. This means living in a loving relationship with God and a loving relationship with God's creation. Such leadership is characterised by self-giving rather than self-seeking and by an open heart for those in need. This love in itself sets people free to be creative.

I give one example, from a visit that I made to the Church of North

India in 2001. I was taken to see a leprosy mission north of Ahmedabad in the state of Gujarat. It was run by a Revd Albert Carpenter, a priest of the Church of North India. He told the following story.

Twenty-six years previously he had been working in a parish in Ahmedabad. Part of his work involved visiting the lepers who camped at the side of the river. They were regarded as outcasts and didn't get many people taking an interest in them. One year there was a flood and the banks of the river overflowed. When Albert Carpenter woke up the next morning and looked out, there was a whole host of lepers camped out on his front doorstep. 'We didn't know where else to go', they said, 'you were our only friend.'

He began to think that they should have somewhere better to live rather than the risky riverbank and so went to the church officers to see what they could offer in terms of alternative housing. After some time of persisting and arguing his cause, the church said that he could have a disused school in a town north of the city. Twenty-six years later he is looking after about hundred people, still often outcast from their families.

We visited not long after the earthquake had hit Gujarat. Some of the buildings of the leprosy mission had been made unsafe and Father Albert, as his people called him, was having to start again with raising money and rebuilding the community. We asked whether he didn't feel daunted after all these years, still having such an uphill struggle. 'The Lord will provide', he said, in his usual gentle way. 'He always has done over these years, why should I doubt him now.'

Here was a leadership rooted in love, that looked at people in need and saw, not an insurmountable problem, but a creative possibility. Because Albert Carpenter's heart was touched by the people in need, he was able to persist, despite all the difficulties in the way, in establishing a new beginning for a whole number of people.

Creative church leadership involves looking with eyes of love on the needs of the world and seeing not problems, but possibilities. It means the life of the leader reflecting the love of God.

Leadership with vision

The primary vision is of God. As we see God, so we are drawn closer to seeing ourselves and the world with his eyes of love. As we grow in our awareness of God, so we grow in our appreciation of the bountiful range of opportunities that God makes possible. Living as people of the Resurrection means that we carry the hope within us that even out of death can come life.

There is a small United Reformed church chapel set in a field in a rural part of Staffordshire. A few years ago it was down to four members. Three out of these four felt that the time had come to close and so voted by a majority of three to one to bring an end to their fellowship. However, the one was not convinced. She went round her family and friends in the few houses scattered down the country lane. Six months later they re-opened and now have a regular fortnightly congregation of 20 and have had baptisms and a wedding.

This one person had a vision that new life was possible, and that the death of the original fellowship was not the end.

Seeing possibilities rather than problems is a central part of being creative in church leadership.

It can be easy, in a time of decline and change, to become inward-looking and focused on problems:

- 'There's not enough money to go round.'
- 'Where are the people who're going to do things?'
- 'Why aren't there more children in the church?'
- 'Why does God only seem to give us awkward people in the church?'

Being creative in leadership in the church means refocusing our eyes on the wider vision and seeing the possibilities.

I remember an elderly lady from the church I first served. One day I got a phone call to say that she was ill with bronchitis. I went round to visit, full of sympathy for her sorry state. When I got there, she opened the door, scarf round her head and paintbrush in hand. 'I thought you were unwell,' I said. 'I can't let a little thing like that get in the way,' she said. 'I thought it would be a good opportunity to do some decorating.' She was also one who, when there was a rise in street crime in the area, said that it wasn't going to put her off coming up to the church at night.

Refocusing our vision in the church means being able to see what God is still making possible:

- Instead of seeing the lack of people, we can look again at reshaping our priorities.
- Instead of seeing the lack of children, we can look at what kind of fruitful work we can do with those of other ages.
- Instead of seeing awkward people, we can look for people's hidden gifts.

Having vision means seeing the church in the wider setting of time and space. It means being open to harvest the richness of the work of God in the saints and across the nations.

The United Reformed Church recently launched a 'Belonging to the

World Church' programme, aimed at giving lay and ordained people an experience of meeting people from different parts of the church internationally, both through visits abroad and through receiving visitors in Britain. Having a vision means seeing with new eyes. International exchanges are one means of opening people's eyes to the work that God is doing in a variety of different places.

A vision that is focused on God and on God's purposes brings with it its own sense of renewal. God is both closer to us than our own breath and yet also other than us and mysterious. This God sustains us in our inner life and calls us to continue to grow in our knowledge and understanding of him and of his loving purpose for the world. Limiting our vision to what we see and know at any one time means limiting God. Having a vision that is of God means continually growing and being renewed in that vision.

This vision of God is not an abstract matter. The creativity of God is poured out in the bounty of creation and seen in the great diversity of the natural world and human inventiveness. Leadership with vision leads into specific ideas about what can actually happen, ideas that inspire people to follow.

Leading and following

It has well been said that there is only successful leadership when there are also followers. While leadership is about having ideas and proposing initiatives, it is considerably limited when there is a vision that is not communicated or ideas that don't take people along.

If the woman at the village church in Staffordshire had not spoken enthusiastically to others of all that she saw was still possible for the church, if her vision hadn't been accepted by those she spoke to, the church would still be closed.

'Following' in this context doesn't mean being led blindly along. It refers rather to the situation where people affirm for themselves the vision and ideas that are being proposed.

There is a balance to be held between seeing the vision and developing the strategy.

There are a number of ways in which the balance between these two can be upset with the result that the vision doesn't take off.

A particular temptation in the church is the development of a 'Messiah' complex. An individual person sees him- or herself as the one who is going to 'save' the people. His or her vision is the right one and the only one. The dilemma in thinking in this way is that it takes away from the focus on God as the one who has the power to save and gives an inflated sense of ego to the individual involved. By focusing over-strongly on one person, this one person can see himself or herself as over against the church rather than as part of a community in which all the members are together responsible to God.

A 'Messiah' complex can lead on to the making of unilateral decisions, often followed by a certain bewilderment as to why these decisions aren't being followed by others. Or it can lead on to a desire to 'tell others what to do' followed by a certain anger as the 'others' are unco-operative.

Another temptation is to have too many ideas.

I discovered something of the truth of this at a corporate level in the General Assembly of the United Reformed Church. (The Assembly meets annually and is made up of representatives from across the church.) A particular individual or committee would bring a resolution to the Assembly, either urging 'the whole church' to take action on a particular matter or asking each council of the church, from the regional to that of the local congregation, to discuss a specific issue. Eventually there would be a list of such resolutions. By the time these came to the regional or congregational council, people felt that there were too many to tackle and, on occasion, abandoned them all. A year later, the person or committee who initially proposed the significant and important idea in the first place returned, lamenting the lack of action.

The same can happen within a congregation when a leader, lay or ordained, has a number of ideas about what might happen, but finds it difficult to discern which idea is the one to take forward at any particular time. The danger is that the creativity that there is in having a host of ideas is diminished by not being able to implement any particular one of them.

Creative leadership is leadership which takes people along. It is leadership which has a sense of the right kind of balance between the vision and the strategy for implementing the vision, so that people are able to affirm and participate in the vision. This affirmation and participation comes through leadership being shared and gifts being released.

Leading and sharing leadership

One historical picture of God has been as the clockmaker, who makes the clock, winds it up and then leaves it to get on with marking the hours. Other thinkers have developed ideas of God sharing the work of creation with humankind, seeing people as 'co-creators', working with God so that creation may become yet more fruitful. This second picture gives a hint of the possibilities of sharing in leadership.

There is a creativity that comes from the person on her own, working away in the garden shed on discovering a new invention, or from an artist, painting in a studio and creating a new work of art. However, creative leadership in the church inevitably involves other people.

While there will be occasions when it is appropriate to decide matters on behalf of other people who are involved, creative leadership looks to enable people to participate in the thinking about the issues that affect them. This participation can be seen as taking place somewhat bureaucratically. The church can feel overrun by the number of committees that are set up. Indeed, the solution to a particular problem can be seen as setting up a committee.

There are a number of aspects to sharing leadership. It's not about taking away responsibility from a particular leader for holding the vision. It's about how the ownership of the vision is shared and how the strategy for implementing the vision is developed.

Creativity can develop when a particular group of people come together to reflect on the vision and purpose for that group. The exchange of views in such a group can lead on to a bigger vision than was held by any one particular member at the outset.

Sharing leadership means looking for the appropriate people with whom to develop a vision and strategy. Sometimes this group will be found within an existing council of the church. At other times it will be a matter of drawing together people particularly for that purpose. One of the dilemmas for the church is the captivity to existing structures. While these are helpful to keep the institution in being and nurtured, they can also lead to a dependence on past practice rather than a breaking free into new models of shared life.

The building of teams is essential to sharing leadership. Teams don't happen overnight. They take considerable work to sustain. Teams can be of ordained people or lay people or a combination of the two. A good team depends on a high level of communication within the team and openness about the issues that are being faced.

I spent 13 years in Milton Keynes, working in an ecumenical ministerial team of Anglicans, Catholics, Methodists and United Reformed Church. Each member of the ministerial team was also involved in a number of other teams with lay people. The experience of listening and sharing together across a wide range of different perspectives was fruitful and led to much creativity. However, there was also much work to be done on the role of each team member and the interaction between the different people.

Sharing leadership is a fruitful and creative experience. It helps to reduce the temptation to an individualistic 'Messianic' tendency and opens up new possibilities for ways of being church.

Leadership as releasing gifts

God the creator offers creation as gift. The Holy Spirit comes, offering particular gifts to different people.

Creative church leadership is about enabling the gifts of God to go on being released among men and women and children and in the created world.

The church at her best is the place where there is a great outpouring of creativity. Over the centuries, cathedrals have been good places for releasing God's gifts. Stonemasons, artists, carpenters, sculptors, musicians and many others have been commissioned to bring beauty in sight and in sound.

However, there are aspects of the life of the church which work against gifts being discovered and released.

In those parts of the church where decline has set in and taken root, people become more inward-looking. With this sense of being inward-looking comes a diminished view of what's possible. People no longer anticipate that either they themselves or people who are new (who are unlikely to stay in such a congregation anyway) will have gifts that can be used creatively. The 'we've always done things this way' mindset doesn't leave space for new ideas and ways of working to be developed. There are times when the experience of newcomers into a congregation is that they are devalued and put to one side because they don't quite fit in with the prevailing ethos. When new initiatives are proposed, they are quietly sidelined, because they would change the shape of the prevailing culture. New gifts are seen as unnecessary, because all that is needful is already there.

Conforming to particular organisational structures can mean that people's gifts are valued in terms of the way in which they fit into and support these structures. This means that gifts that don't conform become moribund, rather than being released. Gifts are seen as being there to support existing structures rather than to be exercised in ways outside those structures or in the wider community.

Discovering and releasing people's gifts has a number of aspects.

It means being attentive to the potential of each individual and giving time to find what the gifts of each person are. It can be easier to look at the needs of the organisation and see how people fit in to supporting these needs, rather than to look at the individual and ask what gifts they have.

I can remember starting a new period of service in a local church with a fixed idea in my mind that the church should have a play-group. However, there were few children of that age in that community and no one in the congregation who had the gifts needed to undertake the work. Instead I discovered that there were a number of people with catering backgrounds. So the church embarked on coffee mornings and lunches for the passers-by in the town centre. If I had stayed with my original idea I would have ended up frustrated. Looking at the people and the gifts they brought released new energy.

Releasing gifts means people being open to new ways of working. When a newcomer becomes part of a group, a new group is formed. However it's interesting to observe whether the newcomer is absorbed into the prevailing culture, or whether the newcomer brings different gifts which change the culture. Sometimes congregations welcome new people because it means that there will be more of the same, and are shocked when these new people bring new ideas. Newcomers themselves can be a source of creativity, however, as their gifts are released into the congregation, and the previous culture is changed. Congregations can be resistant and need help from creative leaders in order to move on.

The church can fall into the trap of seeing that the gifts people are given are solely there for the building up of the institution, rather than for living out the Christian life in the world. There are times when the church needs to give people 'permission' to exercise their gifts outside the church, rather than making people feel guilty for not fulfilling the functions expected of them inside the church.

At her best the church is the place where people are set free to be fully human as they share in the new creation in Jesus Christ. This can in itself be a challenge to such things as job descriptions and contracts. If the church is to be the place where people are set free rather than being boxed in and where gifts are released, there needs to be a certain flexibility towards formal agreements that try to specify too particularly what the responsibilities of any one individual might be.

At her best, the church is also a community of trust, in which people are trusted to exercise their gifts within the framework of the nurture of the body as a whole.

Leadership and freeing time

God is both the God of the immediate moment and the God of eternity. In the contemporary culture of the West, the immediate moment can take precedence over a sense of eternity. Having an appropriate sense of eternity gives a different dimension to the present moment. This dimension is about experiencing time that is set free from the constraints of diaries and agendas, free for the new and unexpected to break in.

There is a two-fold dilemma in leadership in the church at present. The first aspect of this is the lack of clarity in a time of change about what the church is about. The second aspect leads on from this. In a time when things aren't clear, and when resources are stretched, there is a temptation to be more activist.

There is a lack of people to do what needs to be done. There is a need for greater management of the existing resources. Pressures arise out of the need for buildings to be maintained. Leaders become so busy 'keeping the show on the road' that there is little time to stop and reflect and analyse.

We live in a culture in which there are pressures to work harder and live faster. This is the point where the church faces the challenge of deciding between buying into the culture or of being counter-cultural. It is easy for the church to be as busy as the secular world around and put as much, if not more, pressure on people. Taking time out to slow down and wait upon God can be perceived as a counter-cultural endeavour. Yet it is out of this waiting and this sense of space that the new and unexpected ideas come.

I spent a year as national Moderator for the United Reformed Church. I was struck in this experience by the relentless pressure of moving on from one church to another, and one meeting to another with hardly a break in between to pop home. At the end of the year I found myself dreaming vividly at night, and realised that through the year I had hardly remembered a dream. It was as if the round of activity had squeezed out a particular dimension of life.

A speedy pace of life squeezes out new ways of thinking and of dreaming. Leaders in the church are put under pressure from a variety of different directions. For creativity to emerge, time needs to be set free so that new ideas and ways of living and thinking can bubble up.

The church is in an ideal position to reclaim for our society the rightful sense of time and to offer to people an abundant sense of space. In that space can be found new ideas and renewed joy as well as time for healing of hurts and past wounds.

For the church to be able to set time free, leaders also need free time!

Leadership as future oriented

The church is caught in the tension between history and the future. We believe in the God who goes back to before the beginning of time and has revealed himself particularly in one point in time in Jesus Christ. The church has a rightful sense of being rooted in the past. It is the life of Christ, present in one place and at one time in human history, which has shaped the church and given her life. However, the Christian faith also looks forward to the day when all things will be gathered up into Christ, in the fulfilment of the new creation. The Holy Spirit is both behind us to encourage us and in front of us to challenge us.

Leadership in the church builds on the past, but is oriented to the future. In the midst of the patterns of the past and the pressures of the present, leaders glimpse what might yet be. In a time of intense change the shape of the future world, as well as the shape of the future church, is yet to be discerned. This can feel frightening or it can feel full of promise. If we believe that the God who has been with us across past generations is also the one who holds the future in his hands and beckons us on into that future, we can travel forward with confidence.

Creative leadership for such an age needs energy, enthusiasm and perseverance. Such leadership will think in new ways, within the setting of a loving concern for the church as a body, for the people who make up that body and for the people the church is called to serve.

13 Setting the agenda for leadership

PETER RUDGE

In my book *Management in the Church* I coined a phrase; it was based upon those lines of William Ross Wallace:

The hand that rocks the cradle
Is the hand that rules the world.

My version was: 'The hand that writes the agenda rules the world' (Rudge, 1976, p. 12).

The phrase was used in relation to procedural matters, particularly the preparation of agendas for meetings. It means that the person who designs the format for meetings and arranges the list of items to be considered has an extensive control over the way in which the affairs of the meeting are conducted and the outcomes that might arise.

But the term agenda might be also used in a wider context, not just in reference to meetings but to the whole direction that an organisation takes. That is, the person who writes the charter for an organisation or its mission statement or its aims and objectives has a considerable influence over the way in which it develops and matures. It is worth noting also that, while in the popular mind the term agenda might indicate a list of items to be discussed, the derivation of the word places more emphasis upon doing; and so an agenda, whether at meetings or in the wider life of organisations, refers to what is to be done.

Because the use of the word agenda is normally confined to its context of meetings and their conduct, it has not often been used in studies of management. But there was one significant use of the term in the early days – namely, the 1960s – when the issue of management in the church was beginning to emerge. It was perhaps another indication of a growing ferment in the church. One such contributor to the debate was Bishop John Robinson, whose book *Honest to God* was published in 1963. Amongst other contributions that he was making at the time, I can recall a phrase of his when he said: 'The world is the agenda.' I thought it appeared in his *Honest to God* but in a recent rereading of the book I could not find it, though there were other phrases within it on the same lines. For instance, he said in relation to prayer: 'The "matter" of prayer is supplied by the world' (Robinson, 1963, p. 101). On the purpose and work of the church he said: 'Its charter is to be the servant of the world' (Robinson, 1963, p. 134).

Maybe I had read it in one of his other publications, such as his book *On Being the Church in the World*. His point was that the church should look beyond itself and its own internal interests and reach out to the world to see the human needs there and so shape its work and ministry to meet those needs. That is, the world – if looked at with perceptive eyes and with sympathies for the human condition – would provide the appropriate and relevant agenda for the councils and the assemblies of the church. To do so, it would then be fulfilling its mission and purpose as the bringer of the good news of the gospel to the human situation.

Another indication of openness to the world came in the calling of the Second Vatican Council in 1962 by Pope John XXIII. The impetus of the council was in effect to open a window on the world for the church and to provide a great incentive for it to respond to the evident needs in that world. Hence the council also thought in terms of creating a new agenda far beyond any limits that there might have been in the past. This awakening or reawakening in the Roman Catholic Church was particularly evident in its religious communities. Historically these bodies have had that degree of independence and freedom to act in ways beyond the normal structures of the church and so many of them responded extensively to the new opportunities available to them in the light of the new impetus. It so happened that this development within the religious communities coincided with the development of the relevance of management studies to Christian organisations. One example of this was the establishment of CORAT (Christian Organisations Research and Advisory Trust, set up in 1967) which in due course found about half of its management consultancy work in these very same bodies.

These orders welcomed guidance as to how their new hopes might be achieved, and it was interesting to note how many communities began to have a common perception of what work they might attempt. They concentrated on the needs of the world and of the human situation with such issues as the unemployed, the homeless, the poor and the needy. The outcome, however, was that they all seemed to be seeking to do exactly the same kind of work. They were reaching into the same human areas, whereas historically, according to the divine dispensation expressed in their original purpose or charism, they might well have had variant perceptions of how to meet human needs. But they all tended to end up in the same area and seemingly overlooked what distinctive contribution each might make. For instance, there was one whose original foundation had a cross-Channel English-French orientation and which might have had new opportunities of coordination and reconciliation in such areas; but it tended to look for postulants and outreach work in the already heavily concentrated areas of Ireland – the Ireland prior to its membership in the European Union.

The distinctiveness of the contemplative communities tended not to be so blurred as it was with the active communities. This difference was not based on the isolation of contemplative communities within their strict rule of enclosure and apparent separation from the world; indeed they also had a new perception of apostolic opportunity in relation to the world. CORAT's work with them was under the auspices of an organisation called by the somewhat unusual name of 'The Commission on the Economics of the Contemplative Life'. Its spokesman was a Father Barnabas Sandeman of the Order of St Benedict; and his message to CORAT as well as to the contemplative communities was 'the evangelical witness of the contemplative life'. Thus they also had an agenda of a ministry to the world, although it may take some deep perception to see the mysterious ways in which God works. One obvious example of such a redirection came in the person of Dame Theresa Rodrigues, a Benedictine nun at Stanbrook Abbey in Worcestershire. In keeping with the Benedictine charism which encompasses such things as learning, scholarship, music and the arts, she made a distinctive contribution to the quality of the English language newly used in the public prayers and liturgies of the Roman Catholic Church. No doubt many people who worship in that church or who have been attracted to it have appreciated the rhythm and cadences of the language that is used in its formal worship.

Another of the aspects of this renewed emphasis upon openness to the world came in one word in the vocabulary associated with it. The word 'discern' came into much greater use at the time. The word is not a distinctive biblical word. It is used quite sparingly in the Bible and comes as a translation of several Hebrew and Greek words, notably as used in 1 Corinthians 2.14 and Matthew 16.3.

Discern is a good word for indicating the kind of perceptions needed in making assessments of worldly or human situations and it is a characteristic to be desired in and developed in those who aspire to leadership. It came into considerable popular usage at the time. For instance, it appears in the first paragraph of the Preface to Bishop

Robinson's *Honest to God* and it was widely used in the Roman Catholic Church after the Second Vatican Council.

I used it myself once in the title of a paper presented to an international conference on the sociology of religion. The title of the paper was: 'Discerning the Degree of Discontinuity'. It provided the occasion for one of my most embarrassing moments because this Peter F. Rudge was mistakenly identified as Peter F. Drucker, the famous American management guru. There was a reason for such an error in that the title of my paper was partly based on Drucker's then recently published book *The Age of Discontinuity*. His point was that we are living in a changing world. We cannot expect the same conditions to prevail unchangeably in the future; and any consideration of management issues should take into account discontinuity and not continuity as the norm of human experience – and not least in the world of management.

The point of my paper was that an essential skill in management, in management consultancy and in the exercise of leadership was that fine perception of the degree of discontinuity necessary in any forward thinking. It could not be assumed that the same stable situation could continue indefinitely in the future. There was change and it was necessary to estimate the extensiveness of that change. At the other extreme is the situation of complete discontinuity which might be found in the common experience of waking out of a dream wherein all that took place in the dream vanishes and normal life resumes. But what is the degree of discontinuity? How extensive is the change to be?

In one consulting situation I recall Stuart Snell, the Director of CORAT and later the Bishop of Croydon, working with me in accumulating a massive dossier of facts and pages of documentation about the past experiences of our client. He then, as it were, picked them all up and set them aside, asking the question: 'Where do we go from here?' Hence it was a matter of assessing the degree of discontinuity – on this occasion very extensive because in this Christian organisation about 90 per cent of the donated funds had been absorbed in the administration of the organisation rather than used in its outreach missionary work.

There is a psychological dimension to this issue of discerning the degree of discontinuity. I attempted to explore this in my book *Order and Disorder in Organisations*, especially on pages 120–2. There are basic psychological dispositions appropriate to the several schools of management. For instance, in that view of life called the traditional, the emphasis is upon the subconscious psychological activity; whereas, in the view of management called the classical or mechanistic or bureaucratic, the assumption is that the mind is working at the conscious and rational level. But what facet of consciousness might be appropriate where the dominant feature is the awareness of the world outside and the changes taking place in it?

I endeavoured to express this dimension by coining the term extra-conscious, by which I meant extra- not in the sense of something additional but in the way it is used in such words as extra-mural. That is, the extra- refers to what is outside. Is it possible that some people may have the capacity in their minds for the extra-conscious – the awareness of what is taking place outside in a way that is sensitive and perceptive – more so than might be the case with many other people? Such a capacity is essential for one who is to be a leader and who is to set the agenda for leadership in the church as in other organisations as well. Perhaps there are those with training and expertise in psychology who might be able to explore this question further and throw light on a potential dimension of the mind.

Another factor that had a bearing on the nature of agendas in the 1960s and onwards was a development in management studies. Hitherto the dimensions of such studies were well expressed by Douglas McGregor in his 1960 book entitled *The Human Side of Enterprise*. In that book he delineated what has now become famous as Theory X and Theory Y. The former is the standard classical, bureaucratic or mechanistic view of management whereas the alternative Theory Y places great emphasis upon the significance of human relations within an organisation.

Much management thinking has involved these two extreme positions which are set over against each other; or there has been a presentation of a sliding scale between these two extremes devised by Robert Tannenbaum and Warren H. Schmidt. They suggested there could be a shading in of the two major emphases: on the one hand the boss-centred emphasis on authority and at the other end the subordinate-centred emphasis upon freedom. The sliding scale between those two positions indicated the varying degree of these two significant elements expressed in their extreme form in McGregor's Theory X and Theory Y. The significant point, however, was – whether taken as a dichotomy or as a continuum – the focus of thinking within these bounds was on what was internal to the organisation. Hence the agendas of managers were confined to matters inside the church or whatever other organisation was involved; that is, the external world was by definition excluded from consideration.

Nevertheless these restricted views of organisation were overtaken by the changes in the world of such magnitude that management thinking had to come to terms with them and so introduce a new dimension to the way that an organisation's affairs were conducted. One school which expanded on this view was the Tavistock tradition in which serious account was taken of the need to encompass the outside world as part of the purview of managers. In fact, it was suggested that, instead of the managers being at the top of the pyramid, their position was on the boundary between the organisation and the outside world. Their tasks then became to understand all the factors that impinged upon an organisation and so interpret them and explain them internally so that the organisation could respond positively and creatively to the whole new environment around it. It was said that not only were managers on the boundary but that they should spend at least half of their time looking outwards, with the other half looking inwards to see how to give effect to the new dimensions.

Thus a new perspective was added to the role of the manager in an organisation and it began to awaken the consideration of the difference between leadership and management. The difference was explored by Professor John Adair at MODEM's 2002 Sheffield Conference. In notes prepared by Sue Jewell of what Professor Adair said, there was this statement: 'Management . . . has nuances of the day-to-day running of things, controlling, administration (once a synonym for management), use of systems and, finally, the husbanding or thrifty use of resources.' He also said: 'The link between leadership and change is a strong one. A leader is one who takes others on a journey.' While there may have been some opportunities for the exercise of leadership when the agenda of organisations was confined to matters internal to such bodies, the real capacity for leadership comes with the emergence of the significance of external factors as they impinge upon what is inside. Hence the development of management thinking that encompasses this new dimension and direction has helped to focus greater attention upon the qualities of leadership rather than upon the more routine operations. Hence the setting of agendas in this new area becomes increasingly important and a significant task in which leaders might exercise their imagination and vision.

Nevertheless it is inappropriate to make an immediate transfer of these insights from the sphere of management studies into the life of the church and the way leadership is exercised there. There has always been a fear of such transposition when management principles are imported into the life of the church without regard for the distinctive nature of that body. Hence there needs to be a theological foundation for this emerging new perception of management and leadership. That is why in my original book *Ministry and Management*

I looked for theological support for this view of management relating an organisation to its environment. I relied heavily upon that classic presentation by H. Richard Niebuhr entitled *Christ and Culture,* a book which has stood the test of time and which provided the theological basis for the type of leadership in the church that recognised the significance of relating to the world around: Christ and culture, church and society, the organisation and its environment – all matching elements of the same focus in leadership.

I was soon made aware of the importance of the relationship between the church and its environment in one of the earliest CORAT-like consultancy assignments. In this I joined my life-long friend Bishop Robert Davies, the Bishop of Tasmania, in the aftermath of the disastrous bushfires in south-east Tasmania in 1967. So much of the countryside was ravaged and the fires reached the streets of the outer suburbs of Hobart. One significant statistic in the assessment of the damage was the fact that in the rural areas 16 local churches were burnt down. Further, it so happened that all the destroyed buildings belonged to the Anglican Church: none to the Roman Catholic Church or the Methodist Church or the Presbyterian Church or any other – all of them were Anglican churches. The question was raised at the time: was this a situation similar to that recorded in this verse of the gospel?

> Those eighteen who were killed when the tower of Siloam fell on them – do you think they were worse offenders than all the others living in Jerusalem? (Luke 13.4)

No! It was not that the Anglicans were greater sinners than other people, but that their understanding of the church's relationship to society was such that it had a physical presence in the form of church buildings in the many scattered rural communities in south-east Tasmania. The Anglican Church saw its role to be fundamentally associated with such communities to provide the base upon which communities could be built, where people could be strengthened by their association with the church and their lives enriched by the power of the gospel; in districts in decline, the church remained as the last surviving focus of community cohesion. Hence it built those many churches in the rural areas and they were the ones that were destroyed in the bushfires. Other churches may have had other perceptions of the relationship between their church and the society around them but that did not involve the building of these small churches in rural communities as the gathering point for their followers.

In view of these several factors described above, everything seemed to be in place for a major step forward in the life of the church and an extension of its ministry and service to the world. There was the stimulus of thinking such as presented in a challenging way by Bishop Robinson. There was the wise counsel and guidance emerging from the Second Vatican Council. The tide of management thinking was turning in the direction that allowed the church to take serious consideration of the world and its needs. A theological basis had been established to give the church confidence in pursuing those lines of management that would enable us to widen its horizons and to respond creatively to the needs of the world. Thus there was a renewed opening for leaders to create a new agenda for the church. There was this period of reawakening to the opportunity but maybe it did not last all that long. One possible indicator was the history of CORAT itself. It flourished and blossomed on the strength of all these factors just mentioned and developed extensively, particularly in the first half of the 1970s, but by the end of that decade its work had diminished and eventually dried up, with some of the strands of CORAT's life being later reincarnated in the emergence of MODEM.

Indeed, if it were the case that the impetus of this change had begun to fade throughout the church, what really happened was the re-establishment of an agenda that had been set for the church a hundred years earlier. That event took place in 1870 with the First Vatican Council, which is primarily famous for the papal decree of infallibility, but the fine print should be noted in the documents of the council that infallibility was 'in defining doctrine concerning faith or morals'. This council may be thought of as a pinnacle in the life of that church but it is not often recognised that there could be an alternative assessment of the situation.

Those who are brought up in the studies of organisational behaviour will well know how common it is for an organisation that is declining in significance and losing its constituency to respond by strengthening its hold upon what little that remains. Maybe this is what happened in the Roman Catholic Church in 1870, greater and greater authority being asserted over a diminishing sphere of influence, resulting in an agenda reduced to two residual items. I drew attention to this point in my 1999 book *The Transfiguration of Human Knowledge*:

What was even more tragic was [that] the impression was given that this was a high point in the history of the Roman Catholic Church; whereas the decree of the First Vatican Council could be represented as the nadir of the church's fortune. It represented the lowest point possible in the influence of the church on human life since the Middle Ages when theology was the queen of the sciences.

The church increasingly lost its grip upon various areas of life, beginning with the politics of Machiavelli and later with art and music and the natural sciences until the point was reached where the church had nothing left upon which to pontificate other than matters of faith and morals. Law had escaped it, as had likewise all the new areas of knowledge, such as psychology and sociology, which had grown up in the same century as the first Vatican Council.

Moreover, such matters of faith and morals as indicated in the decree of the council diminished in the years ahead to matters of private faith and personal morals; and in the latter part of the twentieth century, the question of morals was restricted even further to become mainly questions of sex and reproduction upon which the church may have little competence or credibility. (Rudge, 1999, pp. 101–2)

I have found that this analysis of the church's situation since the First Vatican Council was not new to me when writing in 1999.

In 1980 I reviewed for *The Canberra Times* an enormous two-volume book entitled *Catholicism* by Richard P. McBrien. I began the review with these words:

This massive work must rank high in the progeny of Vatican Council II, not only for its comprehensiveness but for its eirenic spirit.

In its subject matter, it goes beyond the range of the constitutions and decrees of the Council and virtually matches the compass of the *Summa Theologica* of St Thomas Aquinas.

After commending the many virtues of this treatise, I concluded in this way:

In his concern for the Church in the modern world, he seeks to learn from those disciplines which describe the world and the human condition today: the natural sciences, the social sciences, the humanities, all of which are treated in his felicitous precis manner. He comes to the threshold of delineating the questions the world is asking and of formulating a 'theology of human existence' – with the promise that the remainder of his book will provide a modern *Summa* of all knowledge.

He starts . . . and then falters . . . and ends with a dissertation of great length and much virtue but virtually confined to the residual areas of private 'faith and morals', the world – God's world, the world He so loved, the world into which He in Christ came to reconcile to Himself – having slipped through his fingers.

My interpretation of the First Vatican Council and its sequel should not be regarded as a personal diatribe against the Roman Catholic Church because what is said of that church is likely to be true of all the churches. It is simply that the Roman Catholic Church was more open and public and definitive in its statements than other churches might have been in relation to the issues so clearly expressed there.

I was encouraged in taking this view by finding in Bishop Robinson's *Honest to God* a statement by Dietrich Bonhoeffer in his *Letters and Papers from Prison* which was written sometime before his death at the hands of the Nazis in 1945. In it he is clearly indicating the relevance of the view I was expressing about the Roman Catholic Church being applicable to the Christian cause generally; and he provides a similar interpretation of the situation. Here is the passage from Bonhoeffer quoted favourably by Bishop Robinson:

> The movement beginning about the thirteenth century (I am not going to get involved in any arguments about the exact date) towards the autonomy of man (under which head I place the discovery of the laws by which the world lives and manages in science, social and political affairs, art, ethics and religion) has in our time reached a certain completion. Man has learned to cope with all questions of importance without recourse to God as a working hypothesis. In questions concerning science, art, and even ethics, this has become an understood thing which one scarcely dares to tilt at any more. But for the last hundred years or so it has been increasingly true of religious questions also: it is becoming evident that everything gets along without 'God', and just as well as before. As in the scientific field, so in human affairs generally, what we call 'God' is being more and more edged out of life, losing more and more ground. (Bonhoeffer, 1956, p. 145)

Bishop Robinson himself summed up his analysis of what Bonhoeffer had said and of the situation of the church in these words:

> [T]he God who has been elbowed out of every other sphere has a 'last secret place', in the private world of the individual's need. This is the sphere of 'religion' and it is here that the Churches now operate, doing their work among those who feel, or can be induced to feel, this need. (Robinson, 1963, p. 38)

So much then for the agenda of the church. What possibility is there for the church to be relevant in its ministry and its service when the topics that might be on that agenda are by nature residual, marginal, private and personal?

Currently the church appears to have three items on its agenda: worship, education, service. But they all isolate the church from the real world: worship – where provision is made for its own members; education – mainly for those on the inside and only noticed when a controversial issue such as the creationist view of science is taught and when there are scandals about child abuse; service – widely welcomed but the church is so focused on meeting consequential humanitarian needs that it precludes itself from dealing with the real causes of the problems in the political and economic fields.

I value the reference in the quotation from Bonhoeffer about the time-frame of the church's history from the thirteenth century until now. That was the period, as he said, when almost everything slipped through the fingers of the church. I take it even further in relation to that eight-century phase of Christian history. There were two earlier eight-century periods in the history of human knowledge. I said in my book on transfiguration:

> Some seven or eight centuries had passed from the beginnings of the culture of the ancient Greek world up to the transfiguration given to it by St Augustine. A further seven or eight centuries then followed to the point where a new impact was made by St Thomas Aquinas on the direction of the totality of human knowledge . . .
>
> Now in this modern age, some seven or eight centuries on from that pinnacle associated with St Thomas Aquinas, there may be an opportunity to shape again the future of human knowledge and give it a new direction as St Augustine did in his transfiguration in the early part of the fifth century. (Rudge, 1999, pp. 233–4)

The possibility of creating a new and relevant agenda for the church at the end of this third period of eight centuries remains a possibility. There may be several ways of creating it. One line to take – amongst various options that may be devised – is that suggested in my transfiguration book, where some thirty major topics are listed. The list includes all the natural sciences as well as a wide array of other subjects from music to mathematics, from law to linguistics, from economics to engineering, from dietetics to demography, from art to aesthetics – all of which have had a somewhat chequered history, particularly in the last eight hundred years, as Bonhoeffer himself indicated in a similar list of items. My hope was that there could be a renewal of involvement in all of these areas if serious thought were taken of the potential of the theology of new creation.

Many people will be aware of the transition from the old to the new in the two testaments that constitute the Bible. The advent of a new age and the newness of the new status of humanity is proclaimed in such verses as 2 Corinthians 5.17 and Galatians 6.15. The cosmic dimensions of such a change are foreshadowed in Romans 8.18–21.

Might not a transformation of similar magnitude be applicable to all areas of life so precisely and carefully depicted by scholars in their respective disciplines and in their summation? Here are some of my words explaining that possibility:

> In the transfiguration of the totality of human knowledge, there still needs to be two minds: the theological mind on the one side and the many minds of scholars in all the respective subjects on the other . . .
>
> At this stage the transfiguration may be no more than a foreshadowing of what is possible, with the substantive nature of the transfiguration to emerge in the decades and possibly centuries ahead.
>
> Such would be a welcome step forward in the destiny of human knowledge – after some seven or eight centuries following St Thomas Aquinas where there had been discord, animosity and conflict . . . That phase may be left behind if a new opportunity is seized by those who have the capacity to do so on the theological side and those scholars in all other areas who see the tremendous potential that is available to them singularly and collectively in the process that has been described as the transfiguration of human knowledge. (Rudge, 1999, p. 234)

Thus there is again an opportunity for creative church leadership matching that which was possible in the 1960s and 1970s.

Besides the setting of new agendas by church leaders, there needs to be the capacity within their organisational structures of giving effect to what is being planned to be done. Churches have their meetings in the form of synods, councils and assemblies. For such meetings there needs to be – if the hand that writes the agenda is to rule the world – an effective way of establishing and using agendas.

Meetings commonly begin with apologies, the minutes of the previous meeting are read, then follows business arising from the minutes, inward correspondence, outward correspondence, reports and general business. However, a presentation of this type of agenda tells virtually nothing about the substantive issues that are to be considered at a meeting. Nor does such an agenda indicate the order in which items are to be considered. It is not uncommon for a significant item of business to be included in business arising, in the correspondence inwards and outwards, in reports and also in general business – with little indication at what point in the course of the meeting that the issue is to be considered in a way that takes account of all the locations where it might occur in the agenda paper. Participants at meetings have to switch their minds quickly from one unrelated item to another, not knowing whether there will be another reference to the issue elsewhere in the agenda and not knowing whether the topic is there for information only, for reflection or for decisive action. No wonder the real agenda is lost in the pursuit of a traditional format for the conduct of meetings!

I coined that aphorism about agendas in my book *Management in the Church* where the conduct of meetings was being considered. I drew attention to an alternative format for the shaping of business at a meeting. The author of this different arrangement was Olan Hendrix, an American management consultant and lecturer who specialised in the voluntary and charitable range of organisations. He conducted a number of seminars under the auspices of CORAT for those in executive positions in many Christian organisations. His alternative pattern for an agenda was to arrange the issues under three headings:

Information Items
Study Items
Decision Items

The first included only items of factual information but it contained all that might be relevant to whatever followed later on. The second item was where long-term issues were raised for consideration though not necessarily at this stage for decision. Definite decision items in the form of motions were listed under the third heading.

There was a psychology behind this: people following this format would tend to be in the same frame of mind in each of the three areas. When information items were presented, what was needed by members was open, attentive and receptive minds. Then when moving on to study items there was scope for creative and imaginative thinking. Finally, when people had warmed to this sequence of mental attitudes, there came the decision items which required quick, decisive and balanced minds.

Those who wish to follow this issue further might look to the writings of Edward de Bono who is famous as the originator and populariser of what is called lateral thinking. His most relevant book for this purpose is that entitled *Six Thinking Hats*, in which he uses various colours to indicate the appropriate attitude of participants in meetings. For instance, he thinks of the white hat as that being appropriate for the quiet receptive attitude when considering all the facts and figures. The red hat involves people expressing their emotions and feelings, even their anger. The black hat is designed to indicate negativity in the querying of information or of decisions and presenting a contrary viewpoint of why things are not working. The green hat is the one associated with creative thinking, and so on. Edward de Bono's point is that the proceedings of meetings can be greatly disrupted when it is not recognised under which hat people are speaking. It is desirable that at any one stage of the meeting that all should speak with the same attitude and then move on to other phases and attitudes of expression; and so the Hendrix formula would involve the white hat for information items, the green hat for study items, and some black hat contributions in the consideration of decision items.

In Figure 13.1 there is a comparison between the two types of agendas, the traditional on the one hand and that of Olan Hendrix on the other, together with an indication of how the traditional agenda might be transposed into the new format.

With the Hendrix version, the work of the secretary is greatly simplified. In the course of the meeting there is minimal work to do under Information Items; it is only a matter of noting any corrections or additions. Fuller notes will be needed for recording the discussion of what is considered in Study Items. Then for the Decision Items, it is little more than a cross or a tick unless there are amendments or additional motions. After the meeting the writing up of the minutes may take only minutes. The minutes should be headed: 'Minutes of the meeting dated . . . to be read in conjunction with the agenda papers'. Under Information Items, the secretary simply writes: 'Noted', with any corrections or additions. There will be more writing involved in reporting on the Study Items. But with the Decision Items, the record consists of the numbers of the items with an indication whether the motions are agreed or rejected.

Should this format be adopted, there is considerable scope for the translation of the ideas of a leader into practical effect. Extensive information is allocated to the Information Items. Where there is one or several major issues to be explored, the issues can be outlined in the agenda papers in the section dealing with Study Items; and any decisions to be taken immediately can be listed precisely. Thus leaders

Traditional Agenda	*Hendrix's Counterpart*
1. Apologies – usually called for at a meeting.	Written in attendance book.
2. Minutes – usually read out and confirmed immediately.	Circulated in advance in Information Items; confirmed later in Decision Items.
3. Business arising from the minutes – a string of unrelated items.	
4. Correspondence inward – read out – a string of unrelated items.	For 3, 4, 5: Grouped by subject and set out in Information Items.
5. Correspondence outward – read out – a string of unrelated items.	Significant letters photo-copied for inclusion. Include also faxes, e-mails, telephone calls, notes of interviews and consultations.
6. Financial statement and accounts for payment – usually read out; sometimes distributed at a meeting.	Circulated in advance in Information Items; confirmed later in Decision Items.
7. Reports – usually read out.	Circulated in advance in Information Items.
8. General business – some items may be listed, others spontaneously introduced; seldom researched and documented in advance.	Information and research documented in advance in Information Items for clear-cut issues. For items longer term and requiring consideration, set out in Study Items. Specific motions listed in Decision Items.

Figure 13.1

have a great opportunity for focusing attention on the issues of major importance together with leading those engaged in discussions in a sequence of psychological attitudes that are appropriate to each phase of the meeting.

The effectiveness of meetings can be analysed by using various techniques including those developed by Peter Bates, now the Honorary Treasurer of MODEM but who in earlier days was one of CORAT's most valued associate consultants. One way was to record the time spent on each item discussed at the meeting, often leading to that not so unfamiliar experience that 'the amount of time spent on an item is in inverse proportion to its significance'. Further analysis can be made of who spoke and for how long; the criss-cross of debate can also be traced; and, in the light of de Bono's point, which thinking hat did people have on when they spoke.

Another analytical skill that Peter Bates introduced into CORAT's work was called activity sampling. By means of listing a series of random times based about half an hour apart, more or less, during the course of a day and spread out over a significant period such as a fortnight, it was possible for people in Christian organisations to record how they allocated their time. The resulting analysis would indicate the length of their working days and the amount of attention given to various aspects of their work, whether reading or prayer or study or meetings or whatever else they were engaged in. Such evidence could support or contradict the earlier suggestion that leaders might spend half of their time looking outwards, matching the half of their time looking inwards. Time is a very precious commodity: it is important that leaders trusted with the responsibility of setting the agendas in fact allocate their time adequately for fulfilling that purpose and are not distracted by marginal or less important matters.

An important issue in the management of time is the appropriate use of a diary. A sizeable diary is essential and it is often most helpful to have one that has a week at an opening so that it is possible to glance quickly at the commitments for the whole week. It is not just a matter of listing the fixed appointments: it is helpful to have three columns. On the left side, where the hours of the day are indicated, insert the fixed appointments that must be honoured; in the middle column list the matters that need to be dealt with in the course of the day even though they are not at fixed times; then in the right-hand column include matters that would desirably be dealt with in the course of the week. As the week proceeds, these last items can be inserted into the middle column and if necessary into the left-hand column. Further, it is helpful that the diary be looked at last thing in the day to see what lies ahead for the morrow – either fixed or variable – and perhaps list those more urgent items in the middle column that should take precedence over other issues.

An additional tool for leaders who are creating agendas is an adequate filing system. It is commonplace to arrange files according to the subject matter, with folders being placed in alphabetical order.

That is fine where work is being done on a number of major issues, with information as it comes to hand being slotted in to the relevant subject file. But for busy people with many commitments and appointments an additional filing system may be appropriate. It was found to be so in CORAT's work in a series of bishops' secretariats. It is called a chronological system, whereby a drawer in the cabinet is set up with files for each day of the next three months. Into each relevant file is inserted the papers relating to appointments scheduled for that day so that the relevant file can be quickly picked out together with information that may have been gathered in the course of the preceding weeks, before the relevant appointment. Then, as each day of the current month disappears, a new file is opened for the matching day of the month three months down the track.

In the above text from the consideration of meetings onwards, there are a number of useful tools that are available to church leaders to assist them in their work, especially in providing the practicalities of translating their ideas into action.

There remains for those engaged in creative church leadership that they give their full attention to the setting of agendas that will enable the church not only to be sensitive to the world but also to be ready and committed to its ministry and service in it. Such agendas may well be wider and more extensive than hitherto if the church is to recover from that narrowing of its horizons and to move on to a greater openness and comprehensiveness in its outlook. The hand that writes the agenda – the right agenda – can indeed rule the world; or, to express the point in less mundane terms, fulfil that prayer to the Father that his Kingdom come and his will be done on earth as it is in heaven.

References

Bonhoeffer, Dietrich (1956), *Letters and Papers from Prison*, ed. Eberhard Bethge, tr. Reginald H. Fuller, London, SCM Press, 2nd edn, 1956.

De Bono, Edward (1967), *Six Thinking Hats*, London, Penguin.

Robinson, John A. T. (1963), *Honest to God*, London, SCM Press.

Rudge, Peter F. (1968), *Ministry and Management*, Tavistock.

Rudge, Peter F. (1976), *Management in the Church*, London, McGraw-Hill.

Rudge, Peter F. (1990), *Order and Disorder in Organisations*, Canberra, CORAT.

Rudge, Peter F. (1999), *The Transfiguration of Human Knowledge*, Canberra, CORAT.

14 The one who builds the path cannot make it straight

PETER PRICE

An African proverb observes that, 'The one who builds the path cannot make it straight.' Sometimes leadership is misunderstood as path-building, and many church leaders lose their way because, instead of mapping out where the path should lead, they spend too much time trying to build it.

Leadership in the contemporary church is a difficult and complex task. There are many varied and frequently conflicting claims upon a leader, alongside expectations that are both false and unrealistic. In part these unreal expectations occur because of a confused understanding of the nature, or model of the church that the leader is expected to lead.

One of the descriptions Jesus gave himself was that of the 'path' or 'the Way'. The first Christians were known as 'Followers of the Way'. The path Jesus spoke of was frequently described as 'narrow and hard'[1] – in contrast to the Roman roads which were broad. Jesus' comparison between his 'path' and the broad roads of the empire, enabling rapid troop movement, economic exploitation through the carrying of goods, tax levies and the like, provides clues to the nature of his leadership, and the consequences of following.

Jesus' concern for the oppressed, afflicted and marginalised of his society[2] and his recruitment of followers who will identify with an alternative existence among such people, led him to conclude that his 'way' that challenged unjust imperial practices and social and religious structures was 'hard'.

Living against the grain, being out of step with the majority, being in tension or conflict with the prevailing powers, is a hard journey. It is not surprising that much contemporary Christianity settles for compromise, expressed in the forms of individuality, personal spirituality and a detachment from the world, rather than an engagement with it.

Models of the church

In seeking to address the issue of creative leadership in today's church, I have chosen to focus on Avery Dulles's *Models of the Church*.[3] Dulles offered the observation that the church was determined by one or other of the following models: *herald, servant, community, sacrament* and *institution*. Each of these models has a dominant paradigm, yet at the same time holds within it the potential for a more radical practice of Christian faith.

Creative leadership in contemporary church life demands of the would-be leader the courage and gifts to take a church beyond its dominant paradigm, enabling holistic Christian living that is both liberated and liberating. In offering a brief synopsis of each of Dulles's models, with the addition of a further one of my own, namely, post-modern, I hope to offer pointers as to how creative leadership might emerge that will enable us to 'build the straight path'.

Herald

The model of the church as herald emerges from the concept of the church as proclaimer of biblical truth. Here the church exists to grab attention and gather people who in turn will 'grab' the attention of others, thus expanding the church. Much contemporary charismatic church life relies upon this model. Leadership in it relies heavily upon teaching and a 'teacher', often a charismatic leader. In addition highly organised structures of groups for prayer, Bible study, witness and evangelism are needed to service the heralding mission.

Leadership in such a church often offers 'star' status to its leading ministers, providing they can satisfy the expectations of the congregation. Such leadership is also demanding because not only do the congregations rely heavily upon someone who will keep on bringing in new people but also there is often a moral pressure to speak of certainties. Such demands can leave the leader remote and isolated, often garlanded with accolades which can lead to a certain pride and separation. Raising questions in such structures, as well as exploring new possibilities in worship or theology, will demand courage and discernment, and often leadership fails at this point.

Such churches frequently get stuck, and genuine activity of the Spirit is thwarted because both leaders and followers become bound in some kind of Faustian bargain which prevents real engagement with the communities and people from whom they draw their membership. 'Building a straight path' requires asking questions about the lived experience of the folk who are being ministered to, in order to explore practical and imaginative ways to overcome the obstacles and meet the opportunities that people face day by day.

'Reinventing' this model of church will take people beyond simply 'knowing God' into some sort of analysis of the locality and circumstances in which people live in order to make faith alive and vital.

Asking questions about where and how people live helps clarify the practice of faith. People need encouragement to be proactive in supporting what is good and life-giving in their communities, as well as help in learning how to discern what is wrong, and bringing the values of God's kingdom to bear on difficult situations.

Where such a church places emphasis on 'gifts of the Spirit' and emphasises 'signs and wonders' as an appropriate faith response to God, it is often hard for a leader to nurture the kind of realism that Jesus encouraged when he advised people not to build without being sure of the foundations, the budget and the builders! Or, not to engage in a battle before assuring a reasonable chance of victory.

Servant

The model of the church as servant is frequently evident in places of evident need. Leadership here involves ministering to people who are often vulnerable, demanding and dependent. Its life is attractive to the outside observer because it is seen to be doing things that are relevant and useful, sanitising the conscience of the rest of the church by caring for those who are on the margins either through homelessness, unemployment, sex, drug or alcohol abuse, or mental illness. Among such communities there is often a quality of fellowship and indeed worship that addresses the real concerns of those present, and folk like them.

Creative leadership that 'makes the path straight' to interdependence, healing and discovering the full stature of humanity, demands a willingness to move beyond charity and dysfunctionalism, towards justice. 'One way of putting it is that the servant leader does not generate the community's agenda, but assists the community in every possible way to implement it.'[4]

Among such communities biblical reflection and prayer is often contextual, particularly in terms of the gospel narratives. 'What would Jesus do?' might be a defining question for these communities in seeking a hermeneutic for working in the community. In such situations, creative leadership may require leading people into something of the numinous, the mystery of the divine, a holiness and spirituality that has the possibility of wonderment and awe, often in the midst of deprivation.

In many contexts understanding of *servanthood* is all too easy. In Singapore I was once asked to address a new congregation set in an affluent part of the city. I asked those who accompanied me to help me see those whom St Luke refers to as the *anawim* – the 'little ones', literally 'the ones who cringe'. Initially there appeared to be none of the poor present, but at the end of the service I spoke to a young woman tending some small children. 'Who are you?' I asked. 'I am nobody,' she replied, 'I am just the maid.'

Understanding *servanthood* in a Western context becomes increasingly difficult. In Jesus' analogy the term most used was that of *doulos* – which most connects to 'slave' or 'domestic slave'. This was a particularly low form of slavery, analogous with the kind of work undertaken by not only the economically most vulnerable but also frequently those with physical or mental limitations too. In our situation parallels with the dispossessed, asylum seeker, the mentally or physically impaired, would hardly be an exaggeration.

The perception of the *servant church* is rarely one that identifies with such groups and persons. Servanthood tends to be associated somewhere in the psyche with the upper echelons of the below-stairs hierarchy of the Victorian and Edwardian social structures! It rarely connects with the experience of those without rights and citizenship, who know exploitation that is financial, social and often sexual.

Creative leadership here requires something of a renewed understanding of the church as a 'counter-cultural' or 'alternative' community. Here we might see the church as St John perceived it, when he has Jesus observe of his followers – 'You are not of this world.' John's use of the term 'world' or *cosmos*, here, has frequently led Christians into 'another worldliness' view that has produced unhelpful forms of piety and exclusivism.

The term *cosmos* might be likened to the word 'system', meaning the prevailing dominant political, social, religious and economic structures. Jesus might have said, 'You are not of this *system*,' meaning that the values, ethics and doctrines of his followers require a different structure to model the alternative world order from that which prevails.

Where people gather as much out of their sense of exclusion from the dominant reality, the creative leader will want to encourage processes of empowerment and a generation of self-worth, often amongst folk for whom such aspirations are unthinkable.

Community

In the model of the church as community, the term 'community' is open to a wide range of interpretations, and used ecclesially is similarly open. In the Catholic tradition it might be the form of church life built upon and around a religious order or community. Within my tradition, which is Anglican, I tend to identify the community church with the *parish* church – that is, a faith community that serves a geographical locality. Such churches frequently reflect a dominant tradition – catholic, evangelical, liberal or central. Many so-called 'house churches' define themselves as 'community' churches. Dulles's definition of some thirty or more years ago has become somewhat elastic.

Most community churches are geographical rather than eclectic. This means that leadership requires wise discernment as to the dominant reality within the church. Here 'making room' for those of other persuasions or insights is particularly important, if the church is not to atrophy. Many parish churches leave plenty of space for people who so desire to stay on the edge, unnoticed, and often uncared for. Neglecting such people is often all too easy in a church where a few can take control and to seek to mould it within their preferred image.

Community is part of the language of relationship; it exposes the truth that the self cannot exist in isolation. In its most utopian form, we might say that community provides the environment where mutuality thrives, and where divisions are heated, and reconciliation is made through conversation. *Conversus*, from which our word 'conversation' comes, is that act of turning towards the other, or a new direction in dialogue. As Cowan and Lee observe: 'The noun from *converses* is *conversio*, or in English "conversion". Conversion always involves an interaction with another or with others. It is not a simple, individual "turn around". It is a turn we take in the company of others.'[5]

A creative leader seeking to 'build a straight path' will not only reflect on the meaning of *communitas* and *conversio*, but also call the church to reflect upon the nature of *parish*, which takes its origin from the Greek *paroikos* or *paroikia*. The use of this term in 1 Peter[6] is interpreted as 'foreigners without citizenship', or 'strangers who dwell alongside'. Such people together (*paroikia*) lived their lives frequently without the protection of the law and civil rights. It was from such people that the isolated cells of Christians living in the growing urban sprawls of the empire formed 'church'.

In the social structure of the empire, the Greek word for church, *ecclesia*, also had a sociological definition in relation to political organisation. The *ecclesia* was the gathering of free citizens who were tasked with seeking the welfare of the neighbourhood.

By making use of these definitions for our times we might say that the *parish church* is the 'gathering of called-out people who seek in the name of Jesus Christ the welfare of the strangers who dwell along-side'. Creative leadership will seek to move the geographically based parish community into one that identifies with those who are on the edge, strangers, refugees, asylum seekers and others marginalised by power.

Sacrament

The model of the church as sacrament does not necessarily represent any particular tradition, catholic or evangelical, but rather will seek to make the gospel visible through its behaviour, rather than its language. The early Christian community in Acts is essentially sacramental, marked by its loving behaviour, the sharing of goods and hospitality, enabling others to join without embarrassment or fear.[7]

At different points in Christian history groups have been known for the attractiveness of their behaviour. The Scottish Covenanters, whose communities, along with those of the Anabaptists, were out-lawed, reflected a grass-roots community movement which became more widely reflected in Congregationalism and early Methodism, as well as among the Society of Friends and Moravians.

The impact of the base ecclesial communities of Latin America and elsewhere in the 1970s and 1980s was not dissimilar to those of the movements that grew in post-Reformation Europe, but in the contemporary Latin-American scene became prominent in the Roman Catholic tradition.

Such movements can be said to model new, or different, ways of doing theology, what one writer has called 'a hermeneutic of the people',[8] or theology from the grass roots. In such churches leadership tends to be more consensual, and the theological focus is on meeting so-called 'felt need'. In such situations creative leadership that beckons people into that which goes beyond lived experience into the realms of doctrine, liturgy and traditional spirituality, though difficult, is necessary in order to prevent the twin dangers of atrophy and self-satisfaction.

Reaching beyond the local, the immediate, is always the challenge that faces the Christian community and its leaders. As in other forms of church the dangers of self-containment and satisfaction are always present.

Institution

With the model of the church as institution, many new forms and patterns of church life are emerging from movements as varied as religious orders, communities such as Iona and Taizé, as well as house churches, and other ecclesial structures emerging from charismatic ministries. All such movements eventually have to face the reality of their continuation, and they move from being charismatic entities to institutions in some form.

Canon 6 of the Council of Chalcedon required priests and bishops to be ordained to a specific community, otherwise ordination was invalid. Much of the debate about creative models of leadership in the contemporary church concerns authority, and many who are experimenting with different patterns of church life find difficulty in accepting the inevitable constraints of church rules on these matters. Where the church is 'new', that is, not tied into a denominational structure, the problem paradoxically is no less, for inevitably questions about who is authorised to preach, minister the sacraments and other charisms arise.

A helpful contribution to this discussion has been made by Lee and Cowan,[9] who see the larger institutional structures and interests as representing *societas* with the organised counter-, or more marginal, movements in the church as representing *communitas*.

> When a large new idea appears, most people say, 'It's dangerous, it's untried, it's not orthodox, it should be left alone.' But if it hangs around and does well in the second stage of its career, people are less un-nerved and say, 'It's nothing unusual, what's the big deal, take it or leave it'; but they are not fighting it tooth and nail. In its third career, when a new idea has in fact been found both interesting and fruitful, those who found it dangerous in the first place now claim to have discovered it.

Postmodern

I offer the model of the postmodern church with some sense of trepidation, in that it might well be argued that each of the models highlighted so far *are* postmodern representations of the church. I am interpreting 'postmodern' as that which is defined to some degree by relativism, namely, the absence of absolutes, the right of the individual not only to choose, but also to express a view that 'my story and outlook is as good and valid as yours'.

In each of the models so far defined, some form of framework exists. Though neither dogma nor ecclesiology have been over-defined in the presentation of these models, it is clear that they are not truly postmodern, in that boundaries are defined and credal faith is required at some level at least.

I simply want to draw attention to the phenomena that while Christians do not buy into the relativism that defines postmodernism in a philosophical sense, whole areas of their lives are influenced by it, including patterns of church membership and attendance.

People increasingly 'pick and mix' their preferences for church life, seeking that which meets their individual needs at given moments of time. For many contemporary Christians 'I' has become the most important agenda there is. This is not so different from the *societas* around. Creative leadership in such a church requires the courage to confront such individualism and relativism, with the perspective that, as Elizabeth Templeton has put it, 'The sanctified person is one who is no longer separated from anyone or anything.'[10]

What the church in a postmodern world faces is a certain degree of what might be called 'unmanageability'. People's allegiances to local-ity, tradition and attendance are less important. New forms of church are emerging with little or no economic, social or doctrinal loyalty or links to their founding traditions. Such bodies are more difficult to bring under former patterns of discipline.

Michael Hill, Bishop of Bristol, sees these emerging churches as the ecclesiastical equivalent of teenage adolescents, believing that where discipline is required the 'mother' or 'parent' church should be prepared to say, 'If you want to stay "home" you need to accept there are ground rules. If you cannot keep the rules, leave, but do not expect support from the parents.'

What Hill and to some degree Elizabeth Templeton point to in a postmodern church is that while rightly there is a wider exercise of freedom, there are, however, limits to freedom. God after all is limited to 'being God', and Jesus' freedom to do and be what he was and is comes precisely because he is in the image of God. Freedom in this sense brings greater responsibility. Paradoxically the more a person or community realises they are loved, the less freedom there is.

Creative leadership, the 'building of the straight path' in our post-modern world and church, requires both a willingness to set aside the more prescriptive patterns of leadership, to encourage responsibility and interdependence, while at the same time accepting that, where unity and harmony cannot be achieved, some measure of separation may be the only 'adult', hopefully temporary, option.

All separation or dissonance should be seen as less than ideal, for the church is called to both image and enact a future in which God calls his people to dismantle everything that divides or separates, for the sake of the world which is God's ultimate salvific project.

The 'new thing' and acting 'as if'

Creative leadership therefore requires the capacity to foresee potential for the 'new thing' that is being done. It requires discernment borne out of the wisdom of years, the courage to take risk, and the imagination to envision new possibilities, and to act 'as if'. By acting 'as if' I mean being able to practise something for the time being 'as if' this was the norm, the pattern of church life. Such provisionality of course must be prepared to take the risk of being challenged. In churches with 'canons', it may very well be these that are used to provide the challenge, or corrective. In essence this is the nature of church discipline; it has to be tested against particular realities.

Creative leadership requires the discernment to know when it is right to insist on the strict letter of the law, and when it is not. The aim of canon law should be the pastoral good of people. This is always the deepest purpose of law. Aquinas spoke of *epikeia*, being a virtue and not a way of evading the law, but of ensuring that the deepest purpose of the law is kept. 'What some have called "the gap virtue" is particularly important for priests and those in pastoral ministries,' observes Megan McKenna,[11] and it becomes increasingly important the greater the gap grows between the official regulations of the church and the demands of pastoral practice. *Salus arlimarum supremo lex* ('the good of the individual is the essential component of the common good'). It is the common good itself that calls for the virtue of *epikeia*.

Mapping and building the 'straight path' for the contemporary church does not mean there is an ideal model, nor that there are not considerable obstacles. The analysis of Dulles's models of church and the subsequent commentary offers not an 'ideal', but components of a vibrant, organic, growing entity. Dulles perceived his models of *herald*, *servant*, *community*, *sacrament* and *institution* not as rigid unintegrated structures, but rather as dominant forms. In each, elements of the other were represented.

My purpose in reflecting on these models 'as if' they were separate entities is to give greater emphasis to the potential for understanding radical creative leadership.

The creative leader as 'refounder' of the church

To some extent the task of contemporary leadership within the church is to be described as 'refounding'. Being a voice for our times, as well as a sign of hope and a focus for discipleship for a new unchurched generation, some 'refounding' is required. This 'refounding' is to some discovery 'rediscovery', bringing out from the gospel's store-house 'treasures both old and new'.

From such treasures Gerald Arbuckle[12] offers the following qualities for the task of 'refounding':

- a prophetic concern for liberation and justice
- an incarnational lifestyle
- a church as community seeking the welfare of those it dwells along-side
- a faith of powerlessness set against the unfaith of power
- discernment and prayer
- an ecumenism of purpose and practice.

To lead such a church Arbuckle offers qualities for what he describes as 'a refounding person'. These he sees as people who:

- have the gifts of the Lord to grasp the heart or vision of the gospel message
- can imaginatively and creatively relate it especially to the dramatic new needs of today's world
- can draw others, through conversion and commitment to the vision, into a believing, worshipping and evangelising community.

Beginning with those whom he calls the 'Covenant re-founding prophets', Arbuckle sees that the qualities that brought Israel out of chaos into hope were the capacity to produce *memories of hope*, offer *creative imagination*, be *community oriented*, have *a sense of humour*, being *people of courage, patience* and *prayer*, and being *skilled in grieving and empathy*.

The leadership of Jesus Christ exemplifies these gifts and adds to them the quality of *apostolic adaptability*. This is the ability to address the real and felt needs of people in every situation and circumstance. By inviting into the liberty of the gospel and the vocation of disciple-ship persons within their context and circumstance, Jesus formed a community of diverse yet complementary gifts. Diversity, of course, exposes conflict and difference. Jesus addressed these through the gospel imperatives of forgiveness, love and reconciliation, seeing these radical qualities as foundation stones for living within the purpose of God.

Qualities for 'refounding'

For the contemporary church, creative leadership requires both persons and qualities for its 'refounding'. Arbuckle sees the qualities of *empathy, courage, humour, grieving, prayer, listening* and *apostolic adaptability* as essential tools for 'refounding'.

Empathy

In a world in which the clamour of voices leads to little real hearing, *empathy* becomes a prerequisite of leadership. *Empathy* is the ability not just to listen to people's words, 'but also their pauses, their hesitations, the nuances of speech of action'. More than just listening, empathy truly appreciates and understands all that makes a people 'what' and 'how' they are in their situation, and learns to stand with them.

This quality of *solidarity* seems to me the most apt here. What people have to 'say' depends so much on where and how they live, and the external pressures and forces which govern those lives. Much contemporary evangelism and mission ignores the grace and work of God's Spirit at work in the world. Many whom the church would seek to capture for Christ are already the subject of grace, their lives, albeit often unconsciously, already infused with the activity of God. The quality of listening is paramount lest, in the enthusiasm to 'bring Christ', we may miss how the grace of the divine has already revealed Christ.

Courage

Courage in leadership is perhaps too obvious a quality to require comment. Nevertheless, besides the courage of risk-taking, of innovation and being decisive, there is the courage to offer hope, occasionally certainty, as well as the ability to allow for, and encourage questioning. Two major challenges face leaders within the institutional church: first, a preoccupation with institutional preservation; second, how to articulate and incarnate life centred on Jesus Christ. In an age of un-faith, and a distrust of institutions, discerning how to facilitate the enquiring and questioning, leading them into whatever of faith they may accept, and beckoning them towards worship and transformational living, requires courageous leadership indeed.

Humour

In his *Screwtape Letters*, C. S. Lewis observes that 'true humour is a sense of proportion and an ability to see oneself from the outside'.[13] There is a lack of humour in the contemporary church in its self-appraisal, and it may not be unreasonable to conclude that this lack in part is due to a pomposity and self-importance that paradoxically rises with the church's declining influence.

Grieving

In part I see this lack of *humour* as being accompanied by a genuine lack of ability to grieve. In a world in which 'I' has become the most important project there is, the paradoxical relationship of grief to the Christian, as well as to the materialist, has become the reality most avoided. In his *Parables of Peanuts*, Robert Short observes,

> 'Good grief' may seem a contradiction in terms. But actually there are two types of grief – good and not-so-good grief; 'For godly grief produces a repentance that leads to salvation and brings no regret, but worldly grief produces death'.[14]

Understanding and addressing the contemporary reality of our world, dominated as it is by violence, fear, hunger, disease and pestilence, is not the stuff of everyday Christian living. The retreat into isolationism, individualism and institutional preoccupation prevents the church from understanding the mysterious power of grief to empower. At the heart of the Christian faith is the 'tree'; the cross 'which is first met as . . . archenemy and final stumbling block, has the amazing ability to become [the] central support and refuge – especially in times of great trouble.'[15]

Creative leadership will not ignore the 'tree' on the path that it seeks to build straight.

Prayer

In an age where method is all, the place of contemplation, reflection and a willingness to search for guidance is frequently lacking even among church leaders. There is something of a renaissance in spiritual-ity among both orthodox and unorthodox believers and searchers. But there is a reticence, bordering on the ambivalent, among many church leaders to recognise the absolute necessity of prayer, and encounter with God, in leadership. Moses, in his reluctance to follow

God's calling to lead, eventually meets the divine in the flames of a desert fire. The encounter leads him to remove his sandals, to touch the earth, to reconnect with reality, and discern God's concern for humanity enslaved and disempowered.

The truly creative leader will not fear to 'go on retreat', to make time to pray, apparently to disengage with reality. For it is in the very act of disengagement that engagement becomes possible. It was from the wilderness, and the conflict with the powers that sought to persuade Jesus to be relevant, spectacular and powerful, that the Christ appeared brave enough to take on the arbiters of the status quo, and to announce liberation and perpetual jubilee.[16]

Creative leadership recognises its own limitations, lack of vision and absolute dependence upon God. There is a paradox here, because the leader is widely perceived as the repository of both vision and ability. The leader who really seeks the 'building of the straight path' knows that solitude and the entering into their own piece of desert, provides the only hope of 'making a way in the wilderness' of life.

Apostolic adaptability

It is the *apostolic adaptability* of Jesus that today's creative leader needs to embrace if he or she is to 'build the path straight'. By seeking to imitate Christ, within the infinite possibilities that present themselves for transformation, of relationships, of churches, of society and the wider world, the leader both relates the gospel to the prevailing cultures and helps the process of refounding the church.

Notes

1. Matthew 7.14.
2. Luke 4.18–19.
3. Avery Dulles, *Models of the Church*, New York, Image Books, 1978, pp. 39–50.
4. Michael A. Cowan and Bernard J. Lee, *Conversation, Risk and Conversion: The Inner and Public Life of Small Christian Communities*, New York, Orbis, 1997, p. 53.
5. Cowan and Lee, *Conversation*, p. 3.
6. 1 Peter 1.1, 1.17.
7. Acts 2.42–7.
8. A. William Cook Jr, *Base Ecclesial Communities: A Study of and Re-evangelization and Growth in the Brazilian Catholic Church*, Occasional Bulletin of Missionary Research, Vol. 4 No. 3, July 1980, pp. 113–19.

9. Cowan and Lee, *Conversation*, pp. 56–9.
10. Elizabeth Templeton in a lecture to the House of Bishops, Liverpool, 3 June 2003.
11. Megan McKenna, *Rites of Justice*, New York, Orbis, 1997, p. xi.
12. Gerald A. Arbuckle, *Earthing the Gospel: An Inculturation Handbook for Pastoral Workers*, London, Geoffrey Chapman, 1990. I have expanded these from Arbuckle, who lists *Prophetic concern*, *Incarnational*, *Ecclesial*, *Powerlessness*, *Discernment/Prayer*, *Ecumenical*.
13. C. S. Lewis, *The Screwtape Letters*, London, Fontana, 1970, p. ix.
14. 2 Corinthians 7.10 – the quote is included in Robert Short, *The Gospel according to Peanuts*, Fontana, 1966, p. 82.
15. Short, *Gospel according to Peanuts*, p. 98.
16. Luke 4.18–19.

15 Has God Stopped?
No creative leadership in the Church as long as we have no up-to-date understanding of God's creativity

DAVID JENKINS

My title suggested itself to me when I was asked by the editors-designate of this symposium on Creative Leadership in the Churches to contribute a potential final chapter to this collection. The pressing question which seemed to me to demand investigation was the following: Is it the calling of faithful Christian communities and churches to protect and preserve unchanged understandings of God's revelation *in the past* or to perceive and promote God's promises and calling *for the future*?

The traditionalists, conservatives, fundamentalists and authoritarian sectarians among us seem to believe that we can only be obedient to God if we look backwards and preserve traditions of interpretation, belief, action and discipline fixed from and by the past. But, unless we reject modern science, we all live in what has turned out to be a *process* world and universe.

It is possible that this world, and ourselves in it, have evolved out of nothing much on the way to becoming nothing at all, in which case that is that, but it is also possible that there is sense and hope and promise in this process. It is just possible that we self-conscious personal beings are correctly inspired to think of ourselves as 'in the image of God' – with the corresponding promise, responsibilities and risks of working with this living God for his future.

It seems to me vital that all continuing and realistically faithful believers in this living God must engage with now. Hence my rhetorical question: has God stopped? Can it be that all the important guidance and revelation we may receive from the living God is already stored up and only available through our cherished 'Scriptures', our hallowed 'Tradition' and our historical 'formularies'?

We Christians believe that God was creative and active in and through the people who lived in their world in 'Old Testament' and 'New Testament' times. We seem to have concluded that God's engagement with the world gave out once he had invested himself as the Holy Spirit in the Christian Church and churches and their fragmenting, divisive and perpetually quarrelling successors. Do we really believe that God has stopped and opted out of the world in which we live now? Can the successor Christian churches have nothing to learn from God's activities in our world today?

While I was setting out to write this enquiry, events in the Church of England and its General Synod overtook me in a particularly devastating way. A virulent outbreak of Midsummer Madness over homosexuality, the legitimate and necessary interpretation of particular biblical texts, and matters of church discipline and membership, not only rendered me speechless but also brought me to a near-devastating sense of desolation.

How is it that proponents and opponents in the Church of England can so allow themselves (ourselves?!) to appear as mere neurotic quarrellers who are prepared to threaten to un-church one another over difficulties and delicacies in a certain area of human sexuality? The sight seemed to render the question 'Has God stopped?' irrelevant – a simple, unrealistic evasion. If this is Christianity then it is not a question of God stopping and starting. He never existed.

All the three main theistic religions, which claim to follow a revelation enshrined in Sacred Scriptures (the Torah, the two Testament Bible or the Qur'an), have all repeatedly discredited themselves. The accumulated evidence over the years is devastating – just how devastating was symbolised acutely in the 'Terrorist' attacks on New York and Washington in September 2001. We live in a world where the Qur'an is held to justify violent and deadly attacks as part of a 'Jihad' on the 'Christian' West for its neglect, oppression and exploitation of the Muslim nations. The focusing provocation for these outbursts has been the coming-into-being and manner of existence of the territorial state of Israel. Followers of the Jewish faith, drawing literal equivalence between events depicted in their holy texts that took place two (or three) thousand years ago, and detailed events going on now in what is assumed to be literally the same ground in pursuit of the same literal intentions of the believed-in real God, also commit atrocities and violence they believe to be justified by Scripture.

Sensitive and careful discussion among devout but seeking representatives of the three 'Scriptural' faiths of Judaism, Christianity and Islam is deeply to be desired and needs to be undertaken urgently, and probably fairly privately at the moment. But here I am solely concerned with the current approaches of vociferous Christians in the Church of England to our Christian Scriptures, that is, the Bible.

The immediate issue which I am striving to write about as realistically and hopefully as I can is the use and abuse of scriptural texts among members of the Church of England. What particularly troubles me is the manner in which the debate is carried on with such complete indifference to the widespread case for atheism. If I had not personally believed in the God of the Bible and Jesus in a self-conscious way for nearly seventy years, I do not believe I should be in the least encouraged to believe in him by the current, turned-inward preoccupations of the churches.

As far as I can see, the churches, not least the Church of England, are far more preoccupied with themselves (ourselves) than with God and the world which we believe to be his.

As I drafted this paragraph, Radio 4's *Today* programme was reporting that the General Synod, then assembling at York, was likely to be dominated by issues of unity. I could not help wondering how far our Anglican concerns about our unity promoted the whole Church's call to serve God in the world and for the world? Surely we cannot have deceived ourselves into thinking that the whole purpose of God is to end up with the ghastly and eternal boredom of 'a Church Triumphant' with no other company or activity in eternity?

My enquiry into 'creative leadership' brings me to face the way in which the main religions of theistic revelation discredit themselves. In the focusing light of the events of 11 September 2001 and the reactions thereto, the devastating issue, for us who continue to claim to be actively faithful Christians, seems to me to be the fact that one of the main reasons for the Jews needing a *state* of their own with territorial boundaries and governmental sovereignty is the anti-Semitism of Christian church and communities through much of Christian history.

I am sure that the vast majority of practising Christians did not will the Holocaust but it remains the fact that the New Testament records the betrayer of Jesus as Judas, a name which is all too easily read as 'the Jew' because (in the Fourth Gospel in particular) the Jews of Jerusalem are portrayed as persistently demanding the crucifixion of Jesus. Hence the stigma attached to the Jews as a people and a faith throughout 'Christendom'.

Our post-11 September 2001 situation reveals the discrediting of those religions that claim 'Revelation'.[1] The case is strong for atheism being the intelligent, informed and morally serious way forward for human beings. But the proponents in the June/July 2003 arguments in the Church of England seemed utterly oblivious to this challenging possibility. Dogmatic assertions are bandied about by apparently earnest believers in God as he is in Jesus through the Holy Spirit, without the least sign of awareness that the effect on the world at large is to confirm the already well-established and growing sense that atheism, or at least very reserved agnosticism, is the only truthful and hopeful way forward in our modern, frightening and yet immensely creative world. In a reality where religious faiths are literally a bloody menace, religious controversies are simply too self-indulgent for words.

It seems as if the time has come for all men and women of perception and goodwill to renew the slogan of Voltaire who, exasperated by the horrid treatment of certain troublesome 'heretics' in the middle of the eighteenth century at the hands of the Catholic Church, wrote, 'écrasez l'infame!'; that is: scrub out this infamous nonsense!

If we Christians truly aspire to an effective preaching of the gospel of faith, hope and charity in our twenty-first century we must face up to the fact that no reasonable person could possibly take people who are given to such disputatious and narrowly self-centred arguments as guides to the possible glory of man, let alone to the glorious reality and compassion of God.

The case for utter atheism and total nihilism seems to me to be so strong in the face of actual human behaviour, and the particular, petty and self-centred quarrels of 'the religious', that it haunts me and tempts me to the very verge of despair. Moreover, I have nothing but a *personal* reason for refusing to accept it. But it is a very persuasive personal reason and conviction which I have found I shared with many people in many lands, walks of life and circumstances, and which I find to be particularly and powerfully reflected in the narratives, anguishes and persistent, open-ended experiences of discovery and being found reflected in what I and my like have come to call the Bible.

I have tried to give some sketchy account of my personal pilgrimage in my recently published quasi-autobiography, *The Calling of a Cuckoo*. My summary of the 'seven-fold cord' which binds me to this faith and this pilgrimage of intermittent hope and often near-despair, is described in chapter 14. It cannot be further summarised here. I can only report that what pushes me near to despair in our current controversies in and around the Church of England is the narrow-minded near-bigotry (besmirching the title of 'evangelical' it seems to me) which abuses the Bible in claiming that, first, it is 'the Word of God' and that, secondly, particular selected texts are themselves, in verbal identity and enforced particular meanings, as good as and as absolute as the very words of God and, in consequence, the denial of the selected interpretation of that selected text is to deny, disobey and disgrace God.

This is a deadly reduction. The sacred Scriptures are writings recording the wrestlings, hopes and inspirations of people who have believed themselves to be in touch with God in their own time and age. These reflections and experiences are offered up to those who come after so that they might likewise be helped and inspired by the Spirit of the living and lively God in their subsequent times and age. Demeaning sacred Scriptures by turning particular words from particular verses into particular texts which become, ipso facto, divine mantras and infallible utterances with mysterious and definitive meanings, known only to the priestly or Protestant few, is an utter travesty which can lead only to irrelevant religious incantations and shibboleths, sources of allegedly enforceable religious nonsense.

The Bible gives us glimpses of insight. Knowing ourselves to be touched by God's Spirit we are called to hope that further revelation concerning the realities and possibilities of the world in which we live today are available to us. For it is this world as it is today in which we are called to continue our faithful pilgrimage. We may therefore continue to dare, hope and believe that it is God's world, open to his purposes and relatable to his promises. However, it is absolutely and literally vital that we should realise as clearly as the apostle Paul did that our knowledge is limited.

In the very midst of his incomparable hymn to God as love and charity in his First Letter to the Corinthians, Paul writes:

> We know in part and we prophesy in part. But when that which is perfect is come, then that which is in part shall be done away . . . For now we see through a glass darkly[2] but then face to face: now I know in part; but then shall I know even as I am known. (1 Corinthians 13.9–12)

The essence of true and realistic faith is knowing that God is in touch with us, however often and however much we remain, properly and humbly, unsure whether we are in touch with God. Living faith in the living God reflected and powerful in and through the Bible is nearer to agnosticism than to certainty. People who are sure that they know very much who God is and therefore have absolute assurance about what he essentially and definitely requires are inevitably a destructive, divisive and off-putting menace. And more so than ever now that we know that we live in a world of *process* from beginning to end. People who claim that the Bible, as such, is 'the Word of God' have got to realise that revelation is not a print-out from the divine computer.

It is all to do with a process pursued and sustained by the divine compassion and presence.

It is in the light of considerations such as these that I turn to the Bible for guidance and enlightenment. If we continue to have faith in the reality and love of the God of all, who is the God of Jesus, and of the Spirit of the Future, how can we face the humiliating impasse we have been forced into by the clamour for certainty in faith? A particular bone of contention at the time of writing is, of course, the dogmatic and dismissive assertion that to give any consideration to a possible legitimacy for a range of homosexual practices is 'to deny the Word of God'.

The maintaining of this position is not faithful but faithless, for it is simply and clearly denied by, first, the facts we now know about the Bible and, secondly, by the facts we now know about the world.

First, two hundred years or more of careful, critical and often deeply devout study of the writings and composition of the Bible have made it absolutely clear that it is an amazing collection of writings of a vast variety of thoughts, assembled, passed down, edited and added to, over many years. There are many different layers, strands and strata in it dating from very different times and often added to or amended as time goes on. It is simply not reasonable or realistic to fix on this or that short text, say from Leviticus in the Old Testament or from Paul in the New Testament, and to say dogmatically and decisively that this selection of texts is God's final and last word on the subject. Why choose texts on homosexuality to beat people over the head? Why not choose to reassert the verses in Deuteronomy, for example, where God is said to command Moses to massacre the inhabitants of the areas of Canaan that he has earmarked for the Israelites?[3]

Secondly – and most importantly for faithful realism and modern relevance – we now know that we have *evolved* as self-conscious personal beings over many thousands of years at least. This reality makes confident and dogmatic statements such as, for instance, that God laid it down in Scripture that the marital relationship between a man and a woman was *from creation* ordained as the one and only possible form of sexual human relationships, untenable. In light of our modern discoveries about the world and ourselves, such dogmatic assertions about 'the Word of God' become mere excuses for a religious bullying which surely arises more out of fear and uncertainty than from faith.

Further, taking the dogmatic short-cut by seeking to close arguments about sexuality, as in many other fields of human life, morality and society, with 'authoritative' biblical quotations, renders it almost impossible for the Christian church to play an effective part in this absolutely vital area of human sexuality at a time of rapid change and uncertainty. The mere citations of selected texts effectively seals off religious authorities from entering the arena of destructive sexual promiscuity and irresponsible sexual activity. But the churches at large seem incapable of engaging with these issues. We insist on retaining various shibboleths from the past rather than committing ourselves to negotiating new, decent, responsible and hopeful sexual arrangements and protocols for the future. Insisting on pseudo-'Word of God' instructions is, surely, evasion – almost a displacement activity rather than a creative, honest and realistic engagement with reality, informed and directed by faith.

But the most serious and devastating error is to ignore the basic fact that we are all part of a process of processes through which we have developed an immense and increasing knowledge and have become either partial *creators* of our world – or, possibly, *co-creators*, in which latter responsibility we might surely derive illumination and support from a modern reading of the Bible.

Consider. The first chapter of the biblical collection of documents is Genesis 1. It states the unambiguous claim that 'God saw everything that he had made and, behold, it was very good' (Genesis 1.31). The last chapter of the Christian Bible presents a vision of the heavenly Jerusalem, picturing 'a pure river of water of life' flowing from 'the throne of God and of the Lamb' and on either side of the river the tree of life; 'and the leaves of the tree were for the healing of the nations' (Revelation 22.1 and 2). In other words both the myth at the beginning of the Bible and the vision at the end state the claim (the revelation?) that the God whose dealings with men and women constitute the whole thrust and matter of the Bible is the God of all from beginning to end and that the End of this God is the redeemed and redeeming good of all.

This theme of universalism – that is, that the God of the Bible is the good of all for the future of all – is picked up again and again throughout the Old Testament and powerfully developed in the New Testament. The Resurrection appearances of Jesus at the end of the Gospels and at the beginning of the Acts of the Apostles all end with a command to preach God's good news in and through Jesus to 'all the nations' or 'to the ends of the earth'; and this command is embodied in the Pentecost experiences at the beginning of Acts.

The idea is expanded in the writings of the apostle Paul (e.g. 'There is neither Jew nor Greek, there is neither bond nor free, there is neither male nor female, for ye are all one in Christ Jesus' (Galatians 3.28). It is further to be noted that Paul relates this universal thrust to *Abraham* –

that is the first prophetic figure and 'father of many nations' in the Old Testament.

Historically this potential and godly universalism became stuck in substitute 'Holy Cities' in various Western and Mediterranean parts of the world – for example, Rome, or Constantinople, or Canterbury or Geneva – and the notion became trapped by Christendom and culture. But could we not rediscover the initial and explosive universalism as the renewed offer of God to a globalised and deeply divided world? Might we not humbly ask our potential fellow believers in Judaism and Islam whether we do well for the sake of God and our fellow human beings across the world to over-focus on our particular 'holy cities', whether they be Rome and Canterbury, or Jerusalem or Mecca? In the Epistle to the Hebrews in our Christian New Testament the writer speaks powerfully of the universal pilgrimage of faith and points out, for example, that 'here we have no continuing city, but we seek one to come' (Hebrews 13.14).[4]

Faith in this living God demands pilgrimage. As God is on the move from the beginning of his creation in collaboration with human beings as they have emerged until the very end, we are simply on our way. Revelation, therefore, as I have already written, is a process and not a printout.

God has *not* stopped. He is the living God and he goes on with his revelation, his encounters, his calling, his creativity and his promises. If the Church and the churches are to come to terms with and engage both creatively and constructively in our twenty-first century world, it is necessary for faithful Christians to understand that the living God of the Bible was not effectively switched off in the developing modern world from, say, the seventeenth century onwards.

In 1648, through the Peace of Westphalia, the warring European 'Christians' – divided between Catholics and Protestants – came to an accommodation with one another. Neither side could win and the situation had become intolerable. 'Christendom' was effectively abolished. Protestant 'establishment' continued side by side with the papacy's ineffective universalistic claims. The time was clearly ripe for something more liberating and progressive than the destructive stalemate of opposing Christian camps demanding absolute authority. The accommodation enabled the amazing development of the eighteenth-century Enlightenment and the nineteenth-century advances in science. By 1800 or so the French mathematician Laplace was able to produce a 'theory of the universe' which, when he explained it to Napoleon, led the Emperor to ask, 'But God, monsieur? What do you do with God?' Laplace replied, 'Sire, we have found no need for that hypothesis.' His reply was vindicated by Charles

Darwin in his *Origin of Species* published in 1859. Evolution, it seemed, could explain everything and the human race was free to go on its way without any faith in the so-frequently discredited 'god'.

When some 'liberal' Anglicans got together in 1860 to publish a book entitled *Essays and Reviews*, a collection of pieces that sought to bring together understandings of Christian faith and the developments in science, they were met with a chorus of outraged conservative voices – voices and arguments exactly paralleled by the outraged 'evangelicals' and 'traditionalists' today. Nobody has learnt anything. The churches are still circling through periodic outbreaks of quasi-hysteria over coming to terms with what has been happening for three hundred years or more (i.e. since 1648 at least) about faith and revelation, science and process. I do not say 'science and *progress*' because the urgent human concern today is how science, society and human *progress* can be enabled to develop. This is clearer than ever right now when we live in a very uncertain, troublesome and potentially dangerous time – just as people did in the times of Abraham and the prophets. An essential and continuing element in human historical living is its uncertainties and hopes.

The pressing question of immediate relevance to the churches of today is whether there is this on-going God of the Bible. If there is no living God who is as he is in Jesus through the Spirit, who is involved now – as he ever was – in the history, stories and struggles of on-going human life, then Christians should surely shut up shop and cease their inter-sectarian troubles for they are evidently displacement activities. After all, religions have already caused enough trouble in history.

But if God has not stopped and is living, available and struggling now as he is portrayed as living in the troublesome, uncertain and disastrous times of the Bible and of Jesus, then there is hope indeed, and real and persevering possibilities of faith and love. Then creative and prophetic Christian leadership is called to develop pilgrimage in a universalistic direction; to promote a twenty-first century drive for universality among the faiths and the struggles of human beings for the sake of as decent a future as can be possibly found, on its way to eventual fulfilment in the future planned, pursued and suffered for by God.

My hope would be that these scrappy notes, offered as a postscript to this book on creative leadership, might be developed into a foreword for another book on – *What next for the servants and prophets of the God of the future?* I continue to believe that this God is as he is in Jesus through and in the Holy Spirit. It is clear to me that this can be worked out and suffered through only by engaging in and with the world as it is now with regard to a future as it might be in and through and under God in collaboration with the struggles, inventions and constructions of human beings. As for the Church and the churches, to struggle to preserve a past and unfinished revelation as definitive is most assuredly to betray the God and Father of our Lord Jesus Christ who is at work in his creative Spirit.

Items on the agenda for a forward-looking Foreword to the shape and shaping of our human pilgrimage together with the help of God might include the following at least.

1. *The New Saeculum*: Taking secularity seriously. The churches are still behaving as if we were living in what Augustine in the early fifth century designated as the sixth (i.e. last but one) 'Day' in God's 'seven days' of creation. Jesus Christ had originated the 'sixth day' and Christians had to live by Grace in it, waiting for the *seventh* day when Christ would return and all would be summed up and fulfilled. Nothing could be done about 'the secular', but to live as religiously and faithfully as possible within it. No further developments were to be expected or hoped for until the End. Faith was thus expressed in right belief and right practice and endurance.

   What the developments which have spilled out from the West since '1648' onwards show us is that the nature of things have to be understood very differently. We are not in a changeless world or universe but in an endlessly changing one. Hence we as human beings, emerging in the image of God, have creative contributions to make to the processes of the universe and our human history as we live on earth, developing our humaneness and moving towards God's future. Science is an immense gift, not a threat to faith in God. But just as human opportunities are immensely enlarged, so are the risks. Creativity means freedom, risk and loss as well as wonder, construction and love.

2. This reflection would have to be combined with a *New Ecumenism*. The world is indeed one and we, humanely, have to become one in pooling our spiritual resources, insights and energies to develop *positive* progress and to avoid disasters, destructions and distortions. How, therefore, should men and women of faith and of Faiths collaborate to concentrate on such things – and not on selfish, exclusive or limiting *religious* claims? Is it not possible to move towards working together to develop our humanity, pooling our resources and insights, including our spiritual ones, between men and women of many faiths and many humanist *'unbelievers'* who surely care greatly and take values seriously and also seek a worthwhile future?

3. As a footnote to these enquiries with particular reference to the Church of England, the following consideration occurs to me in the midst of our current disagreements. Should we not in and as the Church of England consider that the expansion of our godly mission and pilgrimage may require that we face up to our sectarian, financial and organisational difficulties?

Perhaps we should begin to plan realistically and hopefully for an organisational breakdown which may well include a schism over mutually contradictory ways of maintaining and pursuing faithfulness to the gospel of God in Jesus through the Spirit. Disestablishment would inevitably follow, but that would be entirely in the spirit of resuming the pilgrimage of the Epistle to the Hebrews and rediscovering that we have no 'abiding' city.

Under God, such a breakdown might well lead to a breakout from our present endless and time-consuming obsession with survival, setting us free to be pioneers and pilgrims contributing to a living church of the future with a living gospel for that future. Does a living faith in the living God really demand that we, the faithful, spend most of our time and energies in the spirit of the Emperor Franz Joseph, who commented sadly as he struggled with the last days of the Hapsburg Empire that he had 'spent his life propping up a tottering edifice'? God is surely a source and inspiration for much more creative activities than that.

Notes

1. Alas, the situation is now no better with Hinduism in India, which has emerged as the vehicle for a violent and dangerous nationalism. But that is another story – although it is equally discrediting to 'religion'.
2. The Greek literally means 'in an enigma' – i.e. as you might say, 'riddle-wise'.
3. E.g. Deuteronomy 7.17–26 or 20.10–18.
4. The Greek is probably a pun which might be rendered 'we have no *abiding* city, we seek an *arriving* one'.

16 Points to ponder or take away

My framework is complete and my own ideas, not always in the correct dress, are on parade. Below I am going to offer you my comments and reflections, for what they are worth, on each of the chapters in this book. I am not going to try and summarise them, still less to pick common themes. Rather I shall pick up points that catch my eye or stimulate my creative thinking.

You may, of course, choose quite different points but that doesn't matter: the function of the book is to stir up your own creativity, which is fun. The fact that I do not comment on most of what the contributors say is not significant: it usually means that I agree completely and they have said it much better than I could have done.

Where possible I have drawn your attention to how you might implement the remarkably coherent philosophy that emerges from this book: the common mind and spirit that shines through 14 very different contributions.

A famous Welsh rugby captain told me last week that if a man puts on the red shirt and runs out in front of 75,000 people in the Millennium Stadium and *still* needs to be motivated he has come down the wrong road. You have the red shirt on and the game is out there to be played. You won't get any motivation from me below, but as I pick the ball up from these gifted players, watch out for a few passes!

Malcolm Grundy

Napoleon once said, perhaps cynically, that 'a leader is a dealer in hope'. Malcolm grounds both hope and creative church leadership in the Resurrection, the greatest sign of creative power of God at work on earth transforming all things – even a death – into new life.

The Resurrection event transforms our view of time, so often seen as empty, unreal and gone. Yet the moments we spend building the Kingdom of God are not time lost but have eternal significance. Malcolm quotes Paul Tillich: 'Through our timing God times the coming of His Kingdom; through our timing He elevates the time of vanity to the time of fulfilment' (p. 20).

The commitment is to face real-life situations and to discover how to put faith into practice. 'Creative Christian leadership will see divine possibilities in situations about which a faithless approach would despair' (p. 20).

Out of the 'wrestling to understand and apply God's actions in Jesus Christ' there can come experiences that 'allow glimpses of God's Kingdom to be located and nurtured in the experiences of everyday life'.

Malcolm's grounding of creative church leadership in the Resurrection rang several bells for me. I can think of one or two examples where a true leader fell to the ground and yet the work was carried on by other leaders whom he had helped to create and inspire – his example and his spirit lived on in them. The fact that these examples tend to be military ones need not deter us from taking them into account, for there is a real sense that the context of the Kingdom's coming on earth is a struggle or war between good and evil, one in which evil can and does win tactical victories but the Resurrection is a sign of the ultimate victory of good.

Let me give you one such example. Xenophon is celebrated as a student of leadership under Socrates, but at the age of 26, against his teacher's advice, he enlisted as a cavalry commander in an array of Greek mercenaries. Known to history as the Ten Thousand, they had been hired by a claimant to the Persian throne. The latter's forces, however, lost the crucial battle near Babylon. The Greeks, still more-or-less intact, found themselves surrounded by a vast array of hostile victors, who ordered them to choose between slavery or death.

In this crisis the senior of the Greek generals, a Spartan veteran called Clearchus, came forward with a bold plan. They would break out and march 800 miles through enemy-occupied territory to the Black Sea and freedom. They began the great fight-and-march. A few days into it the Persians invited the six Greek generals, including Clearchus, to a conference under a safe conduct and then assassinated them.

The Greeks elected another set of generals, among them Xenophon, who was to lead the rear, a key post as it would be under constant attack. He called a general assembly and reminded the soldiers that they were Greeks, free men, living in free states, born of free ancestors. Their enemies were slaves, ruled by despots. 'They think we are defeated because our officers and our good old general Clearchus are dead. But we will show them that they have turned us all into generals. *Instead of one Clearchus they have ten thousand Clearchuses against them.*'

Now the Greeks were drilled to fight in phalanxes, and they had to adapt creatively to fighting on the march and in mountainous terrain or die. The situation that confronted them could be met only by throwing away the rules and regulations that had been drilled into them. What they needed was to draw on all the intelligence and power of initiative every man of them possessed.

With leaders elected by virtue of their superior ability the Ten Thousand freely and willingly maintained the necessary discipline. But each soldier was expected to think for himself, to use his initiative and creativity *as if he was a leader*. Once, when Xenophon sent out a reconnaissance force to find a pass through the mountains, he told them, 'Everyone of you is the leader.'

The Persians had acted on the principle of the proverb that Jesus coined or quoted: *Smite the shepherd and the sheep will scatter.* But both the Persians and later the Jewish authorities encountered another mysterious creative principle at work to confound them: *Unless a seed falls to the ground and dies, it abides alone.* The right seed falling in the right ground at the right time creates ten, a hundred, a thousand more leaders inspired by the same spirit as that which animated Jesus and fired by the same vision.

We should perhaps think of the Church as a community of leaders. We have to transcend the old pastoral model of shepherd-and-sheep, which may carry the unconscious, allegorical assumption that the laity are the 'sheep' in the metaphor and indeed sheep-like in their lack of intelligence or creativity. A Church leader as much as Xenophon is, in the words of Euripides, 'a leader of leaders'.

Charles Handy

Charles classifies a church (or religious) organisation as belonging to the class of voluntary or not-for-profit organisations. These in turn fall into three categories: Mutual Support, Service Delivery and Campaigning. Each category makes different assumptions about the purpose of the organisation, etc.

'Church organisations have traditionally combined all three roles, giving them their own more religious titles such as fellowship, ministry and evangelism' (p. 24). But such a blending of types into one body presents a great dilemma to those who aspire to lead them, at whatever level.

What Charles offers in his ten guiding principles for leaders of mixed organisations is a summary of the practical wisdom that applies to any true leader. From his parable of the rowing eight comes the reminder that many people can contribute to leadership. 'You don't, for instance, have to be called a leader to have a leadership task' (p. 29).

The importance of clarity over purpose stands out. 'Be clear where you want to go, and how you will know when you get there . . . Too many church organisations aren't going anywhere . . . ' (p. 29). Behind his words lurks the image of the journey, the origin of our concept of leadership.

The need for positive change (the sixth principle) could hardly be better or more succinctly expressed. For things to stay the same things need to change, and the time to do it is before you have to. As I would put it, take change by the hand before it takes you by the throat. In my experience, churches lacking what Charles calls wise, counter-intuitive leaders are exceptionally disinclined to change before the bailiffs actually move in to remove the furniture.

From the perspective of creative church leadership Charles's ninth and tenth principles are essential. Good management of time – our most precious resource – is critical for any leader. 'It is not only time for recreation and renewal that is needed but also the opportunity to stand outside the organization, to walk in other worlds, and to see your place as others see it . . . Creativity needs empty spaces to sprout, and is not self-fertilising' (pp. 30–1).

The ability to go on learning is important. Creative leaders are those who 'possess what Keats called a negative capability, to function whilst in the midst of doubts, mysteries and uncertainties'. One possible test of creative leadership for me stands out from Charles's final thoughts about luck: it is the ability to see *opportunity where others see problems*.

Bill Allen

Bill starts off with the assumption that the *raison d'être* of theological colleges is not, as their name implies, just to teach theology to men and woman entering the ordained ministry, but to *equip them for effective leadership in the local church*. His research then explores what perceptions of the qualities and skills of 'good' leadership in the Christian ministry are held by people in congregations.

Bill then divides the 73 'key indicators' derived from this research into six categories: Spirituality, Personal Qualities, Leadership, Management, Communication Skills, and Interpersonal Skills. 'It provides a way', Bill writes, 'to ascertain the key qualities and skills required for ministry from the perspective of the churches and it anticipates the development of a curriculum which takes leadership expectations from the church much more seriously than has happened in the past' (p. 38). That is putting it mildly – it could be revolutionary.

The seven *distinguishing competencies* based on these six areas include *the ability to lead others*. Bill breaks each one down into lesser functions which he calls *functional competencies*. As leadership is the focus of this book, let me remind you what he says on that particular subject:

The ability to lead others

- applying vision, creativity and risk-taking in leadership, in order to achieve real and intended change
- discerning gifts in others and equipping people to use those gifts in mission and service
- leading by personal example and demonstrating professional competence in ministry and mission
- working with others effectively, building and motivating teams
- leading groups, teams and meetings, including church members' meetings, appropriately

That takes us on to Bill's use of a Venn diagram of the three overlapping circles to illustrate the three key elements in education and training for ministry: attaining *knowledge*, acquiring *skills* and developing *personal character and spirituality*. This accords with my own view that what matters in leadership is what you *are*, what you *know* and what you *do*.

I think he is right to see spirituality – the relationship with God – as the centre piece, with vocation as its hub: 'This is where the call to Christian leadership is located and rooted and it is this call which is at the centre of all the learning experiences and holds everything together' (p. 43). Confidence, competence and credibility are the hallmarks.

My hope is that Bill's contribution will spark off a major re-evaluation of training for the ministry. Four reflections:

- Bill's three-circle model applies to all Christian vocation, be it ministerial or lay. The content in the knowledge and skills circles varies, but not character.
- Do students leave with vision? Does the experience of training serve to ignite their creativity?
- If colleges are to be schools for inspiring leaders, where do we find the teachers who can teach leadership? Maybe they are outside the theological colleges.

- If the laity lack understanding of their common Christian calling to build the Kingdom of God on earth and the importance of discovering their individual vocations, what is this saying to us about so-called theological education? Has it become too academic in the pejorative sense?

Martyn Percy

'Anglicanism, *at its best* [my italics], is a community of civilised disagreement' (p. 49). Or so one could argue, Martyn suggests.

Martyn takes as his subject theological education. His thesis is 'the assumption that listening and learning from congregations (and I mean deeply here) is an essential prerequisite for any teaching and directing' (p. 49).

The hidden assumption – one of those barriers to creativity I mentioned – that Martyn is challenging is that 'the congregation is an essentially passive body to which the "professional" Christian leader is called to minister' (p. 49). He notes in passing, and gives two good illustrative case studies, the negative attitudes that the Church of England still shows to operational research into issues relating to the ordained ministry, even when it does not have to foot the bill. No 'research, evaluation and critical reflection', no transformation of the Church of England's ordained ministry.

From my own experience I agree with that assessment. Urgently needed, for example, is research into the selection, development and use of NSMs (Non-Stipendiary Ministers) and Lay Readers, how they can best work together in the teams of tomorrow, and the kind of leadership that the professional church leader will be required to give to such teams. No theological colleges have yet taken on board the fact that they are training leaders of a cluster of parishes which will be the size of a rural deanery. It is pointless to employ people as stipendiary ordained ministers who lack that potential: they would be better employed as self-funded local ministers. We need a lot of research to bridge the gap from where we are now to where we want to be in 20–30 years' time. These are my own thoughts, I hasten to add, and I return now to Martyn's argument.

I like the idea that practical theology is there to enable churches to 'practise what they preach', or, as I would put it, to live the vision and to work out its implications, corporately and individually, in the context of the world as they experience it – listening to what that world is saying to them.

As an example Martyn asks: 'what does Christian tradition have to

say to people who, for whatever reason, fail in Christian ministry?'
(pp. 54–5). (We all roughly know what he means by failure in this
context, so I won't delve into that.)

It is an extremely good question, because it is about the Kingdom of
God. I suggest *creative* church leadership might see the picture in the
following ways:

- It is not you but the Church that should bear the burden of this
  failure. The ministry was not your true *métier* but we encouraged,
  we accepted, we trained you and passed you as fit for service.
- This is not the end, though it may seem like it to you, but a new
  beginning. How can we help you to find your true vocation as a lay
  person? What financial or professional support can we give you to
  make the transition?
- Leaders build on the strengths of others, not their weaknesses. All
  that failure does is to tell you what you are not cut out to do. This
  person may be lost to the ministry of the Church but they have an
  immense potential contribution to make to the Kingdom of God
  and *their experience in the ministry will not be wasted*. What is offered
  to God is never wasted. Turn your failures into your greatest
  ambassadors.

The word *transformation* begins to surface in Martyn's paper –
'ultimate transformation'. I take that to be an abstract reference to the
Semitic concept of the Kingdom of God on earth, but I may be wrong.
Two thoughts occur to me.

An influential and widespread theory of leadership today is
labelled *transformational leadership* (in contrast to *transactional leadership*, which is in fact rather low-level management, not leadership at
all). The current version is that a leader should be so inspirational and
charismatic that he or she *transforms* their group or organisation into
exceptionally high performers. A cynic may say that it's getting more
work out of people while paying them less money – and getting a
great deal more money oneself! In fact the original version of this idea
implied that *both* leader and followers are transformed.

Secondly, last week I heard a Permanent Secretary in the Civil
Service – a good leader – assert his belief in *incremental transformation*,
a phrase that sounds almost like a paradox. But is it? Does not the
metaphor of *building* the Kingdom of God (as if it was a city) point to
gradual step-by-step creation through continued efforts? A builder
forms by ordering and uniting materials – some unlikely ones – by
gradual means into a composite whole. Incidentally this doesn't
imply a completely secular concept of progress. Christians do believe

in progress – indeed their hope is undying. Yet it can be lonely in doing so when rational despair is the order of the day. Christian hope may not be rational but it is realistic: 'Except the Lord build the house, they labour in vain who build it' (Psalm 127.1).

What Martyn has to say about the need for a 'transformative pedagogy' – a more creative approach – in theological education made me think hard. Pedagogy is actually a leadership word – in Greek it means literally to lead children.

Now although church leaders (like Jesus) find themselves on occasion teaching children, the core of their teaching role lies with adults. There a different set of principles and methods comes into play: indeed it is doubtful whether or not words like *teaching* or *learning* are much use. It is more a process of exploring and sharing together – like this book – but, honesty must add, it is actually an art or a skill on the part of the leader. If it shows, you are not doing it well enough, for, as Alexander Pope once said:

Men must be taught as if you taught them not
And things proposed as things forgot.

The essence, then, of *adult* education – not that it doesn't apply to children – is *dialogue*, two-way rather than a *monologue*. In a leader's work a monologue does have an occasional part to play – a military commander speaking to his troops before battle, a head teacher addressing the school, or a minister preaching a sermon. But these 'set pieces', valuable as they are if done at the right time and in the right place and in the right way, are not to be confused with mutual or creative learning, a core activity of leadership.

The neglect of this principle has cost the Church of England (and I suspect all other churches) dear. Despite a rediscovery of the theology of the laity in the late 1950s and some pioneering work towards much more effective adult educational methods based on *dialogue* in the context of shared local or parochial ministry, the Church of England let that golden opportunity walk away from it. The main reason, I am afraid, was lack of creative leadership at episcopal level.

The Parish Life Conference, as it was called, was developed by Canon Harold Wilson, then the Church of England's Adult Education Officer, from some innovative church group work in America based on the 'Growing Dynamics' movement there. Harold recruited and trained two or three of us to lead these events. They had a remarkable power to transform parishes from inward-looking to outward-looking communities. I led 10 or 12 of them, embracing about 20 parishes, and they were remarkably effective and enjoyable. But the clergy were either uninterested in lay involvement in ministry to the community or incapable of leading it, and bishops remained indifferent.

So we continued to produce clergymen who were incapable of leading a level-ground discussion with their laity about the problems and opportunities of ministry – that is, the service of the Kingdom of God on earth – in the context of their local wider community. Even worse, some of them acted as if they were threatened by the laity. Whoever heard of a shepherd being afraid of his sheep?

In the course of time this generation of clergy became a bench of bishops who were incapable of, say, inviting a dozen lay leaders of all persuasions or none in their cities or shires to join them for supper in order to discuss the nature and practice of good leadership and leadership for good within the community – a discussion which could be transformative for both parties and serviceable to the Kingdom.

'Can church leaders learn to be learners again?' Martyn asks us. 'And can its leaders learn to truly teach, rather than simply indoctrinate?' (p. 60).

What do you think?

Robin Gill and Derek Burke

Robin and Derek address the issue of church leadership in the context of both institutional decline – a compound of churchgoing decline and a worsening financial position. They noted, too, an apparent marked reluctance on the part of so-called church leaders to face or confront the situation; those who do seem to be at a loss when it comes to doing something about it. In *Strategic Church Leadership* (1996) they outlined the stresses and strains now afflicting the parochial system. 'Resentment is growing amongst congregations about the new financial burden arising from clergy stipends and pensions being increasingly placed upon them' (p. 63). Since 1996 both 'churchgoing statistics and finances within the Church of England are sadly more precarious' (p. 63).

OK, what should church leaders who take the evidence 'very seriously indeed' be doing about it? Robin and Derek suggest that they should show some strategic leadership, which they break down into four key areas.

Setting priorities

The setting of priorities, or the structured way of making choices, isn't happening, they say. Here they introduce their key assumption about the purpose of the Church (of England), focused upon worship as the vertical feature matched by a double-edged horizontal feature – outreach and social action. This led them to a 'mission statement' (or definition of purpose):

> The central aim of churches in modern Britain is the communal worship of God in Christ through the Spirit, teaching and moulding as many lives and structures as deeply as possible through this worship. (p. 67)

It is extremely helpful to have it formulated like that because – setting theology or theory aside – that is just what a pragmatic observer from Mars of the parochial system in the Church of England (and other churches) would conclude that the churches are for – what their purpose actually *is*. But do you think this really is the vision?

If we view the purpose of the Church of England as the maintenance of *communal worship* (vertical plus the horizontal riders), then despair at the decline in churchgoing and the ever greater burden of supporting professional leaders of communal worship becomes more intelligible. And as the tasks of reversing the decline in churchgoing and funding more full-time clergy are impossible ones, we sentence ourselves to decades of low morale, mutual accusations between clergy and laity, and the unfair blaming of bishops for 'lack of leadership'. When in trouble, always blame your leaders!

Yes, the maintenance of opportunities for communal worship is a legitimate aim for a Christian church, especially given our inheritance of glorious buildings. But should we 'bet the company' on it? Perhaps God had a point when he tried to persuade a pilgrim people to stick to their tents, as he was content with his – and not, repeat not, get into the business of building a stone temple with all the manifest and latent consequences of that act.

Determining objectives: opportunities and threats

Robin and Derek explain what they mean by a SWOT analysis, a useful tool for any strategic leader. It could be an extremely useful framework at congregational level to engage everyone – clergy and laity – in thinking, thinking hard, about the realities of their situation.

Unless you determine purpose clearly, however, you will have only a hazy idea of what constitutes a *Strength* or a *Weakness*, an *Opportunity* or a *Threat*. For the Kingdom of God is to us a paradox, an 'Alice in Wonderland' world where strengths prove to be weaknesses and weaknesses strengths, where threats are opportunities and some opportunities are threats.

Strategic planning

Is strategic planning appropriate to the churches? It helps to bear
in mind the distinction between strategic thinking and strategic
planning. Strategic thinking is about what is *important* and relatively
long-term. Poor strategic leaders don't do it because the *urgent* drives
out the *important*, and the short-term is easier to address than the long-
term (by which time, I shall have moved elsewhere or retired).

Unless you take counter-steps the more an institution slides into
crisis – the more *urgent* the survival or maintenance issues become –
the less time church leaders will be spending on strategy. See Charles
Handy.

Ownership and accountability

A sense of ownership and a sense of responsibility (accountability is a
quasi-legal term) is engendered, the authors argue, by involving
people in decisions as much as possible, that is, to secure as much
consensus as one can short of a sometimes elusive, real, unanimous
agreement. True, and the art of sharing decisions in this way can be
taught.

There is, as they say, a case for local budget-holding. Elsewhere, for
example, Martyn Percy has argued that parishes should be given
ownership of their assets. Although I don't expect the Church of
England to adopt a polity akin to, say, the Baptist Church, it will see
decisions about the ordained ministry required – and supportable –
being pushed down to a regional, if not local level. An identified
element of the 'parish quota' will go to financing that ministry. We
shall also see the diocesan and national segments of the tax falling as
those parts that do not 'add value' are quietly axed and the various
synods are halved in size. That will release more funds to support
what Robin and Derek have called outreach and social action as well
as for investing in the young leaders of tomorrow.

While recognising (with Martyn) the diffusion of power within the
Church of England (both a strength and a weakness) which makes the
proper management of change so problematic, Robin and Derek still
urge the relevance of the concept of strategic church leadership.
Without it we are in trouble. 'In short, deep concerns remain about how
effectively changes (or lack of changes) are being monitored within the
Church of England and about who has the power to reverse decisions
even when they are acknowledged to be wrong' (p. 73). More positively, strategic leadership is 'a way for the Church to set priorities
carefully and then to follow them through effectively' (p. 74).

Wesley Carr

Wesley puts his finger on a longing for better church management and more effective leadership, yet without selling out, as he puts it, to secular notions of either term.

Not that it is easy to separate the truths from their clothes. Take the idea that Wesley borrows from Charles Handy, that 'a leader shapes and shares a vision which gives point to the work of others' (p. 78). If one did not detach some of the secular hidden assumptions we would end up with every church leader feeling that he or she had to shape their own vision for the institution or organisation. But that is not appropriate to the Church for it uniquely has a living, yet invisible, acknowledged leader whose vision is the Church's *raison d'être*. A church leader needs the humility of not needing to be original. True of the model leader too. As George Macdonald wrote, 'Jesus never thought of being original.' Yes, but by seeking and serving a truth outside himself Jesus *was* original.

The shared vision is there, deep in the DNA of Christianity. All that a true leader has to do is to evoke it. You don't need charisma; or, rather, all the charisma you need is in the congregation or its equivalents.

Notice Wesley's important point about an unconscious mindset that can afflict church people. It is a logical error, and, he says, can make his point clearer in the form of a syllogism:

> God has infinite resources and God loves us.
> We are short of money and other resources.
> Therefore God will eventually provide and so *we have no need to plan.*

The logical errors are, yes, God has all things in his hand, but he may choose to give more to other more profitable servants than the churches. He may not love the churches less but he may love other institutions as much. His agenda may not be our agenda. As Wesley aptly puts it, 'mere human beings should not presume to manage God' (p. 82). We are expected to get on with the managing ourselves. There is nothing intrinsically holy about disorder, incompetence, waste, inefficiency or wallowing like hippos in the muddle-in-the-middle.

What, then, is the task of the institution, Wesley asks. Yes, indeed, he writes, 'Which of us has not been involved in interminable debates about these topics?' Yet it is still an inescapable question. Wesley's answer is deceptively simple: 'one task that will emerge in some form is that *churches are there to be used*' (p. 82).

Not the practical use of buildings for various purposes but something more profound. Wesley once asked a group, 'Who uses your church?' It was one of the great churches of England. After a lively discussion he pointed out that the chief 'user' was in fact God. The resultant work and activity was remarkable (p. 87).

This task of being used, Wesley continues, is 'itself congruent with the model of Jesus' ministry' (p. 83). The concept of 'task', he adds, directs our attention always to our context and the interaction of a church with it. We don't do things to that context: on the whole, we do things with and sometimes for it.

Leadership involves awareness of others, understanding of groups and skills towards achieving the task. But, Wesley concludes, 'increased sensitivity and understanding are means, not ends: the end is service of the church as servant of the Kingdom of God' (p. 86).

Philip Mawer

How do institutions or organisations grow leaders? One can point to the whole raft of methods – courses, conferences, programmes, selection, mentoring, coaching and so on. We know, too, that the influence and example of the top person and the senior leadership team is most important: one of the seven generic functions of an effective strategic leader is to ensure that today's and tomorrow's leaders are properly selected and developed. But as significant, if not more so, than all these factors is the corporate *culture*. Some cultures grow leaders and others stunt them. Paradoxically, the latter often have leaders at the top but they are the wrong sort. As the Indian proverb says, 'Under the banyan tree nothing grows.'

A critical factor in the *culture* is whether or not leadership is part of the value system. Is it accepted and valued? Institutions like the National Health Service, the Police Service, the Civil Service and the entire secondary education system have woken up late to this factor in the last four or five years, and they are doing their best to make leadership part of their value system. It is work that takes years: there is no such thing as instant leadership.

Turn to the Army, Royal Navy or Royal Air Force and the value is there already within the culture, as Montgomery's letters to me (quoted above, p. 3) illustrate. It is not a theological college but Sandhurst that has as its motto *Serve to lead*. Why is leadership part of their value system? Because leadership is integral to success in that field. As Euripides said, 'Ten men wisely led/Will beat a hundred without a head.' Can we lay our hands on our hearts today and swear that the Church will fulfil its purpose at any level or in any situation *without* leadership? Who will make that case? A difficulty in the past, however, is that misconceptions about leadership – that it is male, military and Western – prevent institutions such as churches from taking it on board as a core value. There is, as Wesley Carr said, a nervousness about it. Is it some Trojan Horse full of secular ideas and assumptions?

In his paper Philip sketches out or outlines a concept of leadership that truly belongs to the Church; it sits fair and square with the Christian values, attitudes and way of life. He sees it as grounded firmly in the model of Jesus Christ as the servant leader. The challenge for us now is to change the culture within our churches so that they encourage, support and sustain servant leaders – as portrayed by Jesus – and with just a mustard seed or two of his creativity!

Norman Todd

The more metaphors we have for leadership the richer, deeper, wider our concept will become. Someone preparing for the ordained ministry may start out with in-house leadership metaphors: *servant* and *shepherd*, perhaps *prophet* – those leaders of Israel from marginal positions. And the metaphor of the *manager* will also be in the frame.

As a general principle, the wider your span of relevance (or analogy) the more creative you tend to be. Sir Isaac Newton, for example, could see a connection between a falling apple and a falling planet. Those with the narrowest span of relevance are wary of any new metaphor. Norman puts us all to the test by comparing the Church to a *circus* and the CCL (I hope I'll be able to forget his labels of DCLs and CCLs!) as a *circus owner* or *ringmaster*.

It helps. A careful basic distinction can be made between *families* and *hunting parties*. Writ large, the former becomes the *community* (tribe, nation) and the latter the *organisation*. The patterns of human relations and headship differ considerably between the two. How many churches operate on the family/community model, where *being* together matters more than *doing*? How many churches conceive themselves on the organisational model with a common task or purpose, a *result* to be realised or a *destination* to be reached at the journey's end? But, in Gillian Stamp's words (p. 21), is this an Either/Or or a Both/And situation?

Traditionally, a *circus* transcends the division. The performers and owners are all related, one big family, and yet they are also a working company. The best teams of oxen, it is said, are made up from animals related to each other.

Circus is a way of life. No one is clown and juggler, acrobat and ringmaster. Each individual or team has a different, complementary contribution to the whole: each combines the three ingredients of skill, creativity and personality.

Sounds crazy, doesn't it? Yet the Cathedral of St John the Divine in New York City's Artist-in-Residence for nearly two decades is the highwire artist Philippe Petit, who told the story of his incredible wirewalk with no safety harness between the twin towers of the World Trade Center in 1974 in *To Reach for the Clouds* (2003). He has been arrested more than five hundred times for street juggling. It is the best book on leadership I have read for a long time. He quotes Dean Emeritus James Morton, 'my spiritual father', as saying 'Philippe does not believe in God, but God believes in Philippe'. Now that's what I call a true *ringmaster* in God's circus.

Pauline Perry

Socrates once said that where women know more than men they will be accepted as leaders, and he gave as examples a group of musicians and the weaving industry in Athens.

The recognition of the equal value or worth of women as individual persons in the world – long developed and far from complete – is a veiled sign of what Christians would interpret as the slow forming of the Kingdom of God on earth. It is part of a shift in world values, the fresh air of progress from an unseen land.

My own view is that seeds of this new view of women are evident in the vision and practice of Jesus, contrasting quite sharply in places with the patriarchal culture in which he lived. New wine in old wineskins. Or it may be that we creatively read our own spirit and values into the record, like the reader of a novel who brings their imagination to complete the creative act of the writer. Imagination or Spirit – or both?

It will always seem odd to me that in this respect the Church of England has insisted on being the last to 'enter the Kingdom of God', way behind the Royal Navy and the Army, for example, which are both – as I can testify – stuffed with tradition and male-centred culture. It's a case, as Jesus said, that sometimes the children of this generation are wiser than the children of light. Which reminds me to add that a sense of humour is absolutely essential in any one who aspires to be a creative church leader.

'The saying is sure: If anyone aspires to the office of bishop, he desires a noble task' (1 Timothy 3.1). It is not ambition in the pejorative sense to apply to be a bishop. All that you are doing is advancing a hypothesis that your talent for leadership, which will have become apparent to the discerning eye, will be better employed in that particular role. Of course that is only half of the story: the other half is that the institution in question has to make a choice between the available candidates, and that it has to do so in a fair and above-board way.

It is to the credit of the Church of England that once the Nolan Report had this open and fair method of choosing senior leaders on the agenda, and other public bodies and institutions have begun to implement it, it too has now decided to follow the same path. Pauline points out in a gentle way, however, that there are some really quite demanding necessary conditions that have to be met if the new appointments system is to fulfil the high expectations that the clergy and laity will rightly form about it.

In fact I can see that the eventual implementation of the principles of the Perry Report will be a catalyst for positive change in the Church of England. Apart from getting senior appointments right it will help us to identify those in 'mid-career' with real potential for creative church leadership and to do something about that situation.

My own pioneering experiment in that direction – a four-week programme for selected Church of England clergymen which I designed and led at St George's House in Windsor Castle in 1969 – I look upon as one of the great experiences of my life. (It was briefly described in *The Becoming Church* (1976).) I was astonished by the creativity of those who took part. Their enthusiasm and spirit has sustained me for many a year.

Gillian Stamp

Several decades ago, when I was acting as what was then called a management consultant to the Royal Navy Chaplains' Department, it fell to my lot to attend their annual conference. A speaker there mentioned the two journeys of a leader: the public career and the inner journey. It was a new idea to me – the idea not the experience – and it fell as a seed on my mind. What Gillian has done for us is to explore and identify some features of the four bridleways that our feet find themselves on as we journey through life.

Gillian sets her discussion against a philosophy *both* rather than *either/or, and* rather than *but*. That has a deep resonance in Christian thinking – both Man and God, both Kingdom and world, both body and soul. To some the Church of England is like a ramshackle set of farm buildings, a cheerful English set of compromises erected around the muddle-in-the-middle. To others it is a creative enterprise, a deep 'yes' to both Catholic and Protestant traditions, a church with a vision. The only real *either/or* decision a Christian faces is whether to say 'yes' or 'no' to the Kingdom of God at the journey's start.

When it comes to leadership I confess that I have struggled with Gillian's thesis. I'll tell you why. For me leadership is essentially an other-centred activity. Your focus is on something out there – a common task, a team, a set of individuals, a changing environment. The last thing you do is spend time 'examining your navel'.

You could label this the Classical approach. What has become more fashionable nowadays is what, by contrast, I would call the Romantic approach. I heard a talk, for example, from a strategic leader, a week before writing this chapter, who exemplified it. More than half the time was taken up by the speaker explaining who they were, how they needed to be accepted for what they are, why others should respect their feelings, their problems in maintaining a proper work/ life balance, their relations with their parents, and the various admiring compliments that those working for them had passed about their style of leadership. Not until half an hour had passed did I form any idea of why the organisation existed, and I never discovered where it was going. It is Romantic in the sense that the expression of personal feelings are now centre stage. 'Leadership is just *you*.'

In fact that last remark was made to me by Field Marshal Lord Slim, who was the epitome of the Classical leader. He meant by it, I believe, that each of us fulfils the role and functions of leadership – if we fulfil them – in our own unique and personal way, just as our voice or hand-writing differs from all others. We are all originals, not copies. Like a good sermon, leadership is *truth through personality*. Personality is humble in this equation: it is servant to truth and doesn't try to upstage it.

Yet, strangely, the inner and the outer journeys of leadership do run together and overflow into each other. The reason, as I have come to see it, is that the more you come to know yourself the more you understand others. It works conversely too: the deeper the knowledge we gain of others the more you become aware of what lies within you.

There are several lines of thought I could pursue from this point, but I must choose one only. If a church leader claims that his/her congregation or diocese lacks creativity, does this tell us more than they have yet to discover the God-given creativity within themselves? For we know that although creativity (like leadership or musicality) does vary from individual to individual, it is much more widespread than was conceived to be, say, fifty years ago. How do we give people experiences in theological college and in their continuing professional development that stir up, stimulate and keep alive the creative spark?

Elizabeth Welch

Elizabeth gives us a vivid case study of a creative church leader. Sometimes a simple story is worth a thousand words of leadership theory or Christian theology. It certainly shows us what *servant* leadership is, but why do we read *creativity* into the picture? 'Because', writes Elizabeth, 'Albert Carpenter's heart was touched by the people in need, he was able to persist, despite all the difficulties in the way, in establishing a new beginning for a whole number of people' (p. 137). Creative church leadership involves looking with eyes of love on the needs of the world and seeing not problems but possibilities.

Elizabeth mentions the phenomenon of 'too many ideas'. Can you have too much creativity? Not if you understand the process. Only individuals have ideas. The first step is often to 'brainstorm' – to generate as many ideas as possible without being too critical or evaluative at this stage. The next stage is sieving the ideas with the net of feasibility. Choosing the best ideas in the net and shaping them – often with *both/and* thinking – into results is the work of *innovation*, and it invariably calls for teamwork. Individuals are creative but only teams are innovative. The artist may have an idea for a picture, but canvas, paints, brushes and frame come with the team. A vocational institution works like a team, composed of complementary gifts.

Leadership as releasing gifts and *Leadership as future oriented* sum up for me two of the central themes in this book. The rub, however, is that the gifts to be released are for the Kingdom and not for the benefit of the church you may belong to. Yet there is a strange law at work, that a church that puts the Kingdom first will have the experience of *being* the Church.

Yes, it is indeed said that 'there is only successful leadership when there are also followers'. But I wonder about that. Almost the first thing a creative leader does is to create *partners* out of what others would see as merely followers. Just look at Jesus of Galilee at work: 'No longer do I call you servants, for the servant does not know what his master is doing; but I have called you friends, for all that I have heard from my Father I have made known to you' (John 15.15).

It is as if we are all on equal footing; Jesus presents himself as the first among equals. What the Church treasures and serves is the astonishing vision of Jesus for this world, a vision that is, as

Elizabeth writes, from God and ultimately of God. It is a company of partners.

Peter Rudge

As a modern saying has it, 'Nothing is impossible until it is sent to a committee.' This is especially true of committees that do not plan their work. *Agenda* – a list, outline or plan of things to be done – is the key metaphor in Peter's chapter.

Although it became something of a buzzword or cliché in church circles after it was first coined some decades ago, 'the world sets the agenda' did make church people think. Church leaders who accept that message would need to be looking at the big picture, to be observant, alert, aware, discerning or perceptive. In other words, they need to develop a keen ability to detect the real meaning of a situation. Discernment – this analytical ability to see things clearly – is an aspect of *phronesis*, practical wisdom: the ability to understand situations, anticipate consequences and make sound judgements.

Peter records how historically secularisation reduced the acknowledged domain of the Church to 'faith and morals', all the rest of human interests establishing their own independence.[1] Even 'faith', it might be added, has escaped into spirituality and 'morals' into the branch of philosophy called ethics. Peter quotes Bishop John Robinson to the effect that the churches have retreated to their last bastion: 'the private world of the individual's need' (p. 155). If Peter is right – and broadly I suspect that he is – it is a development we need to challenge firmly now.

I know what he means. There is one dominant interpretation of Christianity – strong in all branches, and in all times from St Benedict to John Bunyan – that the purpose of the Church is to enable the individual soul to journey from a state of hopeless and ingrained sin to a knowledge of its state, redemption by the atoning death of Christ, and to eventual bliss in the Kingdom of Heaven after death ends this earthly pilgrimage. The managing, so to speak, of this private journey of countless individual souls is the business of the churches. Priests or ministers are leaders of that journey. At best they see themselves as called to be leaders by their own example of holy living as well as by precepts. For the way of salvation each individual treads is no easy one.

When it comes to spiritual leadership – living the vision, exemplifying the ideal – some so-called church leaders have failed to come up to minimum Christian standards, let alone excel in this way of life.

Shakespeare puts this prayer to their leader in the mouths of the laity:

> Do not like some ungracious pastors do,
> Show me the steep and thorny way to heaven.
> Whiles, like a puff'd and reckless libertine;
> Himself the primrose path of dalliance treads,
> And recks not his own rede [advice]. (*Hamlet* 1.iii.47)

It may seem difficult to square this concept of the Church's purpose as supporting, encouraging, feeding the *individual* on his or her journey – not least by providing some spiritual company – with the vision of Jesus which centred on the Kingdom of God *on earth*, to which I have been nailing my own colours as to a masthead.

Yet, in the Gospels, it is *individuals* who are challenged, healed, forgiven or called. The pattern of the Kingdom impacting on individuals continues with the Resurrection. Neither the nation of Israel nor the Roman Empire experiences what Christians interpreted as the greatest sign of the coming of the Kingdom of God on earth. It was *individuals*, sometimes alone, sometimes in small groups and only once in a small crowd. But these individuals are set free and called to give themselves to building the Kingdom on earth.

'The Kingdom of God needs to be maintained first and foremost in the lives of individuals,' said Cardinal Basil Hume. But, he continues,

> [S]ociety itself must reflect and foster those qualities and values. Our task is not so much to convince people of their sinfulness but of their dignity and destiny as children of God, made in his image and called in Christ to make all things new.[2]

Peter sees three main items on the agendas of the churches: worship, education and service. But, he says, *they all isolate the church from the real world* (p. 155). These are challenging words. Is worship only a provision made by a church for its own members? Is education concerned as a benefit mainly for those on the 'inside'? Are the services from the churches focused on social symptoms while excluding itself from 'the real causes of the problems in the political and economic fields' (p. 156)? Why not, Peter asks, a 'new and relevant agenda' for the churches at the threshold of this new millennium, one which reflects 'the advent of a new age and the nearness of the new status of humanity' such as we find proclaimed in Paul's letters?

It is fitting that Peter, having shown us such a sublime view from the mountain top, takes us down to earth again, to the importance of

getting right our meetings, procedures and time-management techniques in the churches. From his sensible advice I pick out one key
point. It is not enough to make decisions: 'there needs to be the capacity within their organisational structures of giving effect to what is
being planned to be done' (p. 157). In *Effective Strategic Leadership*
(2000), I suggest that one of the seven generic functions of an effective
leader is *making it happen*.

Coming back to Peter's central metaphor – setting the agenda – how
does creativity relate to it? Creativity is not inimical to planning,
providing one accepts the principle that a plan is simply a very good
basis for changing one's mind if a situation develops in an unpredicted
way. When it came to the agenda by the wayside we all know that it
was the Samaritan – not a model of contemporary piety – who
showed flexibility as well as compassion.

Arguably the setting and developing of the agenda of a Christian
congregation, community or working group, one that is committed
to the Kingdom of God as its first priority, should be essentially a
creative process, not unlike that which threads the life and works of
an artist, writer, sculptor, poet or composer. For the Kingdom of God
is like an unpredictable journey. In *On Creativity* (London, Methuen,
2003), based on interviews with 14 outstandingly creative individuals
in the arts, John Tusa suggests:

> Working on and completing a particular work is not just an end in
> itself, a moment of particular conclusion. The activity of making
> one work opens up possibilities for what is to be done next. Artists
> discover in their current work sometimes what they want to
> express next, sometimes solutions to ideas that have lain around
> unresolved in the past. In the current act of making, an awareness
> of continuity with the next work – which may well be very different
> in nature – lies hidden until it is discovered.
>
> This idea of a seamless, instinctive continuum to the creative
> process is very strong. Each work throws up fresh ideas, new
> problems and the possibility of new solutions. Continuity involves
> continuous and instinctive innovations, but an innovation that is
> evolutionary as well. It points, too, to the very uncalculating way
> that artists move from one type of work to another.

These reflections lead me back to Peter's concluding summary (p. 162),
which is so apposite to the central theme of this book:

> There remains for those engaged in creative church leadership
> that they give their full attention to the setting of agendas that will

enable the church not only to be sensitive to the world but also to be ready and committed to its ministry and service in it. Such agendas may well be wider and more extensive than hitherto if the church is to recover from that narrowing of its horizons and to move on to a greater openness and comprehensiveness in its outlook. The hand that writes the agenda – the right agenda – can indeed rule the world; or, to express the point in less mundane terms, fulfil that prayer to the Father that his Kingdom come and his will be done on earth as it is in heaven.

Which reminds me of John Ruskin's words: 'If you do not wish for this Kingdom, don't pray for it. But if you do, you must do more than pray for it; you must work for it.'

What is that work? That is what churches – ministers and laity – have to struggle to know in general and to discern in particular, a task that calls now for creative or imaginative thinking. That is why God is sending the churches creative leaders. One of the first and greatest of the Church's leaders gives us (in Colossians 4.11) in eight words a definition of what a church today is called to be: 'my fellow workers for the Kingdom of God'.

Peter Price

'The one who builds the path cannot make it straight.' Call me a sceptic. I am a little dubious about the African provenance of Peter's key proverb. (It is not in my *A–Z of African Proverbs*, though it tells me there that an estimated one million of such proverbs, most unwritten, probably exist.) Tracks of trails in Africa are seldom straight and they are made by the innumerable treadings of man or beast. But all that is really irrelevant: the proverb makes its point. The Roman legionaries with their heads down building a Roman road are not the ones to make it straight; the army of unskilled labourers constructing the great railway that links Peter's diocese to London needed an Isambard Kingdom Brunel to plan its route. The latter, incidentally, a true leader, was not above taking a turn with shovel or pickaxe among the men.

For although Brunel's navvies derived their name from *navigator* they were of course not navigators in the sense that Peter believes that church leaders should be. At sea it is the helmsman who steers a straight course in the right direction. In Greek and Roman times the *kybernetes*, steersman, was often the ship's captain and owner. His art or skill, *kybernesis*, is listed by Paul as one of God's gifts to the Church

(1 Corinthians 12). Both navigating by the stars – technical knowledge – and directing the work of crew members – leading people – came within that art of leadership at sea. *Kybernesis* is a near perfect metaphor for leadership. Where it breaks down is that, short of a mutiny, the crew and passengers have no option but to go where the ship's leader takes them!

Peter comments on the paradox of creative church leaders being asked to be or perceived as being repositories of both vision and ability, but knowing in the inner chamber of their hearts that they lack vision and that their ability is small when measured against the needs and demands of leadership.

Yes, it is a paradox. Yet in the episode where Paul experienced shipwreck – no trained sea captain but a natural leader, Paul himself stepped into a leadership vacuum and steadied the nerves of the crew and passengers – it is clear in this case that the *kybernetes* and the owner of the ship are two different persons (Acts 27.11). As it happens, the former is incompetent and the latter irresponsible.

The paradox fades, then, when we imagine the steersman or navigator and the owner as distinct individuals. We can picture a ship's captain who is both a skilled, experienced navigator and a good leader, who shares the owner's vision and has himself a sense of 'ownership' for the ship entrusted to him and its precious cargo. When two eyes are joined in sight, it matters not which has the better vision. And it is a sign of trust if the owner chooses to accompany you in person on a hazardous voyage.

Doubtless the Roman centurion who escorted Paul at sea in that alarming adventure would rather have had his feet on terra firma. The secret of the Roman roads, he would know well, lay in the foundation of large stones overlaid by smaller stones and gravel. Sometimes the *curatores viarum* – those responsible for the roads – needed to rebuild them. Think of the churches as an old and well-established road system. At least in part, Peter asks, as one of the chief *curatores*, should we not 're-found' it? ('Found' and 'foundation' have the same Latin root – *fundus*, base or bottom.) I have to leave that question in the air, however, for it is really addressed to Peter's fellow *curatores*, who may have very different views on road maintenance.

Still, before we leave the road metaphor it is worth mentioning a third word we derive from *fundus* – fundamental. What the Church stands badly in need of now is what Albert Schweitzer once called *fundamental thinking*, and he himself was no mean exponent of it.

Oddly enough, fundamental thinking is related to creativity. For so often, if you get back to the original vision you discover that it is much broader, deeper and higher than you imagined. We tend to 'close down' the general to the particular in our thinking, and all too often the particular solidifies like the cement that Roman soldiers sometimes added to their road foundations. Fundamental thinking leads us back – or forward – from the particular to the general, and that opens up new vistas and avenues for both thought and action.

I may be wrong but I think this is roughly what Matthew was getting at in the parable to which Peter refers us (13.52). Here Jesus compares 'a scribe trained in the Kingdom of heaven' (Matthew's characteristic circumlocution for Kingdom of God) to 'a householder that brings out of his treasure what is new and what is old'. In that parable of Jesus lies a charter for creativity as well as wisdom in church leadership.

Thinking creatively, Peter tentatively suggests a new model of his own to add to the five he discusses – the Postmodern Church. As 'Postmodern' and 'Post-Christian' are often regarded as synonymous, that may seem to some a contradiction in terms. What have Relativism and Individualism to do with classic Christianity? Yet, when I thought more about it, for Jesus the only absolute seems to have been God; everything else – Law (which many regarded as absolute), Temple, even Jesus himself – is relative. He stands out too, supremely as an individual as he affirms this but denies that – by what authority, they asked. And it is to individuals that the Kingdom of God comes in his day. Perhaps the Postmodern Church predates 'Postmodernism'![3]

A suggested motto for road builders of the Kindom: *Either we will find a way or we will make one.* Which reminds me of a seventeenth-century song:

> Over floods that are deepest,
> Which Neptune obey,
> Over rocks that are steepest,
> Love will find out the way.

David Jenkins

'Fine mess you have got us into now,' Ollie Hardy was wont to say to Stan Laurel in the comedy films of my youth. Some will interpret David's chapter as a leading 'liberal' saying as much to a selection of target groups among the 'traditionalists'. Under such an attack, Stan – the thin, bullied and confused one – would then scratch his head, look blank and dissolve into tears. It is most unlikely, I must add, that the 'traditionalists' – with their tanks already drawn up on the lawns of Lambeth Palace – will react in quite that way!

David shares with us his thoughts and feelings – passionate feel-ings – about all this: the present controversies in the Church of England, the inward-lookingness of churches in general, and the scandalous civil wars between the three great Abrahamic religions. Had he not got a seven-stranded personal anchor-line holding him to the reef, he tells us, the mounting spectacle would have tipped him over into atheism. Strong words coming from a theologian and bishop of his stature. And no less powerful are the questions he poses – speaking for myself, they have given me cause to think long and hard. Here are some first thoughts.

Once, at St Thomas's Hospital in London, I led a discussion on the 'management of change'. 'The only person here who brings about any change', one senior medical consultant said, 'is so-and-so (who wasn't present). *He is the only one who is willing to be changed himself.*'

I thought of this story when reflecting on the *New Ecumenism*. Each of the three great religions needs to move away from exclusive monotheism to inclusive monotheism. Which, I wonder, will be open to being changed first. Those in Islam and Judaism who might want to go in that direction face formidable internal obstacles, for religions are inherently and intensely conservative. So is Christianity: the intellec-tual room for manoeuvre within it is actually very small. They are all locked in their histories. Have the keys been irretrievably lost?

It may be simply incurable optimism on my part, but I think that the Church does potentially have the power to transcend Christianity. (By *transcend* I do not mean abandon or alter but to rise above or go beyond the limits of.) That is because it has still within its DNA the vision of Jesus, namely, the 'Word of God' (Luke 5.1) that he both pro-claimed and taught concerning the presence in power of the Kingdom of God on earth. For that founding vision transcends without remov-ing the divide between sinner and righteous, Jews and Gentiles, male and female, religion and society. Moreover, the vision of God implic-it in it reveals a law of love, which in our day transcends, distils and sometimes tests the various 'ways of life' that form the core in each of the three religions.

Giving up things often implies loss and – if it is with some unse-cured gain in mind – risk. David talks about it in terms of cities as symbols of churches or religions. Christians as archetypal humans – wanderers like the bedouin in their tents in our brief sojourn on earth – ought to be least wedded to bricks-and-mortar.

The City is a powerful metaphor alongside that of the Kingdom of God. The City is something constructed – we have to build it together – it is not just a natural growth. It allows for personal freedoms – choice of occupation, friends, interests, groups, societies. It may be set within a particular nation, indeed be its capital, but its doors are open to people from many other places. The City of God is envisioned as a place into which all nations of the world will bring their treasures.

Yet the universal City, the commonwealth of humanity, the 'city laid up in heaven',[4] to which all of us – by dint of being individual human beings or persons – can claim citizenship, is an ideal, like the Kingdom or its servant the Church. We all know that actual cities and actual churches fall short of the ideal and always will, for we are inescapably human. As T. S. Eliot writes in 'The Hollow Men':

> Between the idea
> And the reality
> Between the motion
> And the act
> Falls the Shadow

Here we come close to the mystery of the Kingdom. For man it is impossible: reason tells us that. Yet we are called to follow one who believed and lived the faith that for God all things are possible.

So we can dream of a day when the Rock in Jerusalem – that threshing-floor which David bought as an altar – will become the common symbol of the three great religions of the Book, an open house under the graceful domed tent of stone that the Caliph Omar erected over its forlorn site so many centuries ago.

> And he taught and said to them, 'Is it not written, "My house shall be called a house of prayer for all the nations?"' (Mark 11.17)

When the world sees the chief leaders of the Jewish, Christian and Muslim faiths standing in a ring around the Rock, hand-in-hand and united in prayer, then it will see the meaning of **creative church leadership**.

The way ahead

As far as John Nelson and I are concerned, this book has exceeded our expectations. The way that the contributors – without prompting – have revealed a common mind and yet at the same time so interestingly developed their own themes, thereby colouring in at least some of the map for us, has been quite remarkable and exciting. Our thanks to all of them.

They have certainly made me think, and to think deeply about a number of issues relating to leadership and the churches. It may not have that effect on every reader. While checking out Peter Price's

African proverb I came across this cautionary one: 'You cannot teach the paths of the forest to an old gorilla.' Not that old gorillas in their silver-back copes are likely to read this book! Their human counterparts who know and follow the familiar paths of church life might pick it up, puzzle over it and put it down. For it is hard to see what creative leadership means to those following the tramlines of tradition as if by instinct or habit, unrelieved by questions. One of my heroes is the frontier scout and pioneer Daniel Boone. Once, returning from the uncharted forests beyond the Kentucky river, he was asked by a lady if he was ever lost. 'I can't say that I was ever lost, ma'am,' he replied, 'but I was once sure bewildered for three days.' We need to be bewildered as a prelude to finding the way ahead.

This book is an exercise in such trailblazing. Like it or not, the churches are moving into new and unfamiliar territory. Though not lost, there is certainly some creative bewilderment around already. Slowly the generation of old gorilla leaders gives way and younger gorillas take up the baton of leadership – to the distant sound of bulldozers slowly tearing down the comfort of the familiar forest. Actually it's a very good time to stop playing at gorillas!

What emerges from this book for me is a simple but central question: *What is the gospel?* Among our 14 contributors I sense a shared conviction that it has essentially to do with God's creative purpose in and for the world. This has to be our starting point. It is also, they believe, a necessary condition for creative church leadership.

For those familiar with the distinction in logic or science, please note that I say *necessary*, and not *sufficient*, condition. For in Christian faith the sufficient condition is the presence and power of the Holy Spirit, guide and leader of the Church. And the Spirit is free; like the desert wind 'it blows where it will'. All we can do is to build windmills and say our prayers.

Conversely, where a church lacks the vision of Jesus, it should not expect to experience creative leadership. At best it might get from its senior officers what Robert Bridges once called the 'masterful administration of the unforeseen'. But that isn't quite what we mean by leadership, is it?

The more a church turns itself inside out and faces God's needy, suffering and beloved world as it struggles forwards, the more it becomes the Church. And the more it becomes the Church the more it discovers its own inner resources of kindness, love and hope, together with a God-given natural and graceful creativity. Hence a vision of the Church as a 'community of callings' made up of creative people which calls for inspiring leadership that can release that inner greatness. Perhaps John Buchan best summarises the task of creative church leaders in a lecture he delivered in 1930 before the University of St Andrews, the first such lecture on leadership at a university in modern times:

> The task of leadership is not to put greatness into humanity but to elicit it, for the greatness is there already.

Notes

1. For a further exploration of secularisation, I commend Hugh McLeod and Werner Ustorf (eds), *The Decline of Christendom in Western Europe, 1750–2000*, Cambridge, Cambridge University Press, 2003.
2. The full passage from the Cardinal's address on vision and values of a reborn Europe can be found in *The Leadership of Jesus* (2001), p. 159.
3. This paragraph is dedicated to my daughter Kate, who has kindly typed out my contributions for me. As she is the author of a first-class dissertation on 'A quest to unearth the true source of authority of the New Age Movement', which I have read with much interest and profit, I can only hope that what I have written here gets good marks from her!
4. Plato, *Republic*, ix, 592b. Owing largely to St Augustine's *The City of God*, it is under that name rather than 'the Republic' or even 'the New Jerusalem' that the image of the City has taken root in our tradition. Though Augustine holds that citizens of the City of God should bear office in the city of the world he does not envisage that they will change or transform it.

Part 3

17 The Foundation for Church Leadership

MICHAEL TURNBULL

The reasons for the proliferation of organisations concerned with church leadership are not hard to find. In the secular field, business schools and many freelance organisations have long seen the need for developing leadership theory and training in disciplines as diverse as public bodies, large multinational corporations and small businesses. The backcloth of a fast-changing global environment and continual legislative impositions has meant that the Armed Services, the Police, universities, health authorities and global and local commercial enterprises have to ask major questions about how they are led and managed.

At the same time there has been a cultural shift in society as a whole from hierarchical to more corporate ways of doing things. The Church of England is not immune from these changes. It might be assumed that the 'body' and 'Trinitarian' images of Christian theology might have put the church in the forefront of this thinking but in fact the church has itself become locked into an institutional framework which at least *looks* hierarchical, for many *feels* hierarchical and at worst for some is an opportunity to practise authoritarianism of the worst kind.

Two movements within the church have challenged this. First, the growth of active lay participation in the governance of the church during the twentieth century, from the establishment of the Church Assembly to the formation of the General Synod in 1970, has created a diversification of authority. Secondly, the decline in the number of clergy and the creation of multi-benefices has forced the church into thinking of more collaborative ways of leadership. Team and group ministries paved the way for the more recent concept of 'cluster' or 'localities'.

The bishop's role has always been confused by his *pastoral* responsibilities on the one hand and his quasi *legal* role on the other, so it is not straightforward for a bishop to exercise true collaborative leadership, however hard he may try. Hence there is a problem as desire is frustrated by circumstance and expectation. Amongst all this, I dare to add, is that the advent of women priests has enriched our thinking and practice in terms of collaboration rather than competition for authority.

The result is that bishops and clergy have been faced with the dilemma of leading a church which is portrayed as clinging to the concept of hierarchical authority but in reality is working in a much more consultative and collaborative way. So it is time to go back to our roots and ask theological questions about the nature of 'church' and 'leadership' and seek to apply that in a contemporary setting.

As has often happened in the past the initiatives for these enquiries have come from 'voluntary' movements within the church rather than from the church structures themselves. The voluntary principle has great advantages because it provides independence from committee structures and therefore the competing demand for resources; it has greater freedom to be prophetic; and it usually gets things done more quickly and effectively. Nevertheless, in order to be of lasting influence, it needs to have the capacity to infect the structures of the church.

In terms of leadership learning and training, this is already beginning to happen as, for example, many dioceses (and parallel structures in other churches) are using the impetus of voluntary organisations to feed their own programmes of both lay and ministerial continuing education.

The disadvantage of voluntary movements working in the same sphere is that there may be too much repetition and overlap and therefore a possible waste of resources and energy. We need, therefore, to ensure that small but vigorous voluntary organisations, working in the field of leadership in the church, communicate well with each other, share resources of money and manpower where possible and share knowledge, experience and research. Moreover, it is vital that the energy of the voluntary principle is put at the disposal of the church as a whole and contributes to the strategies of the dioceses and synodical structures. The Archbishops and their Council, the House of Bishops and the training officers in the dioceses need to know that the voluntary movements are there to engage with and to supplement their work rather than to protect their parallel independence.

It is with some of this thinking in mind that the Foundation for Church Leadership was formed and became a registered charity in 2003. It has been made possible by a generous donation which will be the impetus for further fundraising. Its small body of trustees is 80 per cent lay people, most of whom are working in the secular sphere and have expertise in leadership training and human resources.

Our purposes are fourfold. First, to identify theologies of leadership by engaging with theologians and leaders of sociological disciplines to bring together a philosophy of leadership which is relevant to, and supportive of, the current mission of the church.

Secondly, we wish to support and sponsor ways of enabling individuals and teams to develop their potential for leadership. We shall try and do this in partnership with others and by discovering and filling gaps in leadership training programmes. We shall listen particularly to the thinking of the Archbishops' Council and seek to support the strategies of the House of Bishops' continuing education programme. We shall have a mind to both corporate learning and individual monitoring of those in positions of leadership and we shall also look to the development of potential leaders at every 'level' of church life.

Thirdly, we hope to encourage a wider use of opportunities for the development of individuals – opportunities that may be within and outside the church. It may be possible, for example, to sponsor individuals on particular courses or to provide financial support for writing and research sabbaticals which focus on leadership.

Fourthly, we shall attempt to provide some evaluation of the outcomes of training and to identify and then support best practices. We are conscious that some of this is going on through other endeavours and therefore providing research about what is being done best and where will be an important aspect of our work.

The trustees are aware that the Foundation is in its early days and we need to be prepared to adapt and change as new needs become apparent. But we are sufficiently confident to believe that we have a distinctive contribution to make in a field that needs urgent and thorough attention. We have plans in hand for the development of our infrastructure and communication, though we wish to keep things simple, travel light, remain focused and scratch where the church itches. Watch this space!

Michael Turnbull
Chairman, Foundation for Church Leadership

Trustees

Part 4

18 A database of resources for church leadership and management from The Lincoln Theological Institute, Manchester University

DAVID A. HARVEY

Introduction

The recognition that management studies and practices are relevant and acceptable fields for the church to be involved in may have been slow in arriving, particularly in the British church. It may still be true that:

> For many people, management may seem to be far removed from the ethos of the church, and they might wonder how a bridge might be built, a relationship established, its relevance shown.[1]

But the publishing of Rudge's[2] book in 1976 demonstrates that, at least in the wider world, there has been a recognition that management techniques have much to offer the hard-pressed parish minister as well as larger church organisations. The publication of the Report of the Archbishop's Commission on the Organisation of the Church of England[3] brought the subject, if not into the public eye, then at least on to the agenda of the 'management' of the Church of England. In response to this report G. R. Evans and Martyn Percy drew together a collection of essays aimed at exploring the relationship between management and order in the church.[4] Whilst acknowledging that 'Individuals do not join Christian communities to be "organized"; they come to serve, worship and participate in the generosity of the life of God,'[5] the authors also recognise that 'Clearly . . . there are problems of governance in the Church at the practical level that go beyond administration.'[6] It is with the intention of assisting to alleviate these problems that this database of material and institutions concerned with managing and leading the church has been constructed. Since the Turnbull Report was published management has become big business, and as with all 'worldly wisdom' the church needs to take care in considering how much management theory and practice it is going to take on board. Again Evans and Percy give us a timely reminder:

> We live in an age in which service has become an industry, is costed and accounted for, and is something society sometimes thinks it cannot afford. Yet Jesus reminds us that service of one another lies at the root of the gospel and of society. No one is so great as to have graduated to a status of being above offering service.[7]

The management resources given here, therefore, should be seen as aids to service and not as ends in themselves.

The drawing up of a database containing the key resources, both written and institutional, of church leadership and management is somewhat like attempting to produce a list of the best eating places in a large city. In the end, virtually all the restaurants, cafés and fast-food outlets have to be included because one man's meat is bound to be another man's poison and in any case people want different food on different occasions. A snack in a food court will do whilst on a shopping trip, but for a business dinner a more sophisticated establishment is required. Not only that, but at any given level of service, there is a great variety of cuisines to choose from. Thus a database of church leadership needs to accommodate not only in-depth works for the serious student, but also lighter resources to give quick and easy help in practical situations. It also needs to cater for a wide range of churchmanship and theologies. It would be possible to group resources into, say, light-, medium- and heavyweight scholarship, and high-, middle- and low-church categories, but this would throw up a multitude of problems concerned with the labelling of both the resources and the intended consumer. A lightweight book of helpful hints is not necessarily to be dismissed as unscholarly; it may be filled with nutritious morsels. Similarly, a theological tome can contain an inordinate amount of indigestible padding. So where then do we start? I have started by allowing that the reader has some understanding and knowledge of the subject and so to a large extent have let the titles, authors and publishers give their own guidance as to the likely content of each work. Where appropriate I have included a very brief indication of what to expect. I have grouped the resources into what I hope will be useful categories for easy reference. I have included institutions and material from the full range of denominations, since in an age of calculating costs it makes sense to share resources as much as possible. For the most part the institutions listed here are restricted to those in the UK; obviously the number of institutions world-wide is enormous and readers wishing to extend their scope are advised to consult the internet or other sources. One or two notable overseas resources are included. Books and articles are from English language publications, mostly from the UK and North America.

In addition to the difficulties of the breadth of material there is the problem of the scope of the subject. Leadership in the church covers an enormous range of skills and gifts. Management has to do not only with organising large workforces such as may be found in a diocese, but also the micromanagement of small groups and even of individuals. The contemporary view of ministry is changing. There is greater participation by lay people, more concentration on teams and wider recognition that ministry is to do with equipping and enabling rather than performing. The concept of the servant leader, flagged by Evans and Percy above and which is referred to in some of the works, is therefore very relevant to today's ministry. The topics in the database attempt to reflect this changing attitude to leadership and to cover as wide a range of areas in which leaders are to be found as possible.

Explanatory notes

Items under each heading are listed in alphabetical order and are not ranked in any way.

Books are given with author, publisher and date of publication. This will enable them to be ordered if required. Most can be found on www.amazon.com where in many cases there is a description of the contents.

Organisations are given with address and telephone number. Readers with web access can find them using the search facility (online resources have a web address given). Information has been gleaned primarily from the *UK Christian Handbook* and the internet. Its accuracy is subject to the reliability of those sources.

Section 1 – Writings on leadership

1a – General books on management and leadership

These are books written on the theory and practice of management. Some are written by Christians but from a secular viewpoint, other authors have no religious stance.

The Age of Unreason, Charles Handy, Random House Business Books, 1995; the future is not inevitable – we can influence it.
Beyond Certainty: The Changing World of Organisations, Charles Handy, Arrow, 1996.
Fundamentals of Project Management, James P. Lewis, Amacom, 2002; step-by-step guidance for projects from idea to completion.
Gods of Management, Charles Handy, Arrow, 1995: Handy uses the gods of Parnassus to illustrate different management types: Zeus = the entrepreneur, Apollo = order and bureaucracy, Athena = craftsmen, Dionysus = artists and professionals.
Handbook of Management Skills, Dorothy M. Stewart, Gower, 1994.
The Inspirational Leader: How to Motivate, Encourage and Achieve Success, John Adair, Kogan Page, 2003; leadership for those who think they are not leaders.
Leadership and the One Minute Manager, Ken Blanchard et al., Harper Collins Business, 2000; effective adaptive styles of situational leadership.
The One Minute Manager, Ken Blanchard, Harper Collins Business, 2000.
Understanding Organisations, Charles Handy, Penguin, 1993; six key concepts for managing organisations: culture, motivation, leadership, power, role play and working in groups.
20/20 Hindsight: From Starting Up to Successful Entrepreneur by Those Who Have Been There, Rachael Thackray, Virgin, 2002.

1b – Management in the Church

Leading and Managing a Growing Church, George G. Hunter III, Abingdon Press, 2000.
Leading, Managing, Ministering, John Nelson, Canterbury Press, 1998.
Management and Ministry, John Nelson, Canterbury Press, 1996; contributions from 24 writers on good management practice in churches.
Management in the Church, Peter F. Rudge, McGraw-Hill, 1976.
Managing the Church: Order and Organization in a Secular Age, G. R.

Evans and Martyn Percy (eds), Sheffield Academic Press, 2000; the
response to the Turnbull Report.

*Ministry in 3 Dimensions: A Theological Foundation for Local Church
Leadership*, Steven Croft, Darton, Longman & Todd, 1999.

Practical Church Management, James Behrens, Gracewing, 1998.

Strategic Church Leadership, Robin Gill, SPCK, 1996; applying the principles of business management to church leadership.

1c – Aspects of ordained ministry

Being a Christian Leader, Fred Bacon, Baptist Union, 1990; Baptist
perspective on leadership.

Being a Priest Today: Exploring Priestly Identity, Christopher
Cocksworth and Rosalind Brown, Canterbury Press, 2002.

The Fire and the Clay, George Guiver, SPCK, 1993.

Freed to Serve: Training and Equipping for Ministry, Michael Green,
Ward, 1989.

An Introduction to Christian Ministry, Gordon Kuhrt, Church House
Publishing, 2000; a historical and contemporary guide to ministry.

Priesthood and Society, Kenneth Mason, Canterbury Press, 2002.

Priests in a People's Church, George Guiver et al., SPCK, 2001.

Transforming Priesthood, Robin Greenwood, SPCK, 1994.

What Is a Minister?, Dorothy Shreeve, Philip Luscombe and Esther
Shreeve, Epworth, 2002; Methodist understanding of ministry.

1d – Pastoral care

It might be argued that pastoral care does not really come under the
auspices of leadership and management. However, the skills used in
the care of vulnerable individuals can certainly be those needed in
managing a church. Careful listening to all sides of an argument,
prioritising demands and problem solving typically come into this
category. Therefore these books are included.

Anchoring Your Well Being: A Guide for Congregational Leaders, Howard
John Clinebell, Upper Room Books, 1997.

Being There, Peter Speck, SPCK, 1988; pastoral care in time of sickness.

The Contemplative Pastor: Returning to the Art of Spiritual Direction,
Eugene H. Peterson, Eerdman's, 1993.

A Critique of Pastoral Care, Stephen Pattison, SCM Press, 2000; healing
and forgiveness in the congregation leading to growth.

A Guide to Pastoral Care, R. E. O. White, Pickering & Inglis, 1976.

Handbook of Pastoral Studies, Wesley Carr, SPCK, 1997.

The Integrity of Pastoral Care, David Lyall, SPCK, 2001.
Pastoral Care Revisited, Frank Wright, SCM Press, 1996.
The Pastoral Nature of Theology: An Upholding Presence, R. John Elford,
    Continuum International, 1999.
*Practical Theology in Action: Christian Thinking in the Service of Church
    and Society*, Paul Ballard and John Pritchard, SPCK, 1996.
Skilful Shepherds, Derek Tidball, Inter-Varsity Press, 1986.
Spirituality and Pastoral Care, Kenneth Leach, Sheldon Press, 1986.

1e – Lay Leadership

The principle of sharing leadership with the laity and of delegating
some aspects of ministry have become an integral part of church life.
In times of rationalisation of resources the training of lay leaders is
becoming increasingly important.

An ABC for the PCC, John Pitchford, Continuum International, 1993.
Equipping the Saints: Mobilizing Laity for Ministry, Michael J.
    Christensen, Abingdon, 2000.
Handbook for Churchwardens and Councillors, Kenneth M. MacMarran,
    Continuum International, 2002.
How to Manage Your Church: A Manual for Pastors and Lay Leaders,
    Edgar Walz, Concordia, 1987.
Lay Leaders: Resources for the Changing Parish, William T. Ditewig, Ave
    Maria, 1991.
The Ministry of a Deacon, Ronnie Aitchison, Epworth, 2003; overview
    of the Methodist diaconate.
*Motivating Your Parish to Change: Concrete Leadership Strategies for
    Pastors, Administrators and Lay Leaders*, Dave Heney, Resource
    Publications, 1998.
Radical Leaders, Paul Beasley-Murray, Baptist Union, 1992; elders and
    leaders in Baptist Churches.

1f – Team and collaborative ministry

Dynamic Local Ministry, Andrew Bowden and Michael West,
    Continuum, 2000; 'Local Ministry' is a Church of England scheme
    to validate lay people for ministry. This is a guide to the scheme.
Fulfilling the Vision: Collaborative Ministry in the Parish, Howard J.
    Hubbard, Crossroad Publishing Company, 1997.
*Leading the Team-based Church: How Pastors and Church Staffs can grow
    together into a powerful fellowship of leaders*, George Cladis, Jossey

Bass Wiley, 1999; covers various team types – e.g. visionary, collaborative, empowering, etc.

Making a Team Work, Steve Chalke, Kingsway, 1995.

The Ministry Team Handbook, Robin Greenwood, SPCK, 2000.

Team Ministry, Dick Iveson, City Bible Publishing, 1989.

Team Spirituality: A Guide for Staff and Church, William Carter, Abingdon, 1977.

1g – Leading small groups

Many churches have small groups. Whether they are Bible study groups, cell groups, activity groups or groups supporting those with special needs, the role of the group leader is vital and particular skills are needed. These books are added to help ministers find the people with the right skills for small group leadership.

Group Dynamics for Teams, Daniel Levi, Sage, 2001; teaching people to work efficiently in teams.

Leading Small Groups: Basic Skills for Church and Community Organisations, Walter W. Turner, Judson Press, 1997; theory and practice of group leadership with practical workshops.

Leading Small Groups That Help People Grow, Henry Cloud and John Townsend, Zondervan, 2003; psychologists Cloud and Townsend provide advice for all small groups to grow spiritually, emotionally and relationally using three key elements: grace, truth and time.

Nine Keys to Effective Small Group Leadership: How Lay Leaders Can Establish Dynamic and Healthy Cells, Classes or Teams, Carl George et al., Kingdom Publishing, 2001.

Paradoxes of Group Life: Understanding Conflict, Paralysis and Movement in Group Dynamics, Kenwyn K. Smith and David N. Berg, Jossey Bass Wiley, 1998.

1h – General leadership qualities

Church Leadership, Lawrence O. Richards and Clyde Hoeldtke, Ministry Resources Library, 1980.

Courageous Leadership, Bill Hybels, Zondervan, 2002; advice on leadership from the leader of the Willow Creek Church, Chicago, USA.

Leaders on Leadership, George Barna (ed.), Regal, 1997.

Leadership, Philip Greenslade, Marshalls, 1984.

Leadership by the Book, Ken Blanchard, Bill Hybels and Phil Hodges, Abingdon, 1996.

The Servant Leader, Ken Blanchard, J. Countryman Books, 2003.
Spiritual Leadership, J. Oswald Sanders, Moody Publications, 1994.
Transforming Leadership, Richard Higginson, SPCK, 1996.
21 Indispensable Qualities of a Leader, John C. Maxwell, Thomas Nelson, 1999.
Understanding Leadership, Tom Marshall, Sovereign World, 1991.

1i – Leadership from specific viewpoints

At your Service, John Leach and Mark Earey, CPAS; a guide to planning services.
Booked Out, Chris Kay, Don Smith, Jenny Richardson and Roy Dorey, CPAS; leadership responding to a 'non-book' challenge.
Congregation: Stories and Structures, James Hopewell, SCM Press, 1988; sociological understanding of congregations.
Ecclesiastical Law, Mark Hill, Oxford University Press, 2001; a comprehensive reference on Church of England Law.
In the Name of Jesus: Reflections on Christian Leadership, Henry Nouwen, Crossroad/Herder & Herder, 1993; a theological look at leadership.
Leading your Church to Growth, C. Peter Wagner, MARC, 1984; leadership from the Church Growth perspective.
Power and the Church: Ecclesiology in an Age of Transition, Martyn Percy, Continuum, 1998; the role of power in the church.
Resident Aliens, Stanley Hauerwas, Abingdon Press, 1989; a cultural view on Christian ministry.
Understanding Congregations, Malcolm Grundy, Mowbray, 1998; a study of how congregations are structured.
What They Don't Teach You at Theological College, Malcolm Grundy, Canterbury Press, 2003; practical helps for ministry.

1j – Series with titles on aspects of leadership

Encounters on the Edge; a series of booklets on church planting produced by The Sheffield Centre (Church Army) 50, Cavendish Street, Sheffield s3 7RZ (0114 272 7451).
Grove Booklets; Grove Books produce an ongoing series of booklets on all aspects of ministry and church life: Grove Books, Ridley Hall Road, Cambridge CB3 9HU (01223 464748).
Some useful titles are:

Approaches to Spiritual Direction
Finding Support in Ministry

Leadership Teams: Clergy and Lay Leadership in the Local Church
Minister – Love Thyself: Sustaining Healthy Ministry
Ministry Leadership Teams: Theory and Practice in Effective Collaborative Ministry
Yes Manager: Management in the Local Church

1k – *Other resources*

Church Leadership (CPAS); a resource pack covering all areas of church leadership.

Directory of Anglican training institutions: www.societies.anglican. org/aocm/directory

Retreats: The Retreat Association, The Central Hall, 256 Bermondsey Street, London SE1 3UJ (020 7357 7736); lists the programmes of all retreat centres.

UK Christian Bookshops Directory www.ukcbd.co.uk

UK Christian Handbook: Christian Research, Vision Building, 4 Footscray Road, Eltham, London SE9 2TZ (020 8294 1989). This contains comprehensive listings of all Christian resources and is available in most public libraries.

UK Directory of Bible Colleges: www.members.truepath.com /biblecolleges/directory

(All ministry training institutions and Bible colleges have libraries; most are willing for ministers to use them with permission and a small fee.)

1l – *Articles in journals*

By their nature journals are periodicals and so relevant articles will appear from time to time. Listed here are some recent articles that may be useful.

'Do Moving Ministers Move Congregations? Rational Choice Theory and Methodist Ministerial Itinerancy', Philip Richter, *Religion* 32 (1), 2002: 39–50.

'The Fate of Anglican Clergy and the Class of '97: Some implications of the changing sociological profile of ordinands', Sophie Gilliat-Ray, *Journal of Contemporary Religion* 16 (2) 2001: 201–25.

'How Pastors Learn the Politics of Ministry Practice', Robert W. Burns and Ronald M. Cervero, *Religious Education* 97 (4) 2002: 304ff.

The following articles from secular journals may prove useful.

'Designing Effective Leadership Interventions: A Case Study of Vocational Education and Training', Ian Falk, *Leadership and Organization Development Journal* 24 (4) 2003: 193–203.

'Emergent Leaders as Managers of Group Emotion', Anthony T. Pescosolido, *The Leadership Quarterly* 13 (5) 2002: 583–99.

'How to Manage Unpaid Volunteers in Organisations', Sunney Shin and Brian H. Kleiner, *Management Research News* 26 (2) 2003: 63–71.

'In Times of Turmoil: Great Leaders Emerge', Glen W. Thomas, *Leadership* 32 (5) 2003: 8–10.

'Keeping the "Dream" in Mind is Indispensable for Successful Leadership', Yoshio Kando, *Managing Service Quality* 12 (3) 2002: 146–50.

'Leadership Development for Learning Organizations', Vana Prewitt, *Leadership and Organization Development Journal* 24 (2) 2002: 58–61.

'The Many Faces of Emotional Leadership', Ronald H. Humphrey, *The Leadership Quarterly* 13 (5) 2002: 493–504.

'A Method for Trainers to Examine Teaching Feedback', James Poon and Teng Fatt, *Management Research News* 26 (1) 2003: 64–8.

'The Origins of Vision – Charismatic Versus Ideological Leadership', Jill M. Strange and Michael D. Mumford, *The Leadership Quarterly* 13 (4) 2002: 343–77.

'A Review of Servant Leadership Attributes: Developing a Practical Model', Robert F. Russell and A. Gregory Stone, *Leadership and Organization Development Journal* 23 (2) 2002: 145–57.

'Spiritual and Religious Diversity in the Workplace', Douglas A. Hicks, *The Leadership Quarterly* 13 (4) 2002: 379–96.

1k – Journals

The journals listed here are all more or less scholarly in tone. More popular magazines with relevance to aspects of leadership are available but are not given here. Journals can be subscribed to, or, alternatively, particular ones may be available in theological college libraries.

Anvil: The Vicarage, Belle Vue Road, Ashbourne, Derbyshire DE6 1AT; Evangelical Anglican journal.

British Journal of Theological Education: Sheffield Academic Press, Mansion House, 19 Kingfield Road, Sheffield S11 9AS (0114 255 4433).

Contact: Business Manager, Newhaven, Junction Road, Lightwater, Surrey GU18 5TQ; interdisciplinary journal of pastoral studies.

Epworth Review: 20 Ivatt Way, Peterborough PE3 7PG (01733 332202).

European Journal of Theology: Paternoster Periodicals, PO Box 300, Carlisle CA3 0QS (01228 512512).

Evangelical Review of Theology: Paternoster.

Expository Times: Continuum International, 11 Tower Building, York Road, London SE1 7NX (020 7922 0923); established journal of Bible exposition.

Heythrop Journal: Heythrop College, Kensington Square, London W8 5HQ (020 7795 6600); Roman Catholic theological journal.

Journal for the Study of the New Testament: Sheffield Academic Press.

Journal for the Study of the Old Testament: Sheffield Academic Press.

Journal of Contemporary Religion: Carfax Publishing, Taylor & Francis Ltd, Rankine Road, Basingstoke, Hants RG24 8PR; journal with a sociological slant on all aspects of religion.

Journal of Education and Christian Belief: Paternoster.

Journal of Feminist Studies in Religion: Sheffield Academic Press.

Journal of Pentecostal Theology: Sheffield Academic Press.

Ministerial Formation: PO Box 2100, 150 route de Ferney, 1211 Geneva 2, Switzerland; World Council of Churches journal.

Modern Believing: Modern Churchpeople's Union, 25 Birch Grove, London W3 9SP (020 8932 4379); liberal view of theology and church life.

New Testament Studies: Theology Faculty Centre, 41 St Giles, Oxford OX1 3LW (01865 270791).

Priest and People: Blackfriars, 64 St Giles, Oxford OX1 3LY (01865 514845).

Review of Theological Literature: Continuum.

The Reader: Church House, Great Smith Street, London SW1P 3NZ (020 7898 1415); journal for Readers in the Church of England.

Scottish Bulletin of Evangelical Theology: 17 Claremont Park, Edinburgh EH6 7PJ (0131 554 1206).

Scottish Journal of Theology: Continuum.

Studies in Christian Ethics: Continuum.

Themelios: Carl Truman (editor), Westminster Theological Seminary, Chestnut Hill, PO Box 27009, Philadelphia, PA 19118, USA; journal of theological and religious studies.

Theology: SPCK, Holy Trinity Church, Marylebone Road, London NW1 4DU (020 7643 0382).

Theology and Sexuality: Sheffield Academic Press.

Transformation: PO Box 70, Oxford OX2 6HB; journal of the Oxford Centre for Mission Studies.

Section 2 – Centres for leadership study and training

As with the writings, so with the centres for study, the variety and breadth available is enormous. The centres listed here are institutions of academic learning and resources offering material of a good standard. There are, of course numerous retreat centres, conference centres and church-based learning activities that are not listed here. Locally available resources can be discovered through denominational centres, Christian bookshops and locally produced news sheets. The publication *Retreat* (listed above) is particularly useful for discovering the availability of one-off courses in leadership and management at retreat and conference centres.

2a – Denominational ministerial training colleges

Sections 2a and 2b contain colleges offering courses validated by a British or Irish University unless otherwise stated. Most offer postgraduate courses and research to suit the individual's requirements. Many colleges accept students from different denominations.

Anglican

Church of Ireland Theological College, Braemor Park, Dublin D14 (01492 3506).

College of the Resurrection, Mirfield, West Yorks WF14 0BW (01924 494318).

Cranmer Hall (St John's College), 3 South Bailey, Durham DH1 3RJ (0191 374 3579).

Oak Hill College, Chase Side, Southgate, London N14 4PS (020 8449 0467).

Ridley Hall, Cambridge CB3 9HG (01223 741080).

Ripon College, Cuddesdon, Oxford OX44 9EX (01865 877400).

St Chad's College, 18 North Bailey, Durham DH1 3RH (0191 374 3364).

St John's College, Bramcote, Nottingham NG9 3DS (0115 925 1114).

St Stephen's House, 16 Marsden Street, Oxford OX1 1JX (01865 247874).

Theological Institute of the Scottish Episcopal Church, Old Coates House, 35 Manor Place, Edinburgh EH3 7EB (0131 220 2272).

Trinity College, Carmarthen SA31 3EP (01267 676767).

Trinity College, Stoke Hill, Bristol BS9 1JP (0117 968 2803).

Westcott House, Jesus Lane, Cambridge CB5 8BP (01223 741000).

Wilson Carlile College of Evangelism (Church Army), 50 Cavendish Street, Sheffield S3 7RZ (0114 278 7020).

Wycliffe Hall, 54 Banbury Road, Oxford OX2 6PW (01865 274200).

Apostolic Church

Apostolic Church Training School, Bryn Road, Penygroes, Llanelli SA14 7PH (01269 832069).

Assemblies of God

Mattersey Hall, Mattersey, Doncaster DN10 5HD (01777 817663).

Baptist

Bristol Baptist College, The Promenade, Clifton Down, Bristol BS8 3NJ (0117 946 7050).

Irish Baptist College, 67 Sandown Road, Belfast BT5 6GU (028 9047 1908).

North Wales Baptist College, Ffriddoedd Road, Bangor LL57 2EH (01248 382079).

Regents Park Baptist College, Pusey Street, Oxford OX1 2LB (01865 288120).

South Wales Baptist College, 54 Richmond Road, Cardiff CF2 3UR (029 2025 6066).

Spurgeon's College, 189 South Norwood Hill, London SE25 6DJ (020 8653 0850).

Church of the Nazarene (Wesleyan Holiness)

Nazarene Theological College, Dene Road, Didsbury, Manchester M20 2GU (0161 445 3063).

Congregational

Scottish Congregational College, 20 Inverleith Terrace, Edinburgh EH3 5NS (0131 315 3595).

Elim Pentecostal

Regents College, London Road, Nantwich, Cheshire CW5 6BR (01270 610800).

Free Presbyterian

Whitefield College of the Bible and Theological Hall of the Free Presbyterian Church of Ulster, 117 Banbridge Road, Gilford, Craigavon BT63 6DL (028 4066 2232).

Interdenominational

Northern College (Methodist, Baptist, URC), Luther King House, Brighton Grove, Rusholme, Manchester M14 5JP (0161 249 6404).

The Queen's Foundation of Ecumenical Theological Training (Anglican, Methodist, URC), Somerset Road, Edgbaston, Birmingham B15 2QH (0121 454 1527).

St Michael's College (Anglican, Methodist, URC), Llandaff, Cardiff CF5 2YJ (029 2056 3379). 'Centre for Ministry Studies' fosters research related to ministry.

Selly Oak Colleges, Central House, 998 Bristol Road, Birmingham B29 6LQ (0121 472 4231).

Centre for Black and White Christian Partnership
Crowther Hall (Church Missionary Society)
Responding to Conflict (For research and study of conflict resolution)
United College of the Ascension (United Society for the Propagation of the Gospel and Methodism)
Westhill (University of Birmingham, School of Education)

Lutheran

Westfield House, 30 Huntingdon Road, Cambridge CB3 0HH (01223 354331).

Methodist

Cliff College, Calver, Sheffield S32 3XG (01246 582321); evangelism studies.

Edgehill College, 9 Lennoxvale, Malone Road, Belfast BT9 5BY (028 9066 5870).

Urban Theology Unit, 210 Abbeyfield Road, Sheffield S4 7AZ (0114 243 5342); ministerial training and postgraduate research centred on urban and liberation theology studies; validated by the University of Birmingham.

Wesley College, College Park Drive, Henbury Road, Bristol BS10 7QD (0117 959 1200).

Wesley House, Jesus Lane, Cambridge CB5 8BJ (01223 741053).

Pentecostal

International Bible Training Institute, Hook Place, Cuckfield Road, Burgess Hill RH15 8RF (01444 233173).

Presbyterian

Christ's College (Church of Scotland), 25 High Street, Aberdeen AB24 3EE (01244 272138).

Reformed Theological College, 98 Lisburn Road, Belfast BT9 6AG (028 9066 0689).

Union Theological College, 108 Botanic Avenue, Belfast BT7 1JT (028 9020 5080).

United Theological College (Church of Wales), Aberystwyth SY23 2LT (01970 272380).

Roman Catholic

Allen Hall, 28 Beaufort Street, Chelsea, London SW3 5AA (020 7351 1296).

Heythrop College (University of London), Kensington Square, London W8 5HQ (020 7795 6600).

Institute of St Anselm, Edgar Road, Cliftonville, Margate CT9 2EU (01843 234700).

Margaret Beaufort Institute of Theology, 12 Grange Road, Cambridge CB3 9DX (01223 741039).

St John's College, Wonersh, Guildford GU5 0QX (01483 892217).

St Mary's Seminary, Oscott College, Chester Road, Sutton Coldfield B73 5AA (0121 321 5000).

St Mary's Strawberry Hill, Department of Theology and Religious Studies, Waldegrave Road, Twickenham TW1 4SX (020 8240 4198).

Scotus College, 2 Chesters Road, Bearsden, Glasgow G61 4AG (0141 942 8384).

Ushaw College, Durham DH7 9RH (0191 373 8510).

Salvation Army

William Booth Memorial College, Denmark Hill, London SE5 8BQ (020 7326 2700).

Seventh Day Adventist

Newbold College, St Mark's Road, Binfield, Bracknell RG42 4AN (01344 407407).

United Reformed Church

Mansfield College (with Congregational Church), Mansfield Road, Oxford OX1 3TF (01865 270988).

Westminster College, Madingly Road, Cambridge CB3 0BJ (01223 741084).

2b – Non-denominational theological colleges

Adelaide College, 3 Nineyard Street, Saltcoats, Ayrshire KA21 5HS (01294 463911).

All Nations Christian College, Easneye, Ware, Herts SG12 8LX (01269 843791).

Belfast Bible College, Glenburn House, Glenburn Road, Dunmury, Belfast BT17 9JP (028 9030 1551).

Birmingham Christian College (Associate of Selly Oak Colleges), 54 Weoley Park Road, Selly Oak, Birmingham B29 6RB (0121 472 0726).

Evangelical College of Wales, Bryntirion House, Bridgend CF31 4DX (01656 645411).

Highland Theological College, High Street, Dingwall, Ross-shire IV15 9HA (01349 780000).

International Christian College, 110 St James Road, Glasgow G4 0PS (0141 552 4040).

London Bible College, Green Lane, Northwood HA6 2UW (01923 456000).

Open Theological College, University of Gloucestershire, Francis Close Hall, Swindon Road, Cheltenham GL50 4AZ (01242 532 837); no postgraduate degrees.

Redcliffe College, Wootton House, Horton Road, Gloucester GL1 3PT (01452 308097).

South London Bible College, Lomond Grove, Camberwell, London SE5 7HN (020 7703 9999); study validated by Carolina University of Theology, USA.

2c – Part-time training courses

Carlisle and Blackburn Diocesan Training Institution, Church House, West Walls, Carlisle CA3 8UE (01228 522573); Anglican, Methodist, URC.

Cranmer Memorial Bible College, PO Box 20, Bexhill-on-Sea TN40 2ZH (01424 734345); Reformed Protestant.

East Anglian Ministerial Training Course, 5 Pound Hill, Cambridge CB3 0AE (01223 741026); Anglican, Methodist, URC.

East Midland Ministry Training Course, Room C90, School of Continuing Education, University of Nottingham, Jubilee Campus, Nottingham NG8 1BB (0115 951 4854); interdenominational.

Free Church College, 15 North Bank Street, The Mound, Edinburgh EH1 2LS (0131 226 5286); Free Church of Scotland.

Missionary Institute, Halcombe House, The Ridgeway, Mill Hill, London NW7 4HY (020 8906 1893); Roman Catholic – validated by University of Leuvan, Belgium and Middlesex University.

Monmouth Ordination Course, The Rectory, 19 Main Road, Portskewitt, Caldicot NP26 5SG (01291 420313); Church in Wales (Anglican).

North East Oecumenical Course, Ushaw College, Durham DH7 9RH (0191 373 7600); Anglican, Methodist, URC.

North Thames Ministerial Training Course, Chase Side, Southgate, London N14 4PS (020 8364 9442); Anglican, Methodist, URC.

St Albans & Oxford Ministry Course, Church House, North Hinksey, Oxford OX2 0NB (01865 208260); Anglican, Methodist, URC.

Sarum College, 19 The Close, Salisbury SP1 2EE (01722 424800); Interdenominational.

South East Institute for Theological Education, Ground Floor, Sun Pier House, Medway Street, Chatham ME4 4HF (01634 846683); Anglican, Methodist, URC.

South West Ministry Training Course, North Petherwin, Launceston PL15 8LW (01566 785545); Anglican, Methodist, URC.

Southern Theological Education and Training Scheme, 19 The Close, Salisbury SP1 2EE (01722 424820); Anglican, Methodist, URC.

West Midlands Ministry Training Course, The Queens Foundation (see section 2a above).

West of England Ministry Training Course, 7c College Green, Gloucester GL1 2CX (01452 300494); Anglican, Methodist, URC.

Woodbrooke Quaker Study Centre, 1046 Bristol Road, Selly Oak, Birmingham B29 6CJ (0121 472 5171).

2d – Universities offering graduate and postgraduate study in religious studies or related subjects

The courses are many and varied and those interested are advised to contact the university for more information.

Aberdeen 01224 273504
Bath Spa 01225 875875
Birmingham 0121 414 5491
Bishop Grossgate College 01522 527347
Bradford 01274 433333
Brighton 01273 600900
Bristol 0117 928 9000
Cambridge 01223 333308
Canterbury (Christ Church College) 01227 782900
Cardiff 0290 874404
Chester College (Univ. of Liverpool) 01244 375444
Chichester Univ. College (Univ. of Southampton) 01243 816002
Durham 0191 334 2000
Edinburgh 0131 650 4360
Exeter 01392 263035
Glasgow 0141 330 4575
Gloucestershire 01242 532825
Greenwich 0800 005006
Heythrop College (Univ. of London) 020 7795 6600
Highlands (Millennium Institute) 01463 279000
Hull 01482 466100
Kent 01227 827272
King Alfred's, Winchester 01962 827234
King's College (Univ. of London) 020 7848 2339
Lancaster 01524 65201
Leeds 0113 343 3999
Leeds, Trinity and All Saints 0113 283 7123
Leo Beck College (Centre for Jewish Education) 020 834 95605
Liverpool Hope 0151 291 3295
Manchester 0161 275 2077
Manchester Metropolitan 0161 247 2000
Newcastle-upon-Tyne 0191 222 5594
Newman College of Higher Education 0121 476 1181
Nottingham 0115 951 6565
Oxford 01865 288000
Oxford Brookes 01865 483040
Queen's (Belfast) 028 9033 5081

Roehampton (Univ. of Surrey) 020 8392 3232
St Andrews 01334 462150
St Mark and St John (Univ. of Exeter) 01752 636890
St Martin's College (Univ. of Lancaster) 01524 384444
St Mary's College (Univ. of Surrey) 020 8240 4029
St Mary's University College (Queen's Belfast) 028 9032 7678
School of Oriental and African Studies (Univ. of London) 020 7074 5106
Sheffield 0114 222 2000
Stirling 01786 467044
Stranmillis University College (Queen's Belfast) 028 9038 1271
Trinity Carmarthen 01267 676767
University College (Univ. of London) 020 7679 3000
Wales (Bangor) 01248 382016
Wales (Lampeter) 01570 422351
Wales (Newport) 01633 432432
Wolverhampton 01902 321000
York St John (Univ. of Leeds) 01904 624624

2e – Institutions that offer training or resources

These often have a particular theological or sociological emphasis.

All Soul's Training, 2 All Soul's Place, London w1b 3db (020 7580 3522); lay training.

Archbishop's Examination in Theology (Lambeth Diploma), 3 The College, Durham dh1 3eq (0191 384 2415); theological study by examination, syllabus or thesis.

Association of Centres of Adult Theological Education, The Old Deanery, Wells ba5 2ug (01749 670777); British Journal of Theological Education.

Bamardi Management & Training; 10 Epping Close, Reading rg1 7yd (0118 939 4900); management training for churches and charities.

Bible Society, Stonehill Green, Westlea, Swindon sn5 7dg (01793 418100); sponsors research into use of the Bible in mission and theology.

Bloxham Project, 29 Leicester Lane, Desford, Leicester le9 9jj (01455 824089); developing and resourcing spiritual education and pastoral care.

British Church Growth Association, Moggerhanger Park, Park Road, Moggerhanger, Bedford mk44 3rw (01767 641001).

Capernwray Bible School, Capernwray Hall, Carnforth la6 1ag (01524 733908); mission studies.

Cardiff Adult Christian Education Centre, City Church, Windsor Place, Cardiff CF16 3BZ (029 2022 5190); ecumenical study centre.

Cell UK, Highfield Oval, Harpenden AL5 4BX (01582 463232); resourcing and training for Cell Church leaders.

Centre for Islamic Studies, London Bible College, Green Lane, Northwood HA6 2UW (01923 456160); training and consultancy in Christian–Muslim relations.

Chillen Christian Training Programme, 175 Dashwood Avenue, High Wycombe HP12 3DB (01494 474788); training for Readers and leaders.

Christian Research, Vision Building, 4 Footscray Road, Eltham, London SE9 2TZ (020 8294 1989); management consultancy.

Clinical Theology Association, 39 Lyndon Road, Olton, Solihull B92 7RE (0121 707 8947); training in Christian pastoral care and counselling.

Cormack Consultancies, King's Gate, St Mary's Tower, Dunkeld PH8 0BJ (01350 728715); strategic consulting and training.

Cornhill Training Course, 140–148 Borough High Street, London SE1 1LB (020 7407 0562); training in lay church leadership.

Equip, Bawtry Hall, Bawtry, Doncaster DN10 6JH (01302 710027); courses and retreats on a variety of issues concerned with church leadership.

Evangelical Alliance – a full list of training institutions belonging to the Evangelical Alliance can be found at www.byfaith.co.uk Apart from those mentioned elsewhere in this list most are unaccredited and independently run.

Lincoln Theological Institute (University of Manchester), Department of Religions and Theology, University of Manchester, Oxford Road, Manchester M13 9PL (0161 275 3602); postgraduate research in religion and society.

MODEM (Managerial and Organisational Disciplines for the Enhancement of Ministry); MODEM CTBI Inter-Church House, 34 Lower Marsh, London SE1 7RL wwww.modem.uk.com

Moorlands Bible College, Sopley, Christchurch BH23 7AT (01425 672369); evangelical ministry studies.

Northern Cornhill Training Course, Christ Church Fulwood, Canterbury Road, Sheffield S10 3RT (0114 230 1911).

Overseas Council for Theological Education and Mission, 52 High Street, Thornbury, Bristol BS35 2AN (01454 281288); leadership training.

St Luke's College Foundation, Heathayne, Colyton, Devon EX24 6RS (01297 552281); grants for advancing higher and further education in theology and religious studies.

Scottish Churches Open College, 18 Inverleith Terrace, Edinburgh EH3 5NS (0131 311 4713); adult education in Scotland.

Unlock, 336a City Road, Sheffield S2 1GA (0114 276 2038); training and resources for churches in urban areas.

Urban Ministry and Theology Project, Newcastle East Deanery, Participation Building, Welbeck Road, Walker, Newcastle-upon-Tyne NE6 4JS (0191 262 1680); theological reflection and training in the context of social and economic regeneration.

2f – Religious educational resource centres and organisations

These offer a variety of resources and services for loan or purchase.

Administry, Mega Centre, Bernard Road, Sheffield S2 5BQ (0114 278 0090); resources for church administration.

Alban Institute, Suite 1250 West, 7315 Wisconsin Avenue, Bethesda, MD 20814, USA ((301) 718–4407); resources for theological education and reflection for churches.

Archdiocese of Southwark Christian Education Centre, 21 Tooting Bec Road, London SW17 8BS (020 8622 7684).

Bath & Wells Diocesan Educational Resource Centre, The Old Deanery, Wells BA5 2UG (01749 670777).

Birmingham Council for Christian Education, Carrs Lane Church Centre, Birmingham B4 7SX (0121 643 6603).

Bradford Diocese Resource Centre, Cathedral Hall, Stott Hill, Bradford BD1 4ET (01274 725958).

CARE (Christian Action Research & Education), 53 Romney Street, London SW1P 3RF (020 7233 0455); resourcing for Christian social and political action.

Carlisle Diocesan Religious Education Resource Centre, West Walls, Carlisle CA3 8UE (01228 538086).

Chelmsford Diocesan Resource Centre, 53 New Street, Chelmsford CM1 1AT (01245 294400).

Church Pastoral Aid Society, Athena Drive, Tachbrook Park, Warwick CV34 6NG (01926 458458); *Church Leadership Magazine* and resources.

Croydon Religious Education Resource Centre, The Crescent, Croydon CR0 2HN (020 8689 5343).

Gloucester Diocesan Religious Education Resource Centre, 9 College Green, Gloucester GL1 2LX (01452 385217).

Guildford Diocesan Education Centre, The Education Centre, The Cathedral, Stag Hill, Guildford GU2 7UP (01483 450423).

Independent Methodist Resource Centre, Flat Street, Pemberton, Wigan WN5 0DS (01942 223526).

Institute for Study of Christianity and Sexuality, Oxford House, Derbyshire Street, London E2 6HG (020 7739 1249).

London Institute for Contemporary Christianity, St. Peter's Church, Vere Street, London W1G 0DQ (020 7399 9555); resources and research into contemporary issues.

London Mennonite Centre, 14 Shepherds Hill, Highgate, London N6 5AQ (020 8340 8775).

National Christian Education Council, 1020 Bristol Road, Selly Oak, Birmingham B29 6LB (0121 472 4242).

North East Learning Resource Centre Ltd, Carter House, Pelaw Leazes Lane, Durham DH1 1TB (0191 375 0586).

The Olive Branch Christian Resources Centre, 5 Cleveland Rise, East Ogwell, Newton Abbot TQ12 6FF (01626 331436).

Ridley Hall Foundation, Ridley Hall, Cambridge CB3 9HG (01223 741080); relating Christian faith to business – seminars and publications.

St Albans Diocesan Education Centre, Hall Grove, Welwyn Garden City AL7 4PG (01707 332321).

St Asaph Diocesan Resource Centre, 20 Rhosnesni Lane, Wrexham LL12 7LY (01978 265967).

Sheffield Christian Education Council, Montgomery Hall, Surrey Street, Sheffield S1 2LG (0114 272 0455).

Welsh National Centre for Religious Education, University of Wales, Bangor, Normal Site, Bangor LL57 2PX (01248 382566).

York Religious Education Centre, University College of Ripon and St John, Lord Mayor's Walk, York YO31 7EX (01904 656771).

2g – Audio-visual resource suppliers

In addition to those listed above, most of which supply videos and cassettes.

Audio Visual Ministries, PO Box 1, Newcastle, Co Down BT33 0DU (028 4376 8007).

Christian Foundation Publications, 45 Appleton Road, Hale, Altrincham WA15 9LP (0161 205 1977).

Christian Resources Project, 14 Lipson Road, Plymouth PL4 8PW (01752 224012).

Kensington Church Videos, PO Box 8207, London W4 1WQ.

Training Image Resource, Mill House, Church Road, Bickerstaffe, Ormskirk L39 0EB (01695 724035); training and support in audio-visual use.

2h – On-line institutions and resource centres

There are many on-line training institutions, which vary widely in their style and provenance. These have not been verified as to the quality of their output or the recognition of their qualifications. Some examples are given here, others may be found by searching the World Wide Web.

> www.christianleadershipcenter.org Christian Leadership Center.
> www.churchlink.com.au Church Link. Resources for ministry and training.
> www.cl-academy.com Christian Leadership Academy.
> www.clm.org Christian Leadership Ministries. A branch of Campus Crusade for Christ concentrating on mission to university professors, but may have some resources on Christian leadership.
> www.cluonline.com Christian Leadership University.
> www.congregationalresources.org The resource site created by the Alban Institute (see above) and the Indianapolis Center for Congregations.
> www.horeb.pcusa.org Christian Education and Leadership Development.
> www.iclnet.org The Internet Christian Library. Christian books online.
> www.iscl.org Institute for Strategic Christian Leadership.
> www.tamcoinc.com Leadership Resources and Counselling.
> www.teal.org.uk Christian Leadership World – leadership training material.
> www.tli.org The Leadership Institute. A Leadership programme based in the International Study Centre, Canterbury and St John's College, Durham, led by Anglican clergy – 'To advance the education of the Anglican Communion worldwide through courses in leadership and Christian management.'

Conclusion

The degree to which a parish priest or local church minister turns herself or himself into a manager is really up to them. In current circumstances, however, some managerial skills are essential. At the very least, the legal requirements for the handling of money, the care of children and the civil responsibilities of marriage and burial have to be adhered to. Beyond that, the proper care of the people demands that good management of personnel, plant and resources is essential for a well-run organisation. Church leaders are, by the very nature of their jobs, managers. They make decisions, organise work and delegate responsibility. Therefore the use of all relevant and available resources not only makes sense but also is incumbent upon the diligent leader. This database should form the basis for a resource file for any church leader; the entries can be used directly, or, in the case of internet sites, links can be followed to many other useful organisations. It is hoped that this resource will be an aid for the 'administration of God's grace' (Ephesians 3.2) in all the churches.

Notes

1. The Archbishop of York and the Cardinal Archbishop of Westminster in the foreword to Peter F. Rudge, *Management in the Church*, Maidenhead, McGraw-Hill, 1976, p. ix.
2. Peter Rudge, at the time of writing, had been an Anglican clergyman, a lecturer in administration at Canberra College of Advanced Education and then Senior Consultant for the Christian Organisations Research and Advisory Trust.
3. The Turnbull Report, *Working as One Body*, London, Church House Publishing, 1995. Not to be confused with the Turnbull Report on Internal Company Controls (1999).
4. G. R. Evans and Martyn Percy, *Managing the Church? Order and Organization in a Secular Age*, Sheffield, Sheffield Academic Press, 2000.
5. Evans and Percy, 'The Church: Management or Service?', *Managing the Church?*, p. 251.
6. Evans and Percy, 'Introduction', *Managing the Church?*, p. 9.
7. Evans and Percy, 'The Church: Management or Service?', *Managing the Church?*, p. 253.

19 A review of leadership literature and leadership development centres from The Centre for Leadership Studies, Exeter University

LINDA DAWSON

When we at the Centre for Leadership Studies were invited to provide guidance for those interested in learning more, we looked for what would be most helpful in the context of creative church leadership. Guidance had to be relevant, of practical utility and represent a range of views and possibilities. Our first step was to embark on an extensive process of consultation. Recommendations were sought, and freely given, from those with a passion for and expertise in leadership from countries as varied in their cultural tradition as India, Sweden, France and Germany. The Anglo-Saxon concept of leadership was represented by views from the United States and Australia as well as the UK. Those consulted included academics, specialists in the field of leadership development, the world of business and, most important-ly of all, from men and women who every day in their professional, business and personal lives practise the art and craft of leadership.

Exeter's choice of key writings

From these recommendations – more than 250 books and articles – the Centre for Leadership Studies made a final choice of 11. In choosing these, the Centre drew on its expertise at the leading edge of contem-porary research, study and teaching about leadership, and on its prac-tical experience of developing leaders in international corporations and non-governmental organisations, large and small, from across the world.

The 11 selected texts

John Adair, *The Inspirational Leader: How to Motivate, Encourage & Achieve Success*, Kogan Page, 2003; ISBN 0 7494 4046 5.

Joseph Badaracco, *Leading Quietly: An Unorthodox Guide to Doing the Right Thing*, Harvard Business School Press, 2002; ISBN 1 57851 4878.

Warren Bennis, *On Becoming a Leader*, Century Business, 1992; ISBN 0 7126 9890 6.

Jim Collins, *From Good to Great*, Random House, 2001; ISBN 0 7126 8709 0.

David L . Cooperrider and Suresh Srivastva, *Appreciative Inquiry into Organisational Life* (23/05/03) (www.appreciative-inquiry.org).

Daniel Goleman, *Emotional Intelligence: Why It Can Matter More Than IQ*, Bloomsbury Publishing, 1996; ISBN 0 7475 2830 6.

Robert K. Greenleaf, *Servant Leadership: A Journey into the Nature of Legitimate Power and Greatness*, Paulist Press, 2002; ISBN 0 80910554 3.

John Kotter, 'Leading Change: Why Transformation Efforts Fail', *Harvard Business Review*, March/April 1995.

Joseph A. Raelin, *Creating Leaderful Organisations: How to Bring Out Leadership in Everyone*, Berrett-Koehler, 2003; ISBN 157675 233 x.

Jeffrey A. Sonnenfeld (ed.), *Concepts of Leadership*, Dartmouth Publishing, 1995; ISBN 1 855521 546 2.

Margaret Wheatley, *Leadership and the New Science: Discovering Order in a Chaotic World*, Berrett-Koehler, 1999, 2nd edn; ISBN 157675 119 8.

All are currently (July 2003) available through libraries, bookshops – real and virtual – or on accessible web sites. Each is intellectually engaging, occasionally difficult, and each encourages reflection on your past and present experience and practice of leading and being led.

Recommendations

The recommendations, which encourage both personal reflection and practical development in leadership, are divided into four parts. *Part 1* summarises books and articles which address the *personal leadership endeavour*, the predicament that each of us faces when we wish to extend our repertoire of leadership behaviours. *Part 2* recommends texts that explore the *leadership endeavour of organisations,* a considera-tion of the options available when concern is focused on the leader-ship capacity of an organisation in its whole. *Part 3* answers the question *'where next'* and points readers towards some of the better options for the development of leaders and leadership, places where leadership is explored and developed with the support of experienced teachers, guides and practitioners. *Part 4* gives the *'longlist'*, those books and articles of acknowledged value and merit that came close to inclusion in our final selection. We at the Centre for Leadership Studies would like to share these with you too.

Part 1: The personal leadership endeavour

John Adair, *The Inspirational Leader: How to Motivate Encourage and Achieve Success*

John Adair – co-editor of this book – is the author of many books and articles about leadership. *The Inspirational Leader* investigates a fundamental question: why it is that one person emerges and is accepted as a leader in a group rather than anyone else. His investigation focuses on four themes: what you are, what you know, what you do, and what you believe.

Theme 1: what you are

A leader, suggests Adair, demonstrates the qualities of a good performer in his or her profession, together with certain generic qualities. These include integrity, moral courage, a combination of toughness and fairness, warmth, humility and, above all, enthusiasm.

Theme 2: what you know

Knowledge is what gives leaders their authority. It is broader than professional expertise, for it includes an understanding of human nature, and knowing how to enthuse others.

Theme 3: what you do

Adair next describes the three overlapping needs of every organisation. These are to achieve the common task, to be held together as a team, and those needs personal to each individual. To demonstrate the interactive nature of these needs, Adair draws on his famous three-circle diagram (see Figure 19.1).

Adair is explicit: being a manager is not the same as being a leader.

Figure 19.1

Some situations demand managers and others leaders. The critical factor is change. Change creates a need for leaders: leaders, argues Adair, bring about change.

Theme 4: what you believe

'The Uses of Spirit' is a pivotal chapter, for it is from here that Adair explores the impact of values, what we believe, on the nature of leadership. He likens people to a four-engined aircraft, each engine in turn representing the body, mind, heart and spirit. The spirit is dynamic, each individual possesses it, and we also share it. From this comes inspiration. This leads Adair to suggest that there may be a higher spirit that inspires us to be creative, that guides and strengthens us.

Leaders answer the question 'why' in a way that convinces the intellect and engages the spirit, for it is purpose that gives the task value, the meaning that our spirit seeks. The values of goodness, truth and beauty inspire the spirit.

Above all, great leaders have what Adair terms strategic hopefulness, 'that faith in the inevitable victory of the good'. The greatest are those that face grave difficulties yet stay true to their values, and never relinquish their hold on strategic hopefulness.

Warren Bennis, *On Becoming a Leader*

This book explores the theme of leadership from within. Leaders, says Bennis, are people who are able to express themselves fully: 'they know who they are, what their strengths and weaknesses are, and how to fully deploy their strengths and compensate for their weaknesses'.

On Becoming a Leader is an examination of the three hows: how people become leaders, how they lead, and how organisations encourage or discourage potential leaders. His first how – how people become leaders – suggests that leaders are made, not born, and that this making comes from within. Leaders continue to grow and develop throughout life. They pay attention to their inner voice. But their most crucial and defining characteristic is concern with guiding purpose, an overarching vision, supplemented with passion, integrity, curiosity and daring.

From this essential inner core, Bennis goes on to answer his second how – how successful leaders lead. Effective leaders inspire through trust. It is impossible to lead unless someone is willing to follow. Through their ability to get people alongside, they change the culture of their organisations and make their guiding purpose real. He observes that there are four ingredients that generate and sustain trust:

- Constancy: leaders don't create surprises for the group
- Congruity: what they say is what they do
- Reliability: leaders are there when it matters
- Integrity: leaders keep their promises

And finally, *On Becoming a Leader* turns to the third how – how organisations encourage leadership. As leaders are made through experience, what is required is to provide opportunities for experience, learning and growth. Becoming a leader is simply becoming yourself.

John P. Kotter, *'Leading Change: Why Transformation Efforts Fail'*

On Becoming a Leader is an exploration of the many aspects of leadership, of which leading change is one. John Kotter's article in the *Harvard Business Review* of March/April 1995, 'Leading Change: Why Transformation Efforts Fail', together with his later book of the same name, entirely focused on the problem of what is needed to embed fundamental change. Although written from the negative, 'why transformation efforts *fail*', Kotter's article succinctly describes eight steps to transformation. These are:

Step 1 Establish a sense of urgency
Step 2 Form a powerful guiding coalition
Step 3 Create a vision
Step 4 Communicate a vision
Step 5 Empower others to act on the vision
Step 6 Plan for and create short term wins

Step 7 Consolidate improvements and produce still more change
Step 8 Institutionalise new approaches

Kotter observes that over half of the companies he followed fail at
Step 1. It is hard to shift people from their comfort zones. Those
responsible for the transformation overestimate their success in
communicating urgency. They may be overwhelmed by the risks.

Companies that fail at Step 2 underestimate the power of the status
quo. Change programmes that don't create a powerful coalition will
find that opposition unites to halt change. It is at Step 3 that Kotter
links most clearly with the two preceding authors, Adair and Bennis.
Step 3 introduces Vision, the need to have one, and to communicate it.
He gives a rule of thumb – 'if you can't communicate the vision to
someone in five minutes or less and get a reaction that signifies both
understanding and interest, you are not yet done'.

A communicated and reinforced vision is fundamental to success.
When there is complex, risky and uncertain change ahead, the unexpected happens. A vision of the change and what it is to achieve
reduces the number of mistakes. Fewer mistakes can make the difference between success and failure.

Daniel Goleman, *Emotional Intelligence: Why It Can Matter More Than IQ*

There is a host of literature on managing and improving oneself and
one's relationships. One of the earliest writers on this theme was
Thomas à Kempis in *Imitation of Christ*. For a more contemporary and
populist approach, take a look at Daniel Goleman's *Emotional
Intelligence: Why It Can Matter More Than IQ*. Goleman defines
emotional intelligence to include self-control, zeal, persistence and
the ability to motivate oneself.

There is only one specific reference to leadership – 'Leadership is
not domination, but the art of persuading people to work towards a
common goal.' For all that, his focus on empathy, developed through
self-awareness, self-control, social awareness and social skill has
much that may be of interest to leaders and managers alike.

Goleman contrasts the emotionally intelligent way of working with
the emotionally unintelligent. He uses three common work situations
to contrast the two different approaches – giving negative feedback,
networking and dealing with diversity. He predicts that emotional
intelligence in knowledge-based organisations will become increasingly important – in teamwork, in cooperating with one another, and
in helping people work together more effectively.

And like each of the authors previously discussed, he believes that these things can be taught, giving everyone the opportunity to make best use of their talents.

Joseph Badaracco, *Leading Quietly: An Unorthodox Guide to Doing the Right Thing*

The last book to be reviewed in this section is Joseph Badaracco's *Leading Quietly: An Unorthodox Guide to Doing the Right Thing*. It offers a counterbalance to a prevailing assumption that leadership is synonymous with being a hero. Badaracco takes the contrary view, that the most effective leaders are ordinary, unassuming men and women who possess three quiet virtues – modesty, restraint and tenacity. These quiet virtues are not reserved for special people or extraordinary events.

Badaracco argues that the heroic view of leadership looks at people as a pyramid. On the summit are the heroes, people with strong values who set a compelling example. At the bottom are life's bystanders. In the middle is the overwhelming majority of humanity, people who face life's ordinary everyday events and problems. In the heroic version, they are left in limbo. In reality, hard choices are interwoven with everyday life. Everyone faces difficult, ethical challenges.

Leading Quietly is a user's manual, each chapter presenting pragmatic and specific guidelines that quiet leaders follow when facing hard choices. Some situations call for direct, forceful action, and the quiet leader identifies these and acts accordingly. What usually makes the difference, however, is careful, thoughtful and practical effort by people working far from the spotlight.

> This approach to leadership is easy to misunderstand. It doesn't excite or thrill. It doesn't provide story lines for television dramas . . . [it] shows how – day after day, through countless, small, often unseen efforts – quiet leaders make the world a better place.

Part 2: The organisation's leadership endeavour

This second part of the chapter addresses the question of how organisations develop the collaborative adroitness needed for leadership to be effective. For those who believe that leaders are born, not made, there is little value in creating an environment in which leadership can flourish everywhere. If the focus is on a few, why divert organisational time and money from other priorities. To quote Nancy Badore, former Head of Executive Business Development at Ford Motors in the US, you have to decide whether to focus on the 'critical few or the critical many'.

So, take the alternative view – that almost all of us face situations that require leadership capacity, that almost all of us have leadership talent latent within, that leaders are made, not born, that leadership comes in many guises and styles, and that leadership does make a difference – then developing leaders and the capacity for leadership becomes a critical organisational priority. The next five books in our selection explore how organisations might improve their capacity for leadership.

Margaret Wheatley, *Leadership and the New Science*

In *Leadership and the New Science*, Margaret Wheatley works with an extended metaphor of science to business. With an exploration of theories and discoveries in biology, chemistry and physics, she is alert to the possibility of challenge to our view of the organisations inside which we work. Wheatley encourages us to consider that science – especially that of quantum physics, self-organising systems and chaos theory – gives new ways of understanding the issues that trouble organisations most: chaos, freedom, communication, participation, planning and prediction. Put another way, 'there is a simpler way to lead organisations, one that requires less effort and produces less stress than our current practices'.

Leadership and the New Science proposes that our present ways of organising are entrenched and out of time. Wheatley challenges organisations to face the questions of:

- Where order is to be found
- How complex systems change
- How to create structures which are adaptable and flexible
- How to match personal needs for autonomy and growth with the organisation's needs for accountability and predictability

Everyone who picks up *Leadership and the New Science* will come to different conclusions about how to transform this scientific metaphor into the reality of their own organisation. Margaret Wheatley states unambiguously that it is not necessary to have one single expert interpretation or one single best practice. The metaphor of science gives insight into different ways of seeing and being. How that translates into organisational reality is for each individual reader and organisation to determine. Examples of Wheatley's most recent thinking can be found at www.margaretwheatley.com.

Jim Collins, *Good to Great: Why Some Companies Make the Leap . . . and Others Don't*

Good to Great is in part about the nature of individual leadership. It is anti-heroic, and like Badaracco's leaders discussed earlier, 'quiet'. In researching the differentiators between highly successful and less successful organisations, Collins observed that the most successful had leaders which exhibited what he calls Level 5 leadership, the highest level in a hierarchy of executive capability. He saw that leaders who demonstrated the other four levels in the hierarchy could produce high degrees of success, but that 'Good to Great' transformations simply didn't happen in the absence of Level 5 leadership.

> [T]hroughout our interviews with such executives, we were struck by the way they talked about themselves – or rather, didn't talk about themselves. They'd go on and on about the company and the contributions of other executives, but they'd instinctively deflect discussion about their own role.

The Level 5 Executive builds enduring greatness through a combination of personal humility and professional will. The Level 4 Effective Leader catalyses commitment to and vigorous pursuit of a clear, compelling vision. The Level 3 Competent Manager organises people and resources towards the effective and efficient pursuit of objectives. The Level 2 Contributing Team Member helps achieve group objectives. The Level 1 Highly Capable Individual contributes through talent, knowledge and skills.

Level 5 leadership is an essential but insufficient feature for taking a company from good to great, but personal leadership proved to be only part of the story. Good to great companies also had a culture of organisational leadership, displayed through disciplined people, disciplined thought and disciplined action.

The *right* people turned out to be the most important asset. Level 5 companies attended to people first. Good to Great companies confronted brutal facts, but never lost faith in ultimate success. They focused on what the company could do best, and ignited the passion of its people. They had a culture of discipline. With disciplined people, you don't need hierarchy, bureaucracy or excessive controls.

Like Wheatley, Collins avoids lists of 'how to become'. And in one key area, he disagrees with most of the authors previously discussed.

He is not convinced that Level 5 leadership can be learned. The seed may be dormant, but it's either there or it's not.

It is possible to access Jim Collins's most up-to-date thinking through www.jimcollins.com, where he shares thoughts, research and lines of enquiry.

David L. Cooperrider and Suresh Srivastva, *The Role of Appreciative Inquiry in Organizational Life*

Cooperrider and Srivastva do not espouse a simplistic approach to leadership, one which is common to each and every organisation or each and every leader within it. Instead, they propose an approach which builds upon the unique being that is every organisation. The leader in appreciative inquiry is transposed into the researcher, one seeking to develop the innovative capacity of his or her organisation.

Like Margaret Wheatley, they draw parallels between the possibilities of science and the workings of the 'executive mind' (Srivastva, *The Executive Mind*, San Francisco and London, Jossey Bass, 1983; Srivastva, *Executive Power*, San Francisco and London, Jossey Bass, 1986). They suggest that in the same way leaders inspire people to strive for new possibilities, scientific theory also affects the cultural practices of organisations and the greater community. Cooperrider and Srivastva suggest that it is only by researching – inquiring – into organisational realities that the existing organisation can be transformed.

In Appreciative Inquiry, the leader takes a perspective that facilitates discovery and nurtures innovation. The leader searches for congruence between the values of the organisation and what happens in practice. He searches for knowledge to assist the evolving vision of the organisation.

Appreciative Inquiry assumes that there is always something on which to build, it 'appreciates' those parts of the system that work, and work well. It builds on what is, rather than on what is not. This is an approach embedded in the possibility of action and applicability. Inquiry and innovation are something of benefit only if the results can be implemented.

Appreciative Inquiry, suggest Cooperrider and Srivastva, is a methodology for evolving and then implementing the collective will of an organisation. It creates the possibility of dialogue that encourages social innovation. It offers insight into the organisation, that 'miracle of co-operative human interaction, of which there can never be a final explanation'.

Joseph A. Raelin, *Creating Leaderful Organisations: How to Bring Out Leadership in Everyone*

The central tenet of Raelin's argument is that today's unstable organisations simply can't be coordinated by bureaucratic authority or charismatic personalities. The only way to succeed is for leadership to be located everywhere, in his words 'leaderful'. In these organisations, leadership is concurrent, it is collective, it is collaborative and it is compassionate.

Where there is concurrent leadership, more than one leader operates at the same time. Leaders willingly share power with others. The hierarchical leader becomes a facilitator for the wider team, supporting colleagues and subordinates as they learn to share leadership.

Collective leadership builds on the concept of concurrent leader. There will be many people who are capable of being leaders. The group does not depend on one individual to inspire them to act or to take decisions.

Where collaborative leadership exists, all members of the group are in control of and speak for the entire community. Each becomes a change agent, each influences the direction of the organisation and each engages in dialogue.

Leaderful leaders are compassionate. They act with conscience and within an ethical framework. Like Badaracco's 'Quiet Leaders' and Jim Collins's Level 5 Leaders, they are unlikely to be charismatic. Leaderful organisations acknowledge that success comes from collective endeavour. Salvation does not come from the top.

Raelin quotes the former CEO (Chief Executive Officer) of UPS (United Parcel Service of America), Jim Kelly:

I think CEOs are terribly overrated. The whole concept of the superstar CEO is nuts. When you look at successful companies, there are a whole lot of folks doing a whole lot of things to make them successful . . . Around here, we don't think of ourselves as individuals doing too much on our own. We thinkoooooo of ourselves as people working together to get things accomplished.

Robert K. Greenleaf, *Servant Leadership: A Journey into the Nature of Legitimate Power & Greatness*

Servant Leadership is a collection of essays, talks and articles spanning a period of 20 years from 1966. Based on an intimate understanding of business, education and the Church (he was a practising Quaker),

Greenleaf concluded that the common characteristic of a great leader was that he (or she) was first a servant. Their desire to lead came from a desire to serve. He explores how individuals demonstrate servant leadership, and then considers how organisations can develop servant leadership, paying particular attention to business, education, foundations (charities) and the Church.

Servant leaders have a great dream which excites the imagination and challenges those around them to work towards that dream. Servant leaders act on what they believe, taking the risk of failure along with the chance of success. Their followers grant the leader authority only because he is trusted and has proved himself a servant to them. Authority can never be taken, only granted. Above all, says Greenleaf, the test of greatness in the servant leader is whether those served are growing as persons: 'do they become healthier, wiser, freer, more autonomous, more likely themselves to become servants?'

Greenleaf makes a unique contribution to the canon of leadership thinking. This is articulated in 'Organizing to Serve', his summary of a talk given to the School Sisters of St Francis. He exhorts the Church to become a servant leader in the wider community, declaring that it has a responsibility to create an exemplary institution for and in itself. In an era when institutions are neither trusted nor regarded as being places where good work and good things happen, then the Church must act, must be a living model of how things might be. It should support leadership and the development of leaders in other, secular, institutions. Their model institution will become a thing of beauty as it demonstrates faith at work. As a thing of beauty, it will be a powerful serving force.

Jeffrey A. Sonnenfeld (ed.), *Concepts of Leadership*

The final book is a collection of significant and influential articles from across the range of leadership enquiry. It offers access to a broad, rich and diverse range of views. In one place it gives insight into the role of leaders, how they transform organisations, and how they impact on the people around them. A new stream of thought is introduced through an exploration of where the limits of leadership effectiveness might be found. J. A. Conger's 1990 article 'The Dark Side of Leadership' (*Organizational Dynamics* 19) is of particular interest in this context.

Contributors range from those now familiar with readers of this chapter – Kotter and Srivastva for example – to those who feature in our Longlist (see below), which contains books and articles of merit which missed the final selection.

Part 3: Specialist centres for leadership development

Where to go – the answer depends, of course, on what is needed. In turn, we give options for developing the individual leader, developing leadership in teams, and for developing leadership at the organisational level.

When considering leadership at the individual perspective, just how does one get better? Mainly by doing it, reflecting on the experience, and trying to do things a bit more skilfully next time. This is why coaching is so popular. Much like a sports coach helps an athlete to improve by watching, analysing and encouraging a better style and attitude, a leadership coach focuses attention on one's own behaviour.

But the analogy with sports goes only so far. So much depends on one's own attitude to power, sense of responsibility, desire for recognition, tolerance of others, patience with the unfolding events. A greater understanding of his or her own personality will tremendously help anyone in a position of authority. Personality tests, psychometrics and other diagnostic processes can be very helpful, especially those oriented towards the factors that are relevant to interpersonal and organisational relationships. Instruments such as the 'Myers Briggs Type Indicator' are widely used, well understood and can be illuminating in two ways: they point to relevant aspects of behaviour, encouraging a reflective, self-aware stance, and also provide a language for describing personality.

While personality tests concentrate on the individual, many other interventions focus on team or group interactions. Team-building activities can help a group communicate more openly and effectively, distinguish between strategic and operational concerns, make better use of their time together and devise ways of working within the wider organisation. Although not directly focused on leadership, team-building events can be crucial in enabling the exercise of authority. This is partly because participants get in touch with their own sense of determination and decisiveness, and partly because they recognise the satisfaction of collaborating in ways that enable the appropriate people to take up leadership roles.

Sometimes the problem is at once broader and more specific – some people can see the need for change, but they don't have enough of a following in the organisation or community. Inspiring messages and clear visions can help, but they can also be alienating. Alternatively, if organisation members at all levels are helped to re-examine their own areas of responsibility, they can almost always come up with ideas for improvements. These invariably add up to significant change, and often enhance the plans of the original visionaries. So real advances in leadership can often come about through what is known as 'organisation development' or OD, rather than explicit attention to formal leadership. There are many approaches to OD, and several consultancies specialise in working with congregations, churches and dioceses.

But very often people do want to improve their grasp of the leadership aspects of their job. Some approaches to this are listed below – website addresses and telephone numbers follow at the end.

- Opportunities to network with other leaders from different sectors, to reflect and recharge one's batteries. The Windsor Leadership Trust runs residential retreats for leaders at various career junctures. An excellent alumni network and very skilful facilitation makes this a high-quality experience. The Aspen Institute in the USA offers a similar experience.
- Training courses in conceptual techniques of strategy, company direction, and so forth. Numerous business schools, for example, Ashridge, INSEAD, Henley and the London Business School. These tend to be expensive, and rather oriented towards business, but they often offer bursaries and the cross-sectoral contact can be stimulating.
- Longer term study of one's own leadership style, its relationship to values and the operational context. The underpinning theory of claims made about leadership. The Centre for Leadership Studies at the University of Exeter offers a part-time MA which supports long-term personal development. It includes face-to-face interaction with peers from other sectors, personal coaching and substantial intellectual challenge.
- Experiential exposé of unconscious aspects of attitudes towards authority, leadership and responsibility. For the past 40 years Working Conferences organised by the Grubb Institute and the Tavistock Institute for Human Relations have made substantial contributions to the dynamics of congregations and church organisations. Leaders who want to see things more clearly without reducing the complexity will find these hugely rewarding.
- Basic training in interpersonal and team skills, along with coaching help in taking up authority and developing one's own leadership style. Certificate in Leadership with the Centre for Leadership Studies in partnership with the Chartered Institute for Personnel & Development. Short courses with The Leadership Trust.
- Coaching is available through numerous partnerships and individual practitioners. A very effective variation is a 'Leadership

Exchange', in which individuals observe each other 'doing leadership'. Properly prepared and employing disciplined observation methods, people can gain – and give – a timely, sensitive and imaginative feedback and insight into each other's practice in the real context, in real time. But it does need professional support. Contact the Centre for Leadership Studies or Lead2lead.net at Lancaster University Management School.

• The Centre for Leadership Studies maintains a register of leadership development trainers and consultants, and will be happy to advise on specific situations.

Contact details for dedicated leadership centres

Ashridge Business School: www.ashridge.org.uk; +44 (0) 1442 843491
The Aspen Institute: www.aspeninst.org; +1 970 925 7010
Centre for Leadership Studies at the University of Exeter: www.exeter.ac.uk/leadership; +44 (0) 1392 413018
The Grubb Institute: www.grubb.org.uk; +44 (0) 2072 788061
Henley Management School: www.henleymc.ac.uk; +44 (0) 1491 571454
INSEAD: www.insead.fr; +33 (0) 1 60 7242 03
Lancaster University Management School: www.lead2lead.net; +44 (0) 1524 594038
The Leadership Trust: www.leadership.org.uk; +44 (0) 1989 767667
London Business School: www.london.edu; +44 (0) 20 7262 5050
The Tavistock Institute for Human Relations: www.tavinstitute.org; +44 (0) 20 7417 0407
Windsor Leadership Trust: www.windsorleadershiptrust.co.uk; +44 (0) 1753 272050

Part 4 The longlist

John Adair, *Developing Leaders: The Ten Key Principles*, Spiro Press, 1985.
John Adair, *Inspirational Leadership*, Thoroughgood, 2002.
John Adair, *The Leadership of Jesus*, Canterbury, 2001.
John Adair, *Not Bosses but Leaders*, Kogan Page, 1991.
Bernard M. Bass, *Leadership and Performance beyond Expectations*, Free Press, 1985.
Bernard M. Bass and Ralph M. Stogdill, *Handbook of Leadership*, Free Press, 1990.

J. McGregor Burns, *Leadership*, Harper & Row, 1978.

Howard Gardner, *Leading Minds: An Anatomy of Leadership*, Basic Books, 1996.

Robert K. Greenleaf, *Power of Servant Leadership*, Barrett-Koehler, 1998.

Keith Grint (ed.), *Leadership: Classical, Contemporary and Critical Approaches*, Oxford University Press, 2001.

R. A. Heifetz, *Leadership without Easy Answers*, Belknap Press, 1994.

R. A. Heifetz, 'Managing Yourself: A Survival Guide for Leaders', *Harvard Business Review* (June 2002).

Dee Hock, 'The Art of Chaordic Leadership', *Leader to Leader* 15 (Winter 2000).

Alan Hooper, *Power, Relationships, Identity, Understanding, Spirituality, Imagination*, forthcoming, 2004.

Alan Hooper and John Potter, *Intelligent Leadership: Creating a Passion for Change*, Random House, 2001.

P. Kostenbaum, *The Inner Side of Greatness*, Jossey Bass, 1991.

John Kotter, *Force for Change: Why Leadership Differs from Management*, Free Press, 1990.

John Kotter, *Leadership Factor*, Free Press, 1988.

James M. Kouzes and Barry Z. Posner, *Leadership Challenge*, Jossey Bass, 2002.

Machiavelli, *The Prince*, ch. 17.

Alastair Mant, *Intelligent Leadership*, Allen & Unwin, 1997.

Eric Miller, *From Dependency to Autonomy: Studies in Organization & Change*, International Specialized Book Service, 1994

Nano McCaughan and Barry Palmer, *Systems Thinking for Harassed Managers*, Karnac, 1994.

Harrison Owen, *Spirit Transformation and Development in Organisations*, Abbott, 1994.

Michael Syrett and Clare Hogg (eds), *The Frontiers of Leadership: An Essential Reader*, Blackwell, 1992.

David Taylor, *The Naked Leader*, Capstone, 2002.

A. Zaleznik, 'Managers and Leaders: Are They Different?', *Harvard Business Review* (March 1992).

Relevant journals

Academy of Management Review, published by US Academy of Management.

Leadership Quarterly, published by Elsevier Science.

Part 5

20 MODEM

MODEM was formed in 1993 as a national ecumenical charity to fulfil a role for the churches of exploring managerial and organisational issues. In its first ten years, its role has evolved from a one-way into a two-way role/mission – that of leading and enabling authentic dialogue between exponents of leadership, management and organisation and spirituality, and theology and ministry.

A successor to CORAT

MODEM replaced the former Christian Organisational Research and Advisory Trust (CORAT). In 1991, CORAT decided to call a consultation meeting of all interested parties to review its work over the previous 20 years or so and to determine whether or not it should continue as an organisation. A further meeting agreed to encourage the creation of a new network of communication for individuals and organisations relating to the organisational and managerial aspects of the work of Christian bodies.

Title

The title 'MODEM' was originally an acronym for 'Managerial and Organisational Disciplines for the Enhancement of Ministry'. Subsequently, it has (like British Telecom's 'BT') become a term in its own right, symbolising a two-way facilitator.

Who is MODEM?

MODEM consists of Trustees, Patrons and Members – Emeritus, Individual, Group and Corporate.

Patrons

Baroness Perry of Southwark
Mary Chapman, Director-General of the Chartered Management
    Institute
Raymond Clarke, JP, OBE
Sir John Harvey-Jones
Sir Philip Mawer, Parliamentary Commissioner for Standards
Rt Revd Christopher Mayfield, former Bishop of Manchester
Professor Gillian Stamp, Director of BIOSS, Brunel University
Bishop Tim Stevens, Bishop of Leicester
Revd Dr Norman Todd
Roger Young, Former D-G Chartered Management Institute

Emeritus Members

Professor John Adair
Charles Handy
Revd Dr Peter Rudge

Premier Corporate Member

Chartered Management Institute

Individual Members

MODEM has attracted approaching 300 individual members – clergy
and lay from church and business.

MODEM's Management Committee meets 10 times a year and
    comprises:

Bishop Christopher Mayfield* – Chairman
Alan Harpham* – Vice-Chairman
Revd Dr Bill Allen
Fred Ayres
Peter Bates* – Treasurer
Peter Chiswell
Richard Fox
Ian Hinton
Sue Howard
Sue Jewell – Meetings Secretary
John Nelson* – National Secretary
Revd Arthur Siddall*

MODEM's achievements

Most significantly, MODEM provides a forum for the exchange of experience in the practice of ministry in the secular world and in the church. It has a particular focus on the development of good organisational and leadership models. The strength of its growing numbers in membership demonstrates that a significant number of practitioners wants to associate themselves with MODEM's aims and objectives. New subscriptions outnumber those that are not renewed and we receive frequent positive acclamations about our work.

MODEM is a collaborative organisation. We attempt to involve our members in our activities and in our projects. We also set out to work in co-operation with organisations that have similar interests to ourselves. We are members of a forum of sister organisations which meets regularly. These include the Christian Association of Business Executives, The Industrial Christian Fellowship, The Network of Ministers in Secular Employment and the Ridley Hall Foundation. In the life of our journal we have collaborated in the production and purchase of MINISTRY from the Edward King Institute for Ministry Development. Internationally, we are also co-members of the Association of Spirit at Work and linked to Spirit in Business in the USA and Europe.

Our best-known activity is our publishing. The two books we have produced in association with Canterbury Press have received much attention and have been well reviewed. *Management and Ministry* tackled the issue of churches needing to manage its resources efficiently and effectively. The second book, *Leading, Managing and Ministering*, explored the wider issues of managing in ministry, ministering in management and of both in leading organisations sacred and secular. *Creative Church Leadership*, MODEM's third book, focuses on church leadership.

MODEM has also produced booklets on important church organisational/managerial issues, such as a review of the Turnbull Report on the Church of England's organisation and the Hurd Report of the See of Canterbury.

MODEM is currently discussing with Canterbury Press the introduction of a series of distinctive booklets to cover topical issues and to disseminate best practice. This is intended to appeal to its members to become active contributors.

Our books and other publications have provided the focus for conferences and meetings around the press launches. Our quarterly newsletter, *MODEM Matters*, keeps members and others well informed of our activities and of the achievements of our members.

As a research organisation, we have produced the report *Hope of the Managers*, looking at exactly what it is which energises leadership. Our bi-annual conferences have focused on important topics in the area of leadership and have resulted in the publication of papers from these events.

Our website is fully operational and gives easy access to all MODEM papers and activities. The programme Lead On, accessed from the website, allows senior church people to enter into a review and mentoring scheme related to their work. It has been taken up by a number of denominations.

Impact

MODEM has already made an impact, to quote MODEM's Patron, Sir Philip Mawer – formerly Secretary-General of the Church of England's General Synod and now Parliamentary Commissioner for Standards. He paid tribute to MODEM 'for the way it has carried the torch for the importance of considering issues of leadership and management in relation to those of ministry'.

MODEM is on course to become the voice of leadership, management and ministry.

21: About the contributors

Professor John Adair
Author, teacher and adviser on leadership and leadership development. He became the world's first Professor of Leadership Studies in 1979, and was previously a senior lecturer at Sandhurst and the first Director of Studies at St George's House, Windsor Castle. He holds degrees in history and theology from Cambridge, Oxford and London universities. His books on leadership, translated into 20 different languages, include *How to Find Your Vocation* and *The Leadership of Jesus*, both published by Canterbury Press, and *Effective Strategic Leadership*, published by Macmillan. Emeritus member of MODEM.

Revd Dr Bill Allen
Regional Minister with special responsibility for mission and strategy for the Yorkshire Baptist Association. He is a member of the Baptist Union National Strategy Forum, and was formerly Director of Pastoral Studies at Spurgeon's College, London. He successfully completed his PhD thesis, *The provision of education and training for leadership in the ordained ministry*, under the supervision of John Adair.

Professor Derek Burke
Vice-Chancellor of the University of East Anglia from 1987 to 1995. Before that he was Vice-President and Scientific Director of Allelix, Toronto, Canada, and Professor of Biological Sciences in the University of Warwick. He has served as a member of the Science, Medical & Technology Committee of the Church of England's Board for Social Responsibility, and Chairman of the Working Party that produced *Cybernauts Awake! Ethical and Spiritual Implications of Computers, Information Technology and the Internet*. He was a specialist adviser to the House of Commons Select Committee on Science and Technology and also a member of the EU–US Consultative Forum on Biotechnology. He is currently a member of the European Life Sciences Group, advising Commissioner Busquin.

The Very Revd Dr Wesley Carr
Dean of Westminster since 1997. He has also been dean of Bristol and canon at Chelmsford Cathedral. Apart from theology, his main skill lies in the realm of group relations. He is an influential writer, in particular of *The Priestlike Task* (SPCK, 1985).

Linda Dawson
Senior Human Resources (HR) Specialist at the University of Exeter's Centre for Leadership Studies, who carried out the Review of Leadership Literature and Leadership Development Centres as a Resource for Creative Church Leaders. She specialises in developing leaders and leadership behaviour; behavioural development in virtual and multicultural environments; design and implementation of career management processes; and coaching. She is a Visiting Fellow at Lancaster University's School of Management.

Elaine Dunn
Assistant Director of Exeter University's Centre for Leadership Studies and supervisor of the Centre's Report and Review of Leadership Literature and Leadership Development Centres as a Resource for Creative Church Leaders. Her main interests are in leadership via networking, negotiation and influencing rather than by direct authority.

Professor Robin Gill
Michael Ramsey Professor of Modern Theology in the University of Kent. Previously he held the William Leech Research Chair of Applied Theology at the University of Newcastle. His recent books include *Churchgoing and Christian Ethics* (CUP, 1999), *The Cambridge Companion to Christian Ethics* (CUP, 2001), *Changing Worlds* (T & T Clark, 2002) and *The 'Empty' Church Revisited* (Ashgate, 2003) and, especially, *Strategic Church Leadership* (with Derek Burke, SPCK, 1996). Ordained an Anglican priest in 1968, he continues to be active in pastoral ministry and is now an honorary canon of Canterbury Cathedral and an Area Dean in the Canterbury Diocese.

Jonathon Gosling
Director of the University of Exeter's Centre for Leadership Studies, and previously Director of the Strategic Leaders Unit at Lancaster University. He is a trustee of the Fintry and J. H. Levy Trusts and Visiting Professor at Lancaster University. His own research focuses on leadership and ethics in current strategic changes and on contemporary innovations in leadership development.

Ven Malcolm Grundy

Archdeacon of Craven in the Diocese of Bradford. He has previously been Senior Chaplain of the Sheffield Industrial Mission, Director of Education and Community in the Diocese of London, Team Rector of Huntingdon, and Director of AVEC. He is the author of a range of books on social and community issues and on parish development. He is a non-executive director of the *Church Times*, an Advisory Board of Ministry (ABM) Senior Selector, Bishops' Inspector of Theological Colleges, and the immediate past Chairman of MODEM.

Charles Handy

A writer and broadcaster. His books, which include *Understanding Voluntary Organizations* (Penguin, 1993), have concentrated on the changing shape of work and what that means for our lives and our organisations. They have sold more than one million copies round the world. The son of an archdeacon, he grew up in Ireland but now lives and works in London and Norfolk. Emeritus member of MODEM.

David A. Harvey

Produced the Lincoln Theological Institute's database of resources for church leadership and management. He is currently completing work for a PhD in contextual theology at the Lincoln Theological Institute, Manchester University. After working in the Health Service as a pharmaceutical quality controller, he obtained a BA in theology from Spurgeon's College, London. He then worked in pastoral and evangelical ministry until 1999 when he studied for and gained an MA in biblical studies from Sheffield University.

Rt Revd David Jenkins

Former Bishop of Durham, and to quote *The Times* (13 October 2003), 'remains one of the Church of England's most influential theologians in retirement'. He served as a staff officer in the Royal Artillery in World War Two. He has degrees in philosophy and theology from Oxford University, where he was Chaplain and Fellow of The Queen's College. During 1969–73 he was Director of the World Council of Churches, Geneva. He is a former Director of the William Temple Foundation, Manchester and Professor of Theology at Leeds University. He has published ten books, latterly his autobiography – *The Calling of a Cuckoo* (Continuum, 2002).

Sir Philip Mawer

Parliamentary Commissioner for Standards since March 2002. Prior to that he was for 12 years Secretary-General of the General Synod of the Church of England. He thus combines extensive experience in a leadership position in the Church with similar experience in Westminster and Whitehall. Patron of MODEM.

John Nelson

Anglican layman working as a management consultant with the Diocese of Liverpool. He was Head of the Department of Management Studies at the former Liverpool Polytechnic (now Liverpool John Moores University). He is National Secretary of MODEM and editor of MODEM's first two books, *Management and Ministry* and *Leading, Managing, Ministering*, and co-editor of this book.

Revd Canon Dr Martyn Percy

Director of the Lincoln Theological Institute for the Study of Religion and Society at the University of Manchester, where he is a Reader teaching sociology, modern theology and contemporary ecclesiology. A canon of Sheffield Cathedral and Adjunct Professor of Theology at Hartford Seminary, Connecticut, USA, he is a prolific author and regular contributor to Radio 4, the BBC World Service and the *Independent* and *Guardian* newspapers. He was formerly Director of Studies and Chaplain at Christ's and Sydney Sussex Colleges, Cambridge University. Member of MODEM.

Baroness Perry of Southwark

Pro-Chancellor, University of Surrey and Chair of Council, Roehampton Institute, a Cambridge graduate and formerly HMI. She took up the post of Vice-Chancellor of South Bank University (formerly Polytechnic) in 1987, the first woman to head a polytechnic in the UK. Formerly President of Lucy Cavendish College, Cambridge (1994–2001), she is Co-Chairman of the All Party Parliamentary Universities Group. She holds Honorary Fellowships and degrees from several universities and is the author of an influential report on the selection of senior clergy in the Church of England: *Working with the Spirit: Choosing Diocesan Bishops* (2001). She was made a Life Peer in 1991. Patron of MODEM.

Rt Revd Peter Price

Bishop of Bath & Wells since 2002. A teacher before ordination, he served his title within the Diocese of Portsmouth. He then served in the Diocese of Southwark as a parish priest, then as Chancellor of Southwark Cathedral and Chairman of the Diocesan Board of Mission. In 1992 he was appointed General Secretary of the United Society for the Propagation of the Gospel (USPG). In 1997 he was consecrated as Area Bishop of Kinston, Southwark Diocese.

Revd Dr Peter Rudge

An Anglican priest best known for his definitive book – *Ministry and Management* – which was based on doctoral work at Leeds University. It combined his earlier administrative training at the University of Tasmania with his theological qualifications at St Michael's House, Adelaide and parish experience in the Diocese of Canberra and Goulburn. The book led to his work as a management consultant in churches under the aegis of CORAT (Christian Organisations Research and Advisory Trust). He has continued to develop his insight into the relationship between theology and management. He now lives in semi-retirement in Australia's Gold Coast. Emeritus member of MODEM.

Professor Gillian Stamp

Director of BIOSS International, a world-wide network of institutes that research and develop the well-being of social institutions and the people within them. She has extensive experience with private and public sectors, religions, the military and voluntary organisations in different parts of the world. For more than 20 years she has worked with the Church of England on synodical government, structures, leadership and consultations with newly consecrated bishops. For six years she was a member of the Council of St George's House, Windsor Castle and she is a Fellow of the Windsor Leadership Trust. Patron of MODEM.

Revd Dr Norman Todd

A retired Anglican parish priest, but not a retired priest. He is a graduate in science and theology, with a doctorate in psychology. He was the first Archbishops' Adviser on Bishops' Ministry and is now a part-time freelance consultant on spirituality, psychotherapy and ministry. Patron of MODEM.

Rt Revd Michael Turnbull CBE

Chairman of Trustees of the Church of England's new Foundation for Leadership Studies. He recently retired as Bishop of Durham, and was previously Bishop of Rochester, and a former Archdeacon and Chief Secretary of the Church Army. He served on the Cathedrals Commission, and is Chairman of the Archbishops' Commission on the Organisation of the Church of England which resulted in the Report *Working as One Body* in 1995, and the formation of the Archbishops' Council.

Revd Elizabeth Welch

A third-generation minister. Her father, Clifford Welch, served in the South Pacific and the Central Congregational Church in Johannesburg in South Africa, where she and her brother Lawrence grew up. Her experience under apartheid was of crucial importance for her thinking about the nature of the Church and its involvement in the world. She was ordained in 1976 to St Barnabas United Church and Christian Centre, Langney, Eastbourne. In 1983 she was called to serve at Christ the Cornerstone, part of the growing ecumenical scene in Milton Keynes. In 1996 she became Moderator of the West Midlands Synod, and from 2001 to 2002 she served as National Moderator of the URC. Elizabeth is co-author with Flora Winfield of *Travelling Together: A Handbook on Local Ecumenical Partnerships* (Baptist Union, 1995). Member of MODEM.

22: Survey reports on resources for church leadership

The following two academic institutions were commissioned to produce our two survey reports on resources available on leadership in general and specifically on church leadership (Chapters 18 and 19).

Exeter University's Centre for Leadership Study

Director – Jonathon Gosling (see brief biography on page 272).

The only university-based centre of its kind in the UK. It is a centre of excellence to support leadership in the South West, nationally and internationally.
  Its portfolio includes:

- Study programmes, including MA in Leadership Studies, CIPD Certificate in Leadership, Advanced Leadership Programme, full-time MBA specialising in Leadership, Continuing Professional Development.
- Research, with its general character focusing on:
  – the dilemmas confronting leaders
  – how to improve leadership development
  – exploring new ways of thinking about leadership.
- Consultancy, including in-house tailored programmes and a Monitoring and Evaluation Service.

Lincoln Theological Institute (LTI), Manchester University

Director – Revd Canon Dr Martyn Percy (see brief biography on page 274).

Inaugurated in 1997, the LTI is a research and teaching unit within the University of Manchester. The Institute focuses on postgraduate and postdoctoral research. The primary areas for research include modern ecclesiology, practical theology and religion in contemporary society. Students may enrol through the University of Manchester for Masters and Doctoral degree programmes.

The LTI originated from Lincoln Theological College, founded in 1874 as an ordination training college. From 1997 to 2002, the LTI was based in Sheffield, where as an independent research centre it was also a designated college of the University of Sheffield. Since 2003 the LTI has been a fully integrated academic unit within the University of Manchester. Recent funded research programmes have included: a study of hospital chaplaincy provision in a multifaith society; the reception of women priests in the Church of England; spirituality and care in residential and nursing homes; and religion, economics and debt.